Nail the Resume!

By Ron and Caryl Krannich

CAREER AND BUSINESS BOOKS AND SOFTWARE

101 Secrets of Highly Effective Speakers
201 Dynamite Job Search Letters
America's Top 100 Jobs for People Without a Four-Year Degree
America's Top Jobs for People Re-Entering the Workforce
America's Top Internet Job Sites
Best Jobs for the 21st Century
Change Your Job, Change Your Life
The Complete Guide to Public Employment
The Directory of Federal Jobs and Employers
Discover the Best Jobs for You!
Dynamite Cover Letters
Dynamite Resumes
Dynamite Salary Negotiations
Dynamite Tele-Search
The Educator's Guide to Alternative Jobs and Careers
The Ex-Offender's Job Hunting Guide
Find a Federal Job Fast!
From Air Force Blue to Corporate Gray
From Army Green to Corporate Gray
From Navy Blue to Corporate Gray
Get a Raise in 7 Days
High Impact Resumes and Letters
I Want to Do Something Else, But I'm Not Sure What It Is
Interview for Success
The Job Hunting Guide: Transitioning From College to Career
Job Hunting Tips for People With Not-So-Hot Backgrounds
Job Interview Tips for People With Not-So-Hot Backgrounds
Job-Power Source and *Ultimate Job Source* (software)
Jobs and Careers With Nonprofit Organizations
Military Resumes and Cover Letters
Moving Out of Education
Moving Out of Government
Nail the Cover Letter!
Nail the Job Interview!
Nail the Resume!
No One Will Hire Me!
Re-Careering in Turbulent Times
Savvy Interviewing
The Savvy Networker
The Savvy Resume Writer

TRAVEL AND INTERNATIONAL BOOKS

Best Resumes and CVs for International Jobs
The Complete Guide to International and Careers
The Directory of Websites for International Jobs
International
Jobs for
Mayors and
s of Family
opping and
iland

Treasures and Pleasures of
Treasures and Pleasures of Bali and
Treasures and Pleasures of Bermu
Treasures and Pleasures of China
Treasures and Pleasures of Egypt
Treasures and Pleasures of Hong Kong
Treasures and Pleasures of India
Treasures and Pleasures of Italy
Treasures and Pleasures of Mexico
Treasures and Pleasures of Paris
Treasures and Pleasures of Rio and São Paulo
Treasures and Pleasures of Santa Fe, Taos, and Albuquerque
Treasures and Pleasures of Singapore and Bali
Treasures and Pleasures of Singapore and Malaysia
Treasures and Pleasures of South America
Treasures and Pleasures of Southern Africa
Treasures and Pleasures of Thailand and Myanmar
Treasures and Pleasures of Turkey
Treasures and Pleasures of Vietnam and Cambodia

Nail the Resume!

Great Tips for Creating Dynamite Resumes

Ron and Caryl Krannich, Ph.Ds

IMPACT PUBLICATIONS
Manassas Park, VA

Warning/Liability/Warranty: The authors and publisher have made every attempt to provide the reader with accurate, timely, and useful information. However, given the rapid changes taking place in today's economy and job market, some of our information will inevitably change. The information presented here is for reference purposes only. The authors and publisher make no claims that using this information will guarantee the reader a job. The authors and publisher shall not be liable for any losses or damages incurred in the process of following the advice in this book.

ISBN: 1-57023-233-4

Library of Congress: 2005927436

Publisher: For information on Impact Publications, including current and forthcoming publications, authors, press kits, online bookstore, and submission requirements, visit the left navigation bar on the front page of our main company website: www.impactpublications.com.

Publicity/Rights: For information on publicity, author interviews, and subsidiary rights, contact the Media Relations Department: Tel. 703-361-7300, Fax 703-335-9486, or email: info@impactpublications.com.

Sales/Distribution: All bookstore sales are handled through Impact's trade distributor: National Book Network, 15200 NBN Way, Blue Ridge Summit, PA 17214, Tel. 1-800-462-6420. All special sales and distribution inquiries should be directed to the publisher: Sales Department, IMPACT PUBLICATIONS, 9104 Manassas Drive, Suite N, Manassas Park, VA 20111-5211, Tel. 703-361-7300, Fax 703-335-9486, or email: info@impactpublications.com.

Contents

Preface

WRITING AND DISTRIBUTING resumes in response to job vacancies has been a time-honored tradition for decades. While some people have never had to write a resume – because they completed application forms or were hired on the basis of an interview alone – more and more individuals must write resumes today. From blue collar workers to white collar professionals, resumes are an acceptable and preferred medium for communicating one's qualifications to employers. Even prospective federal government employees now submit resumes in response to federal vacancy announcements.

Contrary to what you may have heard from others, resumes are here to stay, and in a very big way. As the job market becomes increasingly competitive, as employers seek highly skilled and experienced individuals, and as new technology is adapted to recruitment, resumes are playing a much greater role in the employment process than ever before.

At the same time, the structure and content of resumes have changed in light of new employer expectations. No longer are "summary of work history" resumes appropriate for today's job market. Employers are looking for evidence of performance, unusually in the form of achievements or accomplishments – that would good predictors of workplace behavior and future performance. Hiring managers expect a resume to tell them about a candidate's relevant "patterns of performance" and how they will "add value" to the employer's operations.

The **language of resumes** has changed from historical information and statements of formal duties and responsibilities to the use of action verbs, nouns, and other keywords that form coherent statements of motivated abilities and skills (MAS) and patterns of accomplishments. In other words, your resume should be **employer-centered** – tell employers what you have done, can do, and will most likely do for them once you come on their payroll. Unfortunately, most job seekers still write self-centered resumes that communicate the wrong messages to employers. Primarily interested in what employers can do for them – salary, benefits, perks, advancement

– such candidates do not appeal to many employers who are primarily looking for quality employees who are interested in doing a good job and contributing to the success of the company or organization.

The increasing use of technology to scan resumes for keywords means more and more applicants need to develop an effective electronic version of their resume so it can be "read" by computers. As employers increasingly use the Internet to recruit candidates, job seekers are well advised to develop e-mail versions of their resumes as well as learn how to conduct an online job search for researching employers and locating job opportunities.

Recognizing the increasing importance of resumes and sensitive to the expectations of employers, *Nail the Resume!* outlines the major principles for writing, producing, distributing, and following-up resumes in today's highly competitive job market. Unlike many other guidebooks that primarily focus on the writing process or are essentially compilations of resume examples, this book focuses on what's really important when communicating qualifications to employers. We focus on the whole process that produces results for both job applicants and employers. Writing according to principles of good resume writing is only one of many elements that results in desired outcomes. The other three involve **resume production, distribution, and follow-up**. Failure to closely link these three additional processes to the resume writing process often means a well-written resume never achieves it true potential. Indeed, the best written resumes are only as good as the quality of their production, distribution, and follow up activities. Neglect any one of these processes and you may effectively kill your resume.

As you navigate today's job market, make sure you pay particular attention to how you can best distribute and follow up your resume. The good news is that you now have more opportunities to distribute your resume given the increasing use of resume databases and career services available on the Internet. We outline these opportunities in a separate volume, which focuses on using the Internet in the job finding process, *America's To Internet Job Sites* (Impact Publications, 2004).

Whatever you do, make sure you approach today's job market with a dynamite resume that is written, produced, distributed, and followed up according to the many principles outlined in this book. Use our internal and external evaluation forms in Chapter 4 to assess how well your resume meets the expectations of today's employers. Most important of all, follow up, follow up, follow up. Writing, producing, and distributing a dynamite resume without proper and persistent follow-up is both wishful thinking and a waste of time. If you plan to write it right, follow it up frequently. If you observe this simple follow-up rule, you'll be amazed with the results. You'll indeed nail your resume and go on to land a job you really love!

Ron and Caryl Krannich

Nail the Resume!

1

Dynamite Resumes Generate Interviews and Offers

S O YOU NEED TO WRITE, PRODUCE, and distribute a well organized resume that immediately grabs the attention of prospective employers who, in turn, will invite you to job interviews. Congratulations. You are about to join millions of other people who engage in this hopeful yet stressful ritual each year. But unlike most job seekers, who seem to be preoccupied with summarizing their **history** on a one- to two-page resume, you are going to produce a first-class dynamite resume that communicates your key **accomplishment**s to prospective employers. If you nail your resume, you'll get invited to job interviews that will eventually turn into job offers.

That's our mission in the following pages – make sure you produce and distribute an outstanding resume that has a positive outcome for both you and your new employer. We want you to present your best self to prospective employers. Your resume should clearly communicate who you are in terms of your goals, interests, skills, abilities, and predictable future performance. Within the space of one or two pages, it should persuade employers to contact you for a job interview.

Quick and Easy Resumes

Most people would like to avoid writing a resume if they could – it's often hard, unsatisfying, and disappointing work. A highly ego-involved activity, it frequently results in self-deception. Just when you think you've written a great resume, you

1

discover it's really a mediocre product that will have difficulty passing employers' screening tests. Some resume experts, career coaches, and employers may frankly tell you the truth – your home-grown resume really stinks! Others may just thank you for your effort. If you are like most job seekers, you can use some professional help in portraying on paper who you are and what you can do for employers.

We would love to reveal a secret formula that would make this whole writing, production, and distribution process quick, easy, and effective. In fact, you can save yourself a great deal of reading and writing time by spending $300 to $600 to hire a professional resume writer who will do all this work for you – deliver a beautiful resume to your computer or in the mail within a few days. Just contact members of these well respected professional resume writing groups for such services:

- **Professional Association of Resume Writers and Career Coaches**   www.parw.com

- **Professional Resume Writing and Research Association**   www.prwra.com

- **National Resume Writers' Association**   www.nrwaweb.com

You can see some terrific examples of their work by reviewing the following resume books written by professional resume writers, which are available in many libraries, bookstores, or through Impact Publications (www.impactpublications.com):

101 Best Resumes
101 More Best Resumes
Best KeyWords for Resumes, Cover Letters, and Interviews
Best Resumes and CVs for International Jobs
Best Resumes for $100,000+ Jobs
Best Resumes for People Without a Four-Year Degree
Blue Collar Resumes
Expert Resumes for Computer and Web Jobs
Expert Resumes for People Returning to Work
Gallery of Best Resumes for People Without a Four-Year Degree
The Resume Catalog
Resume Magic
Resumes That Knock 'Em Dead

Several of the resume examples found in this book also have been produced by talented professional resume writers whom we work with. After you have completed this book, you may want to contact such experts for assistance (see our references in "Contributors" on page 219).

However, before you contact a professional resume writer, or attempt to creatively plagiarize resumes written by such professionals, we recommend reviewing the many principles and examples outlined in this book. In so doing, you'll learn a great deal about yourself through an exciting process of self discovery (assessment and goal setting), sharpen your communication skills, and learn how to best market your qualifications to employers through key resume distribution principles. Best of all, you'll be able to organize an effective job search as well as better utilize the services of various career professionals, including professional resume writers. Indeed, you'll be able to clearly communicate your goals, skills, and abilities to these professionals and thus maximize their talents to your advantage.

So let's get started on what may well become a very rewarding journey – producing a first-class resume that speaks volumes about your qualifications and persuades employers to contact you for a job interview. Once you put this book into practice, you should be able to write a dynamite resume that will give greater direction and purpose to your job search. You'll know exactly who you are, what you want to do, and what you can and will do for prospective employers. Most important of all, you will be able to clearly communicate on paper, and hopefully in interviews, your goals, skills, and accomplishments to employers who will want to hire you.

Connecting to the Right Employers

The age-old problem of how to connect the right employer with the right candidate has increasingly moved from print to electronic mediums as the Internet now plays a central role in the job search and hiring processes. Indeed, during the past decade, more and more employers and candidates learned an important lesson – top talent tends to congregate in the digital job market that operates via the Internet. If you're not using the Internet to recruit (employer) or identify employers and jobs (candidate), you're not fully utilizing today's most important employment resources and technology for making the best decisions. You may be missing the right places for finding jobs or acquiring top talent. We outline the dimensions of this digital job market, including its positives and negatives, in *America's Top Internet Job Sites* (Impact Publications, 2004).

> *The application of new technology to the hiring process means resumes are playing an increasingly important role in the job search.*

While the job search has increasingly turned digital, the traditional one- and two-page resume continues to play a critical role in the employment process whether produced on paper, displayed on a computer screen, or stored and analyzed in a searchable database. Communication and distribution mediums have changed – moving from the traditional print classified ad and mailed resume to faxes, e-mail, databases, and websites – but the message remains the same for job seekers: **you must clearly communicate your goals and key qualifications to employers**.

For employers, resumes remain the most efficient and effective means of screening candidates for job interviews. If, as a job seeker, you neglect your resume, you may well miss out on some terrific job opportunities in today's job market.

Employers Want to See Dynamite Resumes

Today's job market is especially responsive to dynamite resumes. These resumes follow a particular structure and are read by seasoned employers as well as scanned by search-and-retrieval software and transmitted via e-mail. Indeed, you'll need a dynamite resume to be successful in this job market. Without such a resume – complete with the latest bells, whistles, and buzz words – you are likely to flounder in the newly evolving job market that is redefining the way most people will find jobs today.

Our best advice: You may want to throw away your old resume which may be designed for a different era or a traditional job market that is now becoming obsolete. Start fresh by writing a dynamite resume designed for today's new job market.

The rules and mediums for finding jobs, communicating qualifications to employers, and screening candidates have changed in recent years. No longer do you just type a resume and send it in the mail to an employer. As technology becomes increasingly applied to the employment process, most resume guides using the type-and-mail approach have become outdated. This change has important implications for how you write, distribute, and follow up your resume in your job search. It requires writing a resume that speaks to employers through both paper and electronic mediums. Your resume must be readable by both human beings and the latest resume scanning technology. It also must be designed so it can be accessed through electronic databases, posted on electronic bulletin boards, and be transmitted via e-mail. Above all, your resume must grab the attention of employers, who will then want to invite you to a job interview.

Does Your Resume Speak the Right Language?

Large corporations continue to downsize, outsource, and offshore, permanently laying off thousands of workers each week. At the same time, many of these same companies have difficulty hiring people with the right skills required for their newly restructured operations. Government policies increasingly shift toward creating jobs, retraining workers, and promoting One-Stop career centers (www.careeronestop.org). Even the federal government's application process has shifted toward greater use of the Internet, resumes, and new automated applications for screening candidates (for details, see Kathryn Kraemer Troutman, *Ten Steps to a Federal Job*, and Dennis V. Damp, *The Book of U.S. Government Jobs*).

From the perspective of job seekers, today's **job finding process** – from electronic bulletin boards (www.AIRSdirectory.com) displaying vacancy announcements to resume databases linking candidates to employers (www.monster.com, www.careerbuilder.com, and http://hotjobs.yahoo.com) – is undergoing numerous changes centered on the role of resumes. From the perspective of employers, the **recruitment and screening processes** are finally becoming more scientific, systematic, and predictable. All of these changes point in one direction – the increasingly powerful role resumes play in the employment process, from locating employers and screening candidates to conducting job interviews. If you want to quickly get job offers, you first need to nail your resume as well as nail your letters and job interviews. For information on the two other critical steps to getting job offers, see our companion *Nail the Cover Letter!* and *Nail the Job Interview!*

These momentous changes are enhancing the role of resumes in the job search. If you believed paperless offices would result from the computer revolution, then you might have believed in the coming demise of resumes. We, of course, now know the computer revolution had just the opposite effect – dramatically increased the volume of office paper. So, too, will be a similar fate for resumes – the newly evolving job market will place even greater emphasis on using resumes for finding employment and screening candidates.

Contrary to what many people believed only a few years ago, resumes are here to stay, and in a very big way. Application of new technology to the job search means you simply must write dynamite resumes tailored to the needs of specific employers. You must pay particular attention to the **language** you incorporate in your resume. Carefully selecting a "keyword" language sensitive to optical scanners becomes one of the most important considerations in writing resumes.

Unknown to many job seekers, resumes are playing an increasingly central role in the job finding process. If you want to get a good job in today's job market, your resume simply must be first-class; it should incorporate the major principles found throughout this book. Therefore, you should spend a disproportionate amount of time crafting the very best resume possible.

If you've not already created a dynamite resume, let's spend a few hours sharing some of the inside secrets of writing and distributing some of the most powerful communications for accessing today's rapidly changing job market.

You Can Do Better

When did you last write a dynamite resume? How important was the selection of language to summarize your experience? How well did you write, produce, distribute, and follow up your resume? Who evaluated it and how? Did it immediately grab the attention of employers who called you for interviews? Would it also do well in the face of today's electronic scanning technology? How well did it stand out from the crowd of other resumes? Did it clearly communicate your qualifications and future performance to potential employers? What did it really say about you as both a professional and a person? Did it become your ticket to interviews or did it dash your job search expectations?

Regardless of what resulted from your previous resume efforts, let's turn to your future success, which should include dynamite resumes.

Abused and Misused Communication

Resumes are some of the most abused and misused forms of job search communication. Not knowing how to best communicate their qualifications to employers, many job seekers go through a mindless ritual of writing uninspired documents that primarily outline their work history rather than provide evidence for predicting their future performance and potential value to employers. Lacking a clear sense of purpose, they fail to properly connect their resume writing activities to their larger job search tasks. Rather than communicate their future performance and potential value to employers, they summarize their past employment history which may be relevant to employers' immediate and future needs.

> *Dynamite resumes grab the attention of potential employers who, in turn, invite you to job interviews.*

But writing a resume is really the easiest thing to do. Once producing it, many job seekers don't know how to best manage their resume in relation to potential employers. Most just send it by "snail mail" or e-mail, as if job interviews and offers are primarily a function of increased direct-mail activity. Preoccupied with the magic of writing right, few job seekers engage in effective resume **distribution and follow-up** activities – the keys for getting your resume read and responded to. Instead, they circulate a lot of pretty paper and electronic files that often go to all the wrong people and all the wrong places!

You can do better than most job seekers if you produce dynamite resumes. Unlike other resumes, dynamite resumes are designed with the larger job search in mind – they grab the attention of potential employers who, in turn, invite you to job interviews. You conduct dynamite interviews because your answers and questions are consistent with your resume. Your dynamite resume should:

■ Clearly communicate a sense of purpose, value, professionalism, competence, achievement, honesty, enthusiasm, and likability.

- Consistently observe the rules of good resume writing – demonstrate strong and compelling structure, form, grammar, word selection, categories, punctuation, spelling, inclusion/exclusion, length, and graphic design.

- Specifically link your interests, skills, abilities, and experience to the employer's present and future needs – it must be employer-centered rather than self-centered.

- Be produced in a professional manner, from paper stock to ink, to further communicate your professional image.

- Include the right combination of keywords used by search-and-retrieval software for scanning resumes electronically.

- Get distributed through the proper channels – mail, fax, and e-mail – and delivered to the right people – those who make the hiring decision.

- Regularly get followed up with telephone calls, letters, and interviews.

- Stand out from the crowd by clearly speaking to employers—*"Let's interview this candidate who appears to have what we need."*

Unlike many other resume books, which are primarily preoccupied with presenting proper resume form and content or presenting numerous examples, *Nail the Resume!* focuses on the whole communication process, from producing an outstanding written document (form, content, and production elements) to distributing and following up your resume with maximum impact. We focus on creating resumes that generate concrete **outcomes** – job interviews and offers.

A 30-Second Image Management Activity

Resume writing is first and foremost a 30-second image management activity designed to motivate an employer to take action that results in you being invited to a job interview. After all, it takes employers no more than 30 seconds to read and respond to your resume. If it is scanned and processed electronically, it takes only seconds for the computer software to match keywords on your resume to

> *Most employers spend no more than 30 seconds reading and responding to a resume.*

determine whether or not your resume should be selected for initial human consideration. Therefore, you must quickly **motivate** the reader to take action. Your resume must communicate your best professional image in writing **before** you can expect to be invited to a job interview. How and what you write, as well as which methods you choose to disseminate and follow up your message, will largely determine how effective you are in moving the employer to take action in reference to your qualifications.

Keep in mind that most employers are busy people who must make quick judgments about you based upon your written message. Neglect the importance of a 30-second dynamite resume and you will surely neglect one of the most important elements in a successful job search. Your resume will join the graveyard of so many other ineffective resumes.

You Are What You Write

When writing and sending resumes to strangers, you essentially are what you write. Your one- to two-page resume succinctly says a great deal about your professionalism, competence, and personality that goes beyond just documenting your work history, experience, and education. Your resume must have sufficient impact to move employers to contact you, interview you over the telephone, and hopefully invite you to a job interview that leads to a job offer and renewed career success. If you fail to properly write, produce, market, and follow up your resume, you will most likely conduct an ineffective job search.

> *To strangers reading your resume, you essentially are what you write.*

Resumes Really Do Count

Finding employment in today's job market poses numerous challenges for individuals who seek quality jobs that lead to good salaries, career advancement, and job security. The whole job finding process is chaotic, confusing, and frustrating. It requires a certain level of organization and communication skills aimed at identifying, contacting, and communicating your qualifications to potential employers. If you want to make this process best work for you, you must do more than just send resumes in response to vacancy announcements.

To be most successful in finding employment, you should develop a plan of action that involves these seven distinct yet interrelated job search steps:

1. Assess your skills
2. Develop a job/career objective
3. Conduct research on employers and organizations
4. Write resumes and letters

5. Network for information, advice, and referrals
6. Interview for jobs
7. Negotiate salary and terms of employment

As illustrated on page 10, each of these steps represents important **communication skills** involving you in contact with others. Assessing your skills (Step 1), for example, requires conducting a systematic assessment of what you do well and enjoy doing – your strengths or motivated abilities and skills (MAS) that become translated into your "qualifications" for employers. Conducting research on individuals, organizations, communities, and jobs (Step 4) requires the use of investigative skills commonly associated with library research. Networking and interviewing (Steps 5-6) primarily involve the use of conversational skills – small talk and structured question/answer dialogues – by telephone and in face-to-face encounters.

But it is the critical resume and letter writing step (4) that becomes the major communication challenge for most job seekers. If you lack strong writing skills, your job search is likely to flounder. Indeed, your ability to write dynamite resumes and cover letters largely determines how quickly you will transform your job search from the investigative stage (research) to employer contact stages (networking, interviewing, and salary negotiations). Your writing skills become the key element in moving your job search from the investigative stage to the final job offer stage. Writing demonstrates your competence.

> *In the job search, paper is the great equalizer. Most employers want to first see you on paper **before** meeting you in person.*

In the job search, paper is the great equalizer. Most employers want to first see you on paper **before** meeting you in person. You along with many others must pass the written test **before** you can be considered for the face-to-face test. Whether you like it or not, you must put your professionalism, competence, and personality in writing before your candidacy can be taken seriously. Thus, your writing activities may well become the most critical **transformation step** in your job search. They become your ticket to job interviews that lead to job offers and employment.

For some reason, job search writing skills usually receive little attention beyond the perfunctory *"you must write a resume and cover letter"* advisory. They also get dismissed as unimportant in a society that supposedly places its greatest value on telecommunication and interpersonal skills. Indeed, during the past two decades many career advisors have emphasized networking as the key to getting a job; writing resumes and letters are considered relatively unimportant job search skills. Some even advise job seekers to dispense with the resume altogether and, instead, rely on cold-calling telephone techniques and "showing up" networking strategies.

Job Search Steps and Stages

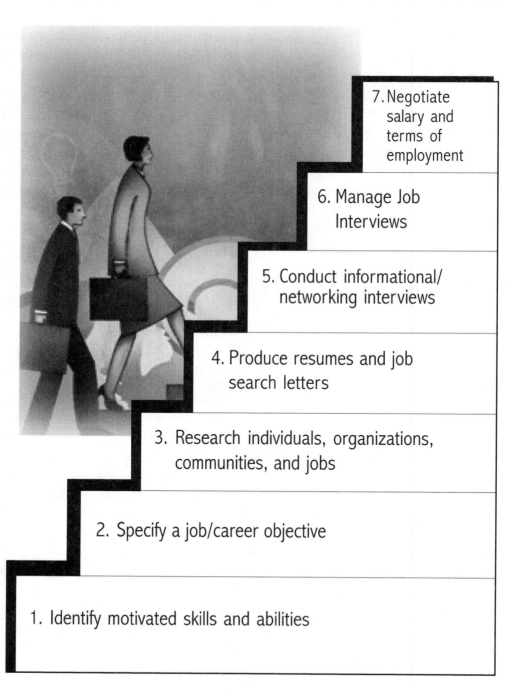

7. Negotiate salary and terms of employment

6. Manage Job Interviews

5. Conduct informational/ networking interviews

4. Produce resumes and job search letters

3. Research individuals, organizations, communities, and jobs

2. Specify a job/career objective

1. Identify motivated skills and abilities

But such advice is misplaced and misses one of the most important points in the job search. Resumes are an **accepted** means of communicating qualifications to employers; they are becoming essential requirements for today's new electronic recruitment operations. Employers expect to receive well-crafted resumes that represent the best professional efforts of candidates. The problem is that hiring officials receive so many poorly written and distributed resumes. Indeed, many candidates might be better off not writing a resume given the weaknesses they demonstrate by producing poorly constructed documents. Failure to develop a well-crafted resume will disqualify you for many jobs.

Resumes do not substitute for other equally important communication activities, but they do play a critical transformational role in your job search. They must be carefully linked to other key job search activities, especially networking and informational interviews which function as important **methods for disseminating resumes**.

You simply must write a resume if you are to be taken seriously in today's job market. And you will be taken most seriously if you write and disseminate dynamite resumes.

While some individuals do get interviews without writing resumes, you can do much better if you take the time and effort to develop a well-crafted resume and disseminate it properly. It should be designed for both electronic and human consumption. Your resume should focus on the employer's needs. It should demonstrate your professionalism, competence, and personality. Without an effective resume, your job search will have a limited impact on potential employers.

Assess and Improve Your Effectiveness

Just how effective are you in opening the doors of potential employers? In addition to writing a dynamite resume, what should you be doing to improve the effectiveness of job search?

Let's begin by identifying your level of job search information, skills, and strategies as well as those you need to develop and improve. You can do this by completing the following "job search competencies" exercise:

INSTRUCTIONS: Respond to each statement by circling which number at the right best represents your situation.

SCALE: 1 = Strongly agree 4 = Disagree
2 = Agree 5 = Strongly disagree
3 = Maybe, not certain

1. I know what motivates me to excel at work.   1   2   3   4   5

2. I can identify my strongest abilities and skills.   1   2   3   4   5

3. I have seven major achievements that clarify a
   pattern of interests and abilities that are relevant
   to my job and career.   1   2   3   4   5

4. I know what I both like and dislike in work.   1   2   3   4   5

5. I know what I want to do during the next 10 years.   1   2   3   4   5

6. I have a well defined career objective that focuses my
   job search on particular organizations and employers.   1   2   3   4   5

7. I know what skills I can offer employers in different
   occupations.   1   2   3   4   5

8. I know what skills employers most seek in candidates.   1   2   3   4   5

9. I can clearly explain to employers what I do well and
   enjoy doing.   1   2   3   4   5

10. I can specify why employers should hire me.   1   2   3   4   5

11. I can gain the support of family and friends for making
    a job or career change.   1   2   3   4   5

12. I can find 10 to 20 hours a week to conduct a part-time
    job search.   1   2   3   4   5

13. I have the financial ability to sustain a three-month
    job search.   1   2   3   4   5

14. I can conduct library and Internet research on
    different occupations, employers, organizations, and
    communities.   1   2   3   4   5

15. I can write different types of effective resumes and job
    search/thank you letters.   1   2   3   4   5

16. I can produce and distribute resumes and letters to the
    right people.   1   2   3   4   5

17. I can list my major accomplishments in action terms.   1   2   3   4   5

18. I can identify and target employers I want to interview.   1   2   3   4   5

19. I know how to use the Internet to conduct employment
    research and network.   1   2   3   4   5

20. I know which websites are best for posting my resumes
    and browsing job postings.   1   2   3   4   5

21. I know how much time I should spend conducting an
    online job search.   1   2   3   4   5

22. I can develop a job referral network. 1 2 3 4 5

23. I can persuade others to join in forming a job search support group. 1 2 3 4 5

24. I can prospect for job leads. 1 2 3 4 5

25. I can use the telephone to develop prospects and get referrals and interviews. 1 2 3 4 5

26. I can plan and implement an effective direct-mail job search campaign. 1 2 3 4 5

27. I can persuade employers to interview me. 1 2 3 4 5

28. I have a list of at least 10 employer-centered questions I need to ask during interviews. 1 2 3 4 5

29. I know the best time to talk about salary with a prospective employer. 1 2 3 4 5

30. I know what I want to do with my life over the next 10 years. 1 2 3 4 5

31. I have a clear pattern of accomplishments which I can explain to employers with examples. 1 2 3 4 5

32. I have little difficulty in making cold calls and striking up conversations with strangers. 1 2 3 4 5

33. I usually take responsibility for my own actions rather than blame other people for my situation or circumstance. 1 2 3 4 5

34. I can generate at least one job interview for every 10 job search contacts I make. 1 2 3 4 5

35. I can follow up on job interviews. 1 2 3 4 5

36. I can negotiate a salary 10-20% above what an employer initially offers. 1 2 3 4 5

37. I can persuade an employer to renegotiate my salary after six months on the job. 1 2 3 4 5

38. I can create a position for myself in an organization. 1 2 3 4 5

TOTAL

Calculate your overall potential job search effectiveness by adding the numbers you circled for a composite score. If your total is more than 90 points, you need to work on developing your job search skills. How you scored each item will indicate to what degree you need to work on improving specific skills. If your score is under 60 points, you are well on your way toward job search success! In either case, this book should help you better focus your job search around the critical writing skills necessary for communicating your qualifications to employers. Other books, the best of which we summarize at the end of this book, can assist you with many other important aspects of your job search.

Get Taken Seriously By Employers

The whole purpose of a job search is to get taken seriously by strangers who have the power to hire you. Your goal is to both discover and land a job you really want. You do this by locating potential employers and then persuading them to talk to you by telephone and in person about your interests and qualifications. In other words, you must sell yourself to people you don't know and who don't know you.

The major weakness of job seekers is their inability to keep focused on their **purpose**.

Being a stranger to most employers, you initially communicate your interests and qualifications on paper in the form of resumes and cover letters. How well you construct these documents will largely determine whether or not you will proceed to the next stage – the job interview.

The major weakness of job seekers is their inability to keep focused on their **purpose**. Engaging in a great deal of wishful thinking, they fail to organize their job search in a purposeful manner. They do silly things, ask dumb questions, and generally waste a great deal of time and money on needless activities. They frustrate themselves by going down the same dead-end roads. Worst of all, they turn off employers by demonstrating poor communication skills – both written and oral.

The average job seeker often wanders aimlessly in the job market, as if finding a job were an ancient form of alchemy. Preoccupied with job search **techniques**, they lack an overall **purpose and strategy** that would give meaning and direction to discrete job search activities. They often engage in random and time-consuming activities that have little or no payoff. Participating in a highly ego-involved activity, they quickly lose sight of what's really important to conducting a successful job search – responding to the needs of employers. Not surprisingly, they aren't taken seriously by employers because they don't take themselves and employers seriously enough to organize their activities around key qualifications that persuade employers to invite them to job interviews. This should not happen to you.

The following pages are designed to increase your power to get taken seriously by employers. Individual chapters provide a quick primer on the key principles involved in writing, producing, evaluating, distributing, and following up your own dynamite resume. It also presents resume examples that illustrate the key principles involved in writing dynamite resumes.

Since the examples in this book are presented to illustrate important resume writing **principles**, they should not be copied nor edited. As you will discover in the following pages, it is extremely important that you create your own resumes that express the "unique you" rather than send "canned" resumes to potential employers.

In the end, our goal is to improve your **communication effectiveness** in the job search. On completing this book, you should be able to write dynamite resumes that result in many more invitations to job interviews.

Do What's Expected and Produces Results

Based on experience, we assume most employers do indeed expect to receive well-crafted resumes. We proceed on the assumption that resumes are one of the most important elements in the job search. Moreover, they are becoming more important than ever given the increased use of resume databases and electronic scanning technology for screening candidates.

The old interview adage that *"you never have a second chance to make a good first impression"* is equally valid for the resume. For it is usually the resume and cover letter rather than your telephone voice or appearance that first introduces you to a prospective employer. Your resume tells who you are and why an employer should want to spend valuable time meeting you in person. It invites the reader to focus attention on your key qualifications in relation to the employer's needs. It enables you to set an agenda for further exploring your interests and qualifications with employers.

Once you discover the importance of writing dynamite resumes, you will never again produce other types of resumes. Your dynamite resume will have the power to move you from stranger to interviewee to employee. It will open many more doors to job interviews and offers!

Choose the Right Resources

If this book is your first job search guide, you'll be surprised to discover many additional print and online resources that can assist you in finding employment. This book is primarily concerned with communicating your qualifications in writing to employers who, in turn, will be sufficiently motivated to invite you to face-to-face job interviews.

Several of our other books deal with the key steps in the job search process as illustrated on page 10:

America's Top Internet Job Sites
Change Your Job Change Your Life
Discover the Best Jobs for You
Dynamite Salary Negotiations
High Impact Resumes and Letters
I Want to Do Something Else, But I'm Not Sure What It Is
The Job Hunting Guide
Job Hunting Tips for People With Hot and Not-So-Hot Backgrounds
Interview for Success
Nail the Job Interview
Nail the Resume!
Salary Negotiation Tips for Professionals
Savvy Interviewing
The Savvy Networker
The Savvy Resume Writer

Others examine specific career fields and focus on the needs of special groups:

The Complete Guide to Public Employment
The Directory of Websites for International Jobs
The Ex-Offender's Job Hunting Guide
Find a Federal Job Fast
From Air Force Blue to Corporate Gray
From Army Green to Corporate Gray
From Navy Blue to Corporate Gray
Job Interviewing Tips for People With Not-So-Hot Backgrounds
Jobs and Careers With Nonprofit Organizations
Jobs for Travel Lovers
Military Resumes and Cover Letters

And still others focus on alternative jobs and careers:

The Best Jobs for the 21ˢᵗ Century
America's Top 100 Jobs for People Without a Four-Year Degree
America's Top Jobs for People Re-Entering the Workforce
Directory of Federal Jobs and Employers

These and hundreds of other career-related books and related resources are available from Impact Publications. For your convenience, many of these titles can be ordered by completing the form at the end of this book or visiting Impact's online bookstore: www.impactpublications.com.

Impact Publications also publishes several catalogs and specialty flyers describing additional job and career resources. To receive free copies of Impact's latest flyers, send a self-addressed stamped envelope (#10 business size) to:

IMPACT PUBLICATIONS
ATTN: Career Flyers
9104-N Manassas Drive
Manassas Park, VA 20111-5211

You also may want to visit Impact's website for a complete listing of career resources, where you also can download over 50 catalogs and specialty flyers: www.impact publications.com. The site contains some of the most important career and job finding resources available today, including many titles that are difficult, if not impossible, to find in bookstores and libraries. You will find everything from additional resume books, to books on self-assessment, cover letters, interviewing, government and international jobs, military, women, minorities, students, ex-offenders, and entrepreneurs. The catalogs and flyers also showcase many videos, DVDs, audio programs, computer software, posters, and games relating to jobs and careers. This is an excellent resource for keeping in touch with the major resources that can assist you with every stage of your job search.

For useful tips and advice on conducting an effective job search, visit our two related websites:

- **WinningTheJob.com**   www.winningthejob.com
- **ExOffenderReEntry.com**   www.exoffenderreentry.com

Individuals interested in international jobs, with an emphasis on VolunTourism, should visit our travel website:

- **Travel-Smarter.com**   www.travel-smarter.com

Put Power Into Your Job Search

You have the power within you to write a dynamite resume that persuades employers to invite you to job interviews. Whatever you do, make sure you acquire, use, and taste the fruits of this job search power. You should go into the job search equipped with the necessary knowledge and skills to be most effective in communicating your qualifications to employers.

As you will quickly discover, the job market is not a place to engage in wishful thinking. It's at times impersonal, frequently ego deflating, and often unforgiving of even simple errors. It requires clear thinking, strong organizational skills, and effective strategies for making the right moves with employers. Above all, it rewards individuals who follow through in implementing each job search step with enthusiasm, dogged persistence, and the ability to handle rejections.

In the following chapters we will address these and many other key principles for nailing your resume. May you soon discover this power and incorporate it in your own dynamite resume!

2

Resume Do's and Don'ts

I F YOU WANT YOUR JOB SEARCH to be most effective, you must follow several principles of effective resume writing, production, distribution, and follow-up. Equally important, you must regularly evaluate your progress and measure your performance. The principles range from obvious elementary concerns, such as correct spelling, punctuation, and placement of resume sections, to more complicated questions concerning when and how to best follow up a resume sent to an employer five days ago. Evaluation involves both conducting self-evaluations and using external evaluators.

Mystery and Ritual

But before putting the principles and evaluations into practice, we need to examine the very concept of a resume within the larger job search. What exactly are we talking about? What is this thing called a resume and how does it relate to other steps in your job search? How do prospective employers typically respond to resumes? What are some of the most common writing errors and mistakes one needs to avoid?

A great deal of mystery and confusion surrounds the purpose and content of resumes. Occupying a time-honored – almost ritual – place in the job finding process, resumes remain the single most important document you will write and distribute throughout your job search. Do it wrong and your job search will suffer accordingly. Do it right and your resume should open many doors that lead to job interviews and offers. The obvious choice is to write dynamite resumes for greater job search success.

Your Resume Has Purpose

What exactly is a resume? Is it a summary of your work history? An autobiography of your major accomplishments? A statement of your key qualifications? A catalog of your interests, skills, and experience? An introduction to your professional and personal style? Your business calling card? A jumble of keywords designed for scanners?

Let's be perfectly clear what we are talking about. A resume is all of these things and much more. It's an important **product** – produced in reference to your goals, skills, and experience – that furthers two important processes – "job search" for you and "screening/hiring" for employers. While it is a basic requirement when applying for many jobs, your resume plays a central role in directing you and your job search into productive information gathering and employment channels. It communicates your goals and capabilities to potential employers who must solve personnel problems – hire someone to perform particular functions and jobs. At the very least, a resume represents the "unique you" to others who may or may not know much about your particular mix of goals and capabilities. It may represent the potential solution to employers' problems.

> *When reviewing your resume, employers look for sound indicators of your probable future performance rather than a summary of your history.*

Better still, let's define a resume in terms of its **purpose** or **outcomes** for you in relation to hiring officials: **a resume is an advertisement for an interview**. In other words, the purpose of writing, producing, distributing, and following up a resume is to get job interviews – nothing more, nothing less. As such, your resume should follow certain principles of good advertising – grab attention, heighten interest, sell the product, and promote action.

Your ultimate purpose in writing a resume is to **get employers to take action** – conduct a telephone interview as well as invite you to the first of several job interviews which will eventually result in job offers and employment. Thus, the purpose of your resume is a specific outcome.

If you define a resume in these terms, then the internal resume structure and specific elements included or excluded – as well as the production, distribution, and follow-up methods you choose – become self-evident. You should only include those elements that will move employers to take action – contact you for an interview.

But what do employers want to see on your resume? They simply want to see sound indicators of your **probable future performance** rather than a summary of your professional and personal history. They want to know if you have a high probability of **adding value** to their operations. Adding value can have several meanings depending on the employment situation – increase market shares, improve profitability, solve specific problems, save money, streamline operations, become more competitive, introduce a new system for improving efficiency.

While the logic here is very simple, it nonetheless needs repeating throughout your job search. After all, many job seekers quickly lose this single-minded focus as they get further into their job search and become distracted by other issues, concerns, and a great deal of wishful thinking.

Since employers will be hiring your future, they are more concerned with your future performance – *"What can you do for me?"* – rather than the "facts" about your past – *"Where did you go to school and what did you do during the summer of 2000?"* Therefore, you must present your past in such a manner that it clearly indicates **patterns of performance** that are good predictors of your future value for your next employer.

Focus on Employers' Needs and Adding Value

Without this central guiding purpose in mind, your resume is likely to take on a different form, as well as move in different directions, than outlined in this book. You simply must keep your resume writing, production, distribution, and follow-up activities focused around your purpose – getting interviews. No distractions nor wishful thinking should interfere with this.

> *You must keep your resume writing, production, distribution, and follow-up activities focused around your purpose – getting interviews.*

Your approach, whether implicit or explicit, to resume writing says something about how you view yourself in relation to employers. It tells readers to what degree you are self-centered versus employer-centered. Are you oriented toward adding value to the employer's operations, or are you primarily concerned with acquiring more benefits for yourself? If you merely chronicle your past work history, you are likely to produce a self-centered resume that says little or nothing about your interests, skills, and abilities in relation to the employers' needs. You say nothing about adding value to the employers' operations. Resumes lacking a central focus or purpose are good candidates for mindless direct-mail approaches – broadcasting them to hundreds of employers who by chance might be interested in your history.

On the other hand, if you thoughtfully develop a job objective that is sensitive to employers' performance needs and then relate your patterns of skills and accomplishments to that objective, you should produce a dynamite resume. Such a resume transcends your history, as it clearly communicates your qualifications to employers and suggests that you know how to add more value to the employer's operations. This type of resume is **employer-centered**; it addresses employers' hiring needs. Such a resume is best targeted toward a select few employers who have job opportunities appropriate for your particular mix of interests, skills, and accomplishments. Therefore, the type of resume you produce tells employers a great deal about you both professionally and personally.

An intensely ego-involved activity, resume writing often goes awry as writers attempt to produce a document that they "feel good" about. Thinking a resume is analogous to an obituary, many writers believe their resume should summarize what's good about them. If the central purpose is to pile on a lot of good information about the individual's past, then a resume becomes a nonfocused dumping ground for a great deal of extraneous information employers neither need nor want. Such a resume may include lots of interesting facts that must be left to the interpretation of the reader who, by definition, is a very busy person; few such readers have the luxury of spending time analyzing and relating someone's chronicle of work history to their specific employment needs. Your resume may end up like most resumes – an uninspired listing of names, dates, and duties that are supposed to enlighten employers about your qualifications. While you may feel good writing such a document, don't expect employers to contact you for an interview. Your resume will likely end up in their "circular files."

Resumes lacking a central focus or purpose are good candidates for mindless direct-mail approaches.

Every time you make a decision concerning what to include or exclude in your resume, and how and when to produce, distribute, and follow up your job search communications, always keep in mind your purpose: **you are advertising yourself for a job interview**. Such a single-minded purpose will serve you well. It will automatically answer many questions you may have about the details of writing, producing, distributing, and following up your resume. It will tell you what is and is not important in the whole resume writing, production, distribution, and follow-up process.

Resume Myths and Realities

Numerous myths about finding employment and contacting employers lead individuals down the wrong resume writing paths. Keep these 11 myths and corresponding realities in mind when writing your resume:

MYTH 1:   **The resume is the key to getting a job.**

REALITY: There is nothing magical about resumes. Indeed, there are many keys to getting a job, from being in the right place at the right time, having a good connection, to conducting an excellent job interview. The resume is only one step, albeit an important one, in the job finding process. A well written application or "T" letter (see our companion *Nail the Cover Letter!*) can substitute for a resume. Other steps depend on well-crafted resumes and cover letters. Remember, your resume is an advertisement for a job interview. Employers do not hire individuals because of the content or quality of their resume; the resume only gets them invited to job interviews. The job interview is the real key to getting the job; it is the prerequisite step for a job offer and employment contract. But you must first communicate your qualifications to employers through the medium of a top quality resume in order to get the job interview.

MYTH 2: **The resume is not as important to getting a job as other job search activities, such as networking and informational interviews.**

REALITY: Resumes still remain one of the most important written documents you will produce during your job search. If you expect to be interviewed for jobs, you simply must produce a well-crafted resume that clearly communicates your qualifications to employers. Whether you like it or not, employers want to see you on paper **before** talking to you over the telephone or seeing you in person. And they want to see a top quality resume – an attractive, error-free document that **represents your best self**. You should pay particular attention to the details and exacting quality required in producing a first-rate resume. Errors, however minor, can quickly eliminate you from consideration. Without such an error-free resume, you seriously limit your chances of getting job interviews. And without job interviews, you won't get job offers.

MYTH 3: **A resume should primarily document your work history for employers.**

REALITY: A resume should communicate to employers how you will **add value** to their operations. You include work history on a resume as evidence that you have a track record of adding value to other employers' operations. The assumption for the reader is that you will add similar value to his or her operations. Be sure you always describe your work history or experience in such value-added terms.

MYTH 4: **Paper resumes are obsolete in today's new high-tech job market. Employment websites and employers primarily want to receive electronic and e-mailed resumes.**

REALITY: You need to produce **both** a paper and an electronic resume. You are well advised to start by producing a paper resume and then create an electronic resume. Electronic and e-mailed resumes are designed by job seekers for high speed distribution to resume databases and employer. They enable employers to quickly store, retrieve, and analyze large numbers of resumes. Paper resumes still play an important role in the job search. Many small businesses prefer working with paper resumes. Job seekers need paper resumes when networking for information, advice, and referrals; when attending job fairs; and when interviewing for a job.

MYTH 5: **It's best to send your resume to hundreds of employers rather than to just a few.**

REALITY: Power in the job search comes from selective targeting – not through numbers. It comes from making a few contacts with the right people who have a specific **need** for your particular mix of interests, skills, and qualifications. While it may be comforting to think you are making progress with your job search by sending resumes to hundreds of potential employers, in reality you create an illusion of progress that will ultimately disappoint you; few people will seriously read an unsolicited resume and thus consider you for employment when they have no need. A resume broadcast or "shotgun" approach to finding a job indicates a failure to seriously focus your job search around the **needs** of specific employers. Your time, effort, and money will be better spent in marketing your resume in conjunction with other effective job search activities – networking and informational interviews. These activities force you to concentrate on specific employers who would be most interested in your interests, skills, and qualifications. These individuals have a need that will most likely coincide with both your resume and job search timing.

MYTH 6: **It's not necessary to include an objective on your resume.**

REALITY: Without an objective your resume will lack a central focus from which to relate all other elements in your resume. An objective gives your resume organization and coherence. It tells potential employers that you are a purposeful individual – you have specific job and career goals in mind that are directly related to your past pattern of interests, skills, and experience as documented in the remainder of your resume. If properly stated, your objective will become the most powerful and effective statement on your resume. Without an objective, you force the employer to "interpret" your resume. He or she must analyze the discrete elements in each resume category and draw conclusions about your future capabilities which may or may not be valid. You force the person to engage in what may be a difficult analytical task, depending on their analytic capabilities. Therefore, it is to your advantage to control the flow and interpretation of your qualifications and capabilities by stating a clear employer-oriented objective. While you can state an objective in your cover letter, it is best to put your objective at the very beginning of your resume. After all, letters do get detached from resumes.

On the other hand, many people prefer excluding an objective because it tends to lock them into a particular type of job; they want to be flexible. Such people demonstrate a cardinal job search sin – they really don't know what they want to do; they tend to communicate their lack of focus in their resume as well as in other job search activities. They are more concerned with fitting into a job (*"Where are the jobs?"*) than with finding a job fit for them (*"Is this job right for me?"*).

One of the major reasons for stating an objective is this statistic from recent surveys of employers: nearly 70 percent indicate they want to see objectives on resumes.

MYTH 7:   **The best type of resume outlines employment history by job titles, responsibilities, and inclusive employment dates.**

REALITY: This type of resume, the traditional chronological or "obituary" resume, may or may not be good for you. It's filled with historical "what" information – what work you did, in what organizations, over what period of time. Such resumes tell employers little about what it is you can do for them in the future. You should choose a resume format that clearly communicates your major strengths – not your historical background – to employers. Those strengths should be formulated as **patterns of performance** in relation to your goals and skills as well as the employer's needs. Your choice of formats include variations of the chronological, functional, and combination resumes – each offering different advantages and disadvantages, depending on your goals.

MYTH 8: **Employers appreciate lengthy detailed resumes because they give them more complete information for screening candidates than shorter resumes.**

REALITY: Employers prefer receiving short, succinct one- or two-page resumes. Longer resumes lose their interest and attention. Such resumes usually lack a focus, are filled with extraneous information, need editing, and are oriented toward your past rather than the employer's future. If you know how to write a dynamite resume, you can put all of your capabilities into a one- to two-page format. These resumes only include enough information to persuade employers to contact you for an interview. Like good advertisements, they generate enough interest so the reader will contact you for more information (job interview) before investing in the product (job offer).

MYTH 9: **It's okay to put salary expectations and references on your resume.**

REALITY: Two of the worst things you can do is to include salary information (history or expectations) and list your references on your resume. Remember, the purpose of your resume is to get an interview – nothing more, nothing less. Only during the interview – and preferably toward the end – should you discuss salary and share information on references. And before you discuss salary, you want to demonstrate your **value** to hiring officials as well as learn about the **worth** of the position. Only **after** you make your impression, gather information on the job, and receive a job offer can you realistically talk about – and negotiate – salary. You cannot do this if you prematurely mention salary on your resume. A similar principle applies to references. Never put references on a resume. The closest you should ever get to mentioning references is a simple statement appearing at the end of your resume:

"References available upon request"

You want to control your references for the interview. You should take a list of references appropriate for the position you will interview for with you to the interview. If you put references on your resume, the employer might call someone who has no idea you are applying for a particular job. The conversation could be embarrassing. As a simple courtesy, you need to ask your references ahead of time whether you may use their name as a reference. At that point, you want to brief your reference on the position you seek, explaining why you feel you should be selected by focusing on your goals and strengths in relation to the position. Give this person information that will support your candidacy. Surprisingly, though, few employers actually follow through by contacting stated references! This is perhaps one reason they often make poor hiring decisions. Many employers are surprised to later discover a problem employee had similar problems in previous jobs.

MYTH 10:   **You should not include your hobbies nor any personal statements on a your resume.**

REALITY: In general this is true. However, there are exceptions which would challenge this rule as a myth. If you have a hobby or a personal statement that can strengthen your objective in relation to the employer's needs, consider including it on your resume. For example, if a job calls for someone who is outgoing and energetic, you would not want to include a hobby or personal statement that indicates that you are a very private and sedentary person, such as "enjoy reading and writing" or "collect stamps." But "enjoy organizing community fund drives" and "compete in the Boston Marathon" might be very appropriate statements for your resume. Such statements further emphasize the "unique you" in relation to your capabilities, the requirements for the position, and the employer's needs.

MYTH 11:   **You should try to get as much as possible on each page of your resume.**

REALITY: Each page of your resume should be appealing to the eye. It should make an immediate favorable impression, be inviting and easy to read, and look professional. You achieve these qualities by using a variety of layout, type style, highlighting, and emphasizing techniques. When formatting each section of your resume, be sure to make generous use of white space. Bullet, underline, or bold items for emphasis. If you try to cram too much on each page, your resume will look cluttered and uninviting. You may make just the opposite impression you thought you were making in an ostensibly well organized resume – you look disorganized!

MYTH 12:   **Once you send a resume to an employer, there is not much you can do except wait for a reply.**

REALITY: Waiting for potential employers to contact you is not a good job search strategy. Sending a resume to a potential employer is only the first step in connecting with a potential job. You should always **follow up** your resume with a phone call, preferably within seven days, to answer questions, conduct a telephone interview, get invited to a job interview, or acquire additional information, advice, and referrals. Without this follow-up action, your resume is likely to get lost amongst many other resumes that compete for the reader's attention.

Taken together, these myths and realities emphasize one overriding concern when writing a resume:

> The key to effective resume writing is to give the reader, within the space of one to two pages, just enough interesting information about your past performance and future capabilities so he or she will get sufficiently excited to contact you for a job interview.

It is during the interview, rather than on your resume, that you will provide detailed answers to the most important questions concerning the job. Those questions are determined by both the interviewer and you during the job interview. Don't prematurely eliminate yourself from consideration by including too much or too little information, or being too boastful or too negative, on your resume before you get to the interview stage. In this sense, your resume becomes an important "window of opportunity" to get invited to job interviews that hopefully will translate into good job offers.

Common Writing Errors and Mistakes

A resume must first get written and written well. And it is at the initial writing stage that many deadly errors and mistakes get made. The most common errors occur when writers fail to keep the purpose of their resume in mind.

Most errors kill a resume even before it gets fully read. At best these errors leave negative impressions that are difficult to overcome at this or any other point in the hiring process. Remember, hiring officials have two major inclusion/exclusion concerns in mind when reading your resume:

- They are looking for excuses to eliminate you from further consideration.

- They are looking for evidence to consider you for a job interview – how much value you will add to their operations.

Every time you make an error, you provide supports for eliminating you from further consideration. Concentrate, instead, on providing **supports** for being considered for a job interview.

Clearly communicate a "pattern of performance" related to the employer's hiring needs.

Make sure your resume is not "dead on arrival." To ensure against this, avoid the most common writing errors reported by employers who regularly review resumes:

1. Not related to the reader's interests or needs.

2. Fails to represent the real candidate.

3. Unrelated to the position in question.

4. Too long or too short.

5. Unattractive with a poorly designed format, small type style, and crowded copy.

Keep your resume short and succinct – one to two pages with crisp language rich in verbs and nouns.

6. Misspellings, poor grammar, wordiness, and repetition.

7. Punctuation errors.

8. Lengthy phrases, long sentences, and awkward paragraphs.

9. Slick, amateurish, or "gimmicky" – appears over-produced.

10. Boastful, egocentric, and aggressive.

11. Dishonest, untrustworthy, or suspicious information.

12. Missing critical categories, such as experience, skills, and education.

13. Unexplained time gaps between jobs.

14. Difficult to interpret because of poor organization and lack of focus – uncertain what the person has done or can do.

15. Too many jobs in a short period of time – a job hopper with little evidence of career advancement.

> *Avoid the use of "canned" resume language or anything that suggests you have not produced your own resume.*

16. No evidence of past accomplishments or a pattern of performance from which to predict future performance; primarily focuses on formal duties and responsibilities that came with previous jobs.

17. Lacks credibility and content – includes much fluff and "canned" resume language.

18. States a strange, unclear, or vague objective.

19. Appears over-qualified or under-qualified for the position.

20. Includes distracting personal information that does not enhance the resume nor the candidate.

> *Include all relevant categories; avoid irrelevant information that distracts from your central message.*

21. Fails to include critical contact information (telephone number and e-mail address) and uses an anonymous address (P.O. Box number).

22. Uses jargon and abbreviations unfamiliar to the reader.

23. Embellishes name with formal titles, middle names, and nicknames which makes the candidate seem odd or somewhat strange.

24. Repeatedly refers to "I" and appears self-centered.

25. Includes obvious self-serving references that raise credibility questions.

26. Sloppy, with handwritten corrections – crosses out "married" and writes "single"!

27. Includes red flag information such as being incarcerated, fired, lawsuits or claims, health or performance problems, or stating salary figures, including salary requirements, that may be too high or too low.

This listing of writing errors emphasizes how important **both** form and content are when writing a resume with purpose. You must select an important form, arrange each element in an attractive manner, and provide the necessary substance to grab the attention of the reader and move him or her to action. And all these elements of good resume writing must be related to the needs of your audience. If not, you may quickly kill your resume by committing some of these deadly errors.

Remember, hiring officials are busy people who only devote a few seconds to reading your resume. They are seasoned at identifying errors that will effectively remove you from further consideration. They want to see you error-free on paper so they can concentrate on what they most need to do – evaluate your qualifications.

Production, Distribution, and Follow-Up Errors

Employers also report encountering several of these production, distribution, and follow-up errors:

1. Poorly typed and reproduced – hard to read.

2. Produced on odd-sized paper.

3. Printed on poor quality paper or on extremely thin or thick paper.

4. Soiled with coffee stains, fingerprints, or ink marks.

5. Sent to the wrong person or department.

6. Mailed, faxed, or e-mailed to "To Whom It May Concern" or "Dear Sir."

7. E-mailed as an attachment which could have a virus if opened.

8. Enclosed in a tiny envelope that requires the resume to be unfolded and flattened several times.

9. Arrived without proper postage – the employer gets to pay the extra!

10. Sent the resume and letter by the slowest postage rate possible.

11. Envelope double-sealed with tape and is indestructible – nearly impossible to open by conventional means!

12. Back of envelope includes a handwritten note stating that something is missing on the resume, such as a telephone number or e-mail address.

13. Resume taped to the inside of the envelope, an old European habit practiced by paranoid letter writers. Need to destroy the envelope and perhaps also the resume to get it out of the envelope.

14. Accompanied by extraneous or inappropriate enclosures which were not requested, such as copies of self-serving letters or recommendations, transcripts, or samples of work.

15. Arrived too late for consideration.

16. Came without a cover letter.

17. Cover letter repeats what's on the resume – does not command attention nor move the reader to action.

18. Sent the same or different versions of the resume to the same person as a seemingly clever follow-up method.

19. Follow-up call made too soon – before the resume and letter arrive!

20. Follow-up call is too aggressive or the candidate appears too "hungry" for the position – appears needy or greedy.

Since the resume is so important to getting a job interview, make sure your resume is error free. Spend sufficient time crafting a resume that shouts loud and clear that you are someone who should be interviewed for a position.

Qualities of Effective Resumes

A well-crafted resume that is properly produced, distributed, and followed up expresses many important professional and personal qualities employers seek in candidates:

- Your sense of **self-esteem and purpose**.

- Your **level of literacy**.

- Your **ability to conceptualize and analyze** your own interests, skills, and abilities in relation to the employer's needs.

- Your **patterns of performance and value-added behavior**.

- Your ability to clearly communicate **who you are** and **what you want to do** rather than who you have been and what you have done.

- Your **view of the employer** – how important he or she is in relation to your interests, skills, and abilities. Are you self-centered?

These qualities are expressed through certain resume principles which you can learn and apply to most employment situations. Your resume should:

- Immediately impress the reader.

- Be visually appealing and easy to -read.

- Indicate your career aspirations and goals.

- Focus on your value in relation to employers' needs.

- Communicate your job-related **abilities** and **patterns of performance** – not past or present job duties and responsibilities.

- Stress your productivity – potential to solve employers' problems.

- Communicate that you are a responsible and purposeful person who gets things done.

- Use a language that clearly communicates skills required by the employer – a "keyword" language that is also sensitive to resume scanning technology.

If you keep these general principles in mind, you should be able to produce a dynamite resume that will grab the attention of employers who will be moved to action – invite you to a job interview. To do less is to communicate the wrong messages to employers – that you may lack purpose, literacy, good judgment, and a pattern of performance.

Always Remember Your Audience and Purpose

When deciding what to include in your resume, always remember these important writing guidelines for creating a dynamite resume:

1. View your resume as your personal **advertisement**.

2. Focus on the purpose of your resume, which is to get a **job interview**.

3. Take the offensive by developing a resume that **structures the reader's thinking** around your objective, qualifications, strengths, and projections of future performance.

4. Make your resume **generate positive thinking** rather than raise negative questions or confuse readers.

5. Focus your resume on the **needs of your audience**.

6. Communicate clearly what it is you **want to do and can do** for the reader.

7. Always be **honest** without being stupid. Stress your positives; never volunteer nor confess your negatives.

If you keep these basic purposes and principles in mind, you should produce a dynamite resume as well as conduct a job search that is both purposeful and positive. Your resume should stand out above the crowd as you clearly communicate your qualifications to employers.

In the next two chapters we'll take an in-depth look at these and several other principles relevant to the whole spectrum of resume activities – writing, producing, distributing, following up, and evaluating.

3

68 Writing, Production, Distribution, and Follow-Up Principles

EFFECTIVE RESUMES FOLLOW certain writing, production, distribution, and follow-up principles that are specific to the resume medium and relevant to the job search. These principles should be incorporated into every stage of the resume writing, production, distribution, and follow-up process. If you neglect to incorporate these resume principles, your job search will most likely fail to reach its full potential.

Writing

Overall Strategy

1. **Do first things first by making sure your resume represents the "unique you":** Avoid creatively plagiarizing resumes written by others, however tempting and easy to do. A widely abused approach to resume writing, creative plagiarizing occurs when someone decides to take shortcuts by writing their resume in reference to so-called "outstanding resume examples"; they basically edit the examples by substituting information on themselves for what appears in the example. The result is a resume filled with a great deal of "canned" resume language that may be unrelated to the individual's goals, skills, and experience.

The best resumes are those based on a thorough self-assessment of your interests, skills, and abilities which, in turn, is the **foundation** for stating a powerful objective, shaping information in each category, and selecting proper resume language. What, for example, do you want to do before you die? Answering this question in detail will tell you a great deal about your values and goals in relation to your career objectives. You may want to incorporate this information into your resume. Do first things first by starting with a self-assessment that will help you build each section of your resume. Numerous exercises and instruments are available for conducting your own self-directed assessment of your interests, skills, and abilities. These are outlined in several other career planning and job search books we and others have written. Several are identified in the "Career Resources" section at the very end of this book. Professional testing centers and career counselors also administer a variety

> *Avoid creatively plagiarizing resumes written by others, however tempting and easy to do. Such a resume will not accurately reflect your qualifications.*

of useful self-assessment devices. Information on such services is readily available through your local community college, adult education programs, or employment services office. For a review of various approaches and recommended self-assessment resources, see our companion volumes: *I Want to Do Something Else, But I'm Not Sure What It Is* and *Job Hunting Tips for People With Hot and Not-So-Hot Backgrounds* (Impact Publications, 2005).

2. **Develop a plan of action relevant to your overall job search:** Make sure your resume reflects your career goals and is part of your larger job search plan. In addition to incorporating self-assessment data, it should be developed with specific goals in mind, based on research, and related to networking and informational interviewing activities. Begin by asking yourself the broader *"What do I want to do with this resume?"* question about the purpose of your resume rather than narrow your focus on the traditional *"What should I include on my resume?"* question.

Structure and Organization

3. **Select an appropriate resume format that best communicates your goals, skills, experience, and probable future performance to employers:** Resume format determines how you organize the infor-

mation categories for communicating your qualifications to employers. It **structures the reader's thinking** about your goals, strengths, and probable future performance. If, for example, your basic organization principle is chronology (dates you worked for different employers), then you want employers to think of your qualifications in historical terms and thus deduce future performance based upon an analysis of performance **patterns** evidenced in your work history. If your basic organizational principle is skills, then you want employers to think of you in achievement terms.

You essentially have three formats from which to choose: chronological, functional, or combination. A **chronological resume** – often referred to as an "obituary resume" – is the most popular resume format but it is by no means the most appropriate. Primarily summarizing work history, this resume lists dates and names of employers first and your duties and responsibilities second. It often includes a great deal of extraneous information. In its worst form – the traditional chronological resume – it tells employers little or nothing about what you want to do, can do, and will do for them. In its best form – the improved chronological resume – it communicates your purpose, past achievements, and probable future performance to employers. It includes an objective which relates to other elements in the resume. The work experience section includes names and addresses of former employers followed by a brief description of accomplishments, skills, and responsibilities rather than formal duties and responsibilities; inclusive employment dates appear at the end. Chronological resumes should be used by individuals who have a progressive record of work experience and who wish to advance within an occupational field. One major advantage of these resumes is that they include the "beef" employers wish to see.

Functional resumes emphasize patterns of skills and accomplishments rather than job titles, employers, and inclusive employment dates. These resumes should be used by individuals making a significant career change, first entering the workforce, or re-entering the job market after a lengthy absence. Since many employers still look for names, dates, and direct work experience – the so-called "beef" – this type of resume often disappoints employers who are looking for more substantive information relating to "experience" and "qualifications." You should use a functional resume only if your past work experience does not clearly support your objective. Otherwise, this can be a very weak resume that may raise negative questions, which will disqualify you from consideration.

Combination resumes combine the best elements of chronological and functional resumes. They stress patterns of accomplishments and skills as well as include work history. Work history appears as a separate section immediately following the presentation of accomplishments and skills in an

"Areas of Effectiveness" or "Experience" section. This is the perfect resume for individuals with work experience who wish to change to a job in a related career field.

Examples of these different types of resumes are included in the remainder of this book. They are illustrated in the resume transformations found in Chapter 5.

4. **Include all essential information categories in the proper order.** What you should or should not include in your resume depends on your particular goals as well as your situation and the needs of your audience. When deciding on what to include or exclude on your resume, always focus on the **needs** of the employer. What does he or she want or need to know about you? The most important information relates to your **future performance**, which is normally determined by assessing your **past patterns of performance** ("experience" presented as "accomplishments," "outcomes," "benefits," or "performance"). At the very least your resume should include the following five categories of information which help provide answers to five major questions:

Information category	Relevant question
Contact information	Who you are/how to contact you.
Objective	What you **want to do**.
Experience	What you **can do** – your patterns of skills and accomplishments.
Work history	What you **have done**.
Educational background	What you **may have learned** and what you might be capable of learning in the future.

Taken together, these information categories and questions provide evidence for answering a sixth unanswered question about future performance:

What will you **most likely do** in the future?

Finding answers to this implicit question is the employer's ultimate goal in the hiring process. Employers must deduce the answer from examining what you said in each category of your one- to two-page resume. Employers must make an important **judgment** about your future performance **with them** by carefully considering what you want to do (your objective), what you can do (your experience), and what you have done and learned (your work history and education). A resume incorporating only these five categories of information should be sufficiently powerful to answer most employers' critical questions.

Other information categories often found on resumes include:

- Military experience
- Community involvement
- Professional affiliations
- Special skills
- Interests and activities
- Personal statement

5. **Sequence the categories according to the principle "What's most important to both you and the employer should always appear first":** You want your most important information and your strongest qualifications to always come first. Recent graduates with little or no relevant work experience, for example, should put education first since it's probably their most important "qualification" at this stage of their worklife. Your educational experience tells employers what you may have learned and thus provides some evidence of a certain knowledge, skill, and motivational base from which you possess a **capacity** to learn and grow within the employer's organization, i.e., you are functionally trainable. Your education also may include important work experience and achievements that indicate a pattern of future performance. Education should also come first in cases where education is an important **qualifying criterion**, especially for individuals with professional degrees and certifications: teachers, professors, doctors, nurses, lawyers, accountants, counselors. Recent graduates with little or no work experience may also want to put education first. The sequence of elements should be:

- Contact information
- Education
- Experience
- Work history

Students or others with little or no work history should omit the "Work history" category (putting little or no information here can be a negative) but convert "Experience" into a new and expanded category: "Areas of Effectiveness" or "Capabilities." This section becomes the central focus that defines a functional resume.

If you have a few or several years of direct work experience that supports your objective, and if education is not an important qualifying criteria, then your "Experience" section should immediately follow your objective. In this case "Education" moves toward the end of the resume:

- Contact information
- Experience
- Work history
- Education

Any other categories of information should appear either immediately after "Work history" or after "Education."

6. **Avoid including extraneous information which is unrelated to your objective or to the needs of employers:** However ego-involved you become in the resume writing process, always remember your goal and your audience. You are writing to a potential employer who by definition is a critical stranger who has specific needs and problems he hopes to solve through the hiring process. You are not writing to your mother, spouse, lover, friends, or former teachers. The following extraneous information often appears on resumes:

- **The word "Resume" at the top:** The reader already knows this is your resume, assuming you have chosen a standard resume format. It's not necessary to label it as such.

- **Present date:** This goes on your cover letter rather than your resume.

- **Picture:** Include a picture only if it is essential for a job, such as in modeling or theater. A picture may indeed be worth "a thousand words," but 990 of those words you don't need distracting from the central focus of your resume! Regardless of what you and your family may think about your picture – even those wonderful glamour shots – it's safe to assume that 50 percent of your readers will like and another 50 percent will dislike your picture. You don't need this type of distraction. Concentrate on the words and information **you** can control.

- **Race, religion, or political affiliation:** Include this information only if these are bona fide occupational qualifications, which they should not be, given current anti-discrimination and equal opportunity laws.

- **Salary history or requirements:** Never ever include salary history or expectations on your resume. If you are forced to submit this information at the initial screening stage, do so in your cover letter. Salary usually is negotiable. The salary question should only arise at the end of the interview or during the job offer – after you have had a chance to assess the worth of the job as well as demonstrate your value to hiring officials. When you include salary information on your resume, you prematurely give information on your value before you have a chance to demonstrate your value in job interviews.

- **References:** Always make your references "available upon request." You want to control the selection of references as well as alert your references that you are applying for a specific position and that they may be contacted.

- **Personal information such as height, weight, age, sex, marital status, health:** Few, if any, of these characteristics strengthen or relate to your objective. Many are negatives. Some could be positives, but only if you are a model, karate instructor, or applying for a position which views these as bona fide occupational qualifications.

- **Negative information:** Employment gaps, medical or mental health problems, criminal records, divorces, terminations, conflicting interests. There is absolutely no reason for you to volunteer potential negatives on your resume. This is the quickest way to get eliminated from consideration. Always remember that your resume should represent your very "best self." If hiring officials are interested in learning about your negatives, they will ask you and you should be prepared to respond in a positive manner – but only at the interview stage.

Since most of this extraneous information is a real negative in the eyes of employers – and has little to do with your supporting your objective as well as answering employers' six critical questions – avoid including this information on your resume.

Contact Information

7. **Put all essential contact information at the very top of your résumé as the header:** The very first element a reader should encounter on your resume is an attractive header. At the very minimum, this header should include your name, address, and phone, fax, or e-mail contact information displayed in one of several alternative layouts:

JAMES LAWSON
8891 S. Hayward Blvd.
Buffalo, NY 14444
Tel. 707-321-9721
LawsonJ@aol.com

| JAMES LAWSON | | LawsonJ@aol.com |
| 8891 S. Hayward Blvd. | Buffalo, NY 14444 | Tel. 707-321-9721 |

JAMES LAWSON

| 8891 S. Hayward Blvd. | | Tel. 707-321-9721 |
| Buffalo, NY 14444 | | LawsonJ@aol.com |

JAMES LAWSON
LawsonJ@aol.com

| 8891 S. Hayward Blvd. | Buffalo, NY 14444 | Tel. 707-321-9721 |

JAMES LAWSON
8891 S. Hayward Blvd.
Buffalo, NY 14444

| | Tel. 707-321-9721 | LawsonJ@aol.com |

We prefer capitalizing the name, although using upper and lower case letters is fine. We also prefer the first header because it introduces a very neat, clean, and eye-pleasing resume layout that is very inviting to readers who quickly survey resumes. We use this format extensively in the examples throughout this book.

8. **Include your complete contact information:** Employers want to know how to contact you immediately should they have any questions or wish to invite you to an interview. Therefore, include only information which enables the employer to make such a quick contact. Be sure to include **complete** contact information – name, address, phone and fax number, and e-mail address. Avoid using P.O. Box numbers; they communicate the wrong message about your housing situation – that you do not have a stable address. Also, include daytime telephone numbers (land line and cell, if you use both) through which you can be reached. If you do not have a telephone, or if your only daytime number is with your present

employer, enlist a telephone answering service or use the number of someone else who will be available and willing to screen your calls. They, in turn, can contact you at work and then you can return the call. Include your first and last name, and maybe your middle initial, depending on your professional style. The use of a middle initial is the sign of greater formality and is most frequently used by established professionals. However, using your full first, middle, and last name together is too formal: ROBERT DAVID ALLAN. If you prefer using your middle name rather than first name, do so either alone or in combination with your first initial: ROBERT ALLAN or J. ROBERT ALLAN. Do not include nicknames (ROBERT "BUDZY" ALLAN) unless you feel it will somehow help your candidacy, which it most likely will not! Include any professional titles, such as M.D., Ph.D., J.D., immediately after your last name: ROBERT ALLAN, J.D. Never begin your name with a formal gender designation: Mr., Mrs., or Ms. Your address should be complete, including a zip code number. It's okay to abbreviate the state (NY for New York, IL for Illinois, CA for California) as well as certain common locational designations: N. for North, SW for Southwest, Ave. for Avenue, St. for Street, Blvd. for Boulevard, Apt. for Apartment. However, it's best to spell out Circle, Terrace, or Lane. Be sure to include your telephone number; you may want to preface it with "Tel." or "Tel:". If you have a fax number and/or e-mail address, you may want to include them immediately following your phone number:

Tel. 819-666-2197
Fax 819-666-2222
AllanB@aol.com

If you are applying for a position abroad, be sure to include a fax number and/or e-mail address. Do not clutter your header with extraneous information, such as age, marital status, sex, height, and weight. Such information is totally irrelevant – indeed a negative – on a resume. It communicates the wrong messages and indicates you don't know how to properly present yourself to potential employers. These are not qualifying criteria for most jobs. Such information should never be volunteered during your job search. Moreover, most is illegal information for employers to elicit from candidates.

Objective

9. Include a job or career objective relevant to your skills, employers' needs, and the remaining elements of your resume: While some resume advisors consider an objective to be an optional item –

preferring to keep it general or place it in a cover letter – or provide little guidance on how to structure an objective and relate it to other resume elements, we strongly recommend including a powerful objective at the very beginning of your resume. Otherwise you neglect the critical issue of **focus**. Your objective should be the **central organizing element** from which all other elements in your resume flow. It should tell employers what it is you **want to do, can do**, and **will do** for them.

Put in its most powerful form, your objective should be employer-centered rather than self-centered. It should incorporate both a skill and an outcome in reference to your major strengths and employer's major needs. Rather than being a statement of wishful thinking ("A position in management") or opportunistic ("A research position with opportunity for career advancement"), it should focus on your major strengths **in relation to** an employer's needs. Take, for example, the following objective statement:

> A position in data analysis where skills in mathematics, computer programming, and deductive reasoning will contribute to new systems development.

This type of objective follows a basic **job – skill – benefit** format:

I want a _____ where I will use my _____
  position/job   skills and abilities

which will result in _____.
                           outcomes and benefits

Restated in this basic format, the above objective would appear in this form:

> A <u>data analysis job</u> where I will use my <u>skills in mathematics, computer programming, and deductive reasoning</u> which will result in <u>new systems development</u>.

An objective based on this originating statement follows a very specific form. The first part of this objective statement emphasizes a specific position in relation to your strongest skills or abilities; the second part relates your skills to the employer's needs. Such an objective becomes a statement of **benefits** employers can expect from you. All other elements in your resume (experience, work history, education, awards) should provide **supports** for your objective. Formulated in this manner, your objective becomes the most important element on your resume as well as in your job search; it directs all other elements appearing on your resume, determining what should or should not be included in each section. It also gives your job search direction, focusing your efforts toward particular employers and helps you formulate well focused answers to interview questions. While formulating such an objective may be very time consuming – your two- to three-line objective statement may take several days to develop and refine – the end result will be a well-focused resume that communicates your value and benefits to employers. If you fail to include an objective on your resume, chances are your resume will reflect the very nature of your job search – it's probably unfocused and disorganized. You're trying to fit into jobs rather than find a job fit for you.

10. **An objective should be neither too general nor too specific:** Many resume writers prefer developing a very general objective so their resume can be used for many different types of jobs. However, highly generalized objectives often sound "canned" or are meaningless ("A position working with people that leads to career advancement"); they may indicate you don't know what you really want to do. Indeed, if your purpose is to apply for many different types of jobs, you are attempting to fit into jobs rather than find jobs fit for you. You appear to lack a clear focus on what you want to do. On the other hand, a very specific objective may be too narrow for most jobs; you may appear too specialized for many positions. Another alternative is to write a separate or targeted objective, responsive to the requirements of each position, every time you send a resume to a hiring official. This approach should result in resumes that are most responsive to the needs of individual employers. However, you may have difficulty doing this unless you have word processing capabilities that allow you to custom-design each resume. An objective that is not too general nor too specific will serve you well for most resume occasions. It should indicate you know exactly what you want to do without being overly specific. Look at our examples in Chapters 5 and 6 for objectives that are neither too general nor too specific.

11. **Relate all other resume elements to your objective, emphasizing skills, outcomes, benefits, and probable future value to the employer:** All other elements appearing on your resume should reinforce your objective. When deciding what to include or exclude on your resume, ask yourself this question:

> "Will this information strengthen my objective, which emphasizes my skills in relation to the employer's needs?"

If the answer is "yes," include it. If the answer is "no," exclude it. Remember, the most effective one- to two-page resume clearly and concisely communicates your objectives and strengths to employers. If you fail to organize your resume in this manner, you are likely to include a great deal of extraneous information that communicates the wrong message to employers – you don't know what you want to do; your interests, skills, and experience are peripheral or unrelated to the reader's needs; you lack a clear focus and thus appear disorganized. These are

> *All elements in your resume should relate to, as well as support, your objective.*

cardinal sins committed by many resume writers who produce self-centered resumes that fail to respond to the needs of employers. Make sure each section of your resume clearly and consistently communicates what it is you **want to do, can do,** and **will do** for employers.

Summary of Qualifications

12. **You may want to include a "Summary of Qualifications" section immediately following your "Objective":** Some resume writers prefer including a short one-line objective but immediately following it with a three- or four-line "Summary of Qualifications" statement. This statement attempts to crystallize the individual's major strengths that are also relevant to the objective. It is usually a synthesis of the "Experience" section. We consider this an optional item to be used by individuals with a great deal of work experience and who choose a chronological resume format. It is most effective on chronological resumes where the objective is weak and the experience sections are organized by position, organization, and inclusive employment dates. The "Summary of Qualifications" section enables you to synthesize in capsule form your most important skills and accomplishments as **patterns of performance**. Especially with chronological resumes, this can be a very effective section. It helps elevate your resume by stressing major accomplishments and thus overcoming the inherent limitations of chronological resumes. An example of such a statement includes the following:

SUMMARY OF QUALIFICATIONS

Twelve years of progressively responsible experience in all phases of retail sales and marketing with major discount stores in culturally diverse metropolitan areas. Annually improved profitability by 15 percent and consistently rated in top 10 percent of workforce.

As noted in our example of Mark Able in Chapter 6, the remainder of this resume, especially the "Experience" section, provides **supports** for this statement. Many resumes may use other terminology to for this section, such as "Professional Profile," "Professional Strengths and Qualifications," "Capabilities," or "Areas of Competencies."

Work Experience

13. **Showcase your work experience with particular emphasis on your special skills, abilities, and achievements:** Next to your objective, your work experience section will be the most important. Here you need to provide key details on your past skills and related accomplishments. To best develop this section, complete worksheets which include the following information on each job:

   - Name of employer
   - Address
   - Inclusive employment dates
   - Type of organization
   - Size of organization/number of employees
   - Approximate annual sales volume or annual budget
   - Position held
   - Earnings per month/year
   - Responsibilities/duties
   - Achievements or significant contributions
   - Demonstrated skills and abilities
   - Reason(s) for leaving

We include several worksheets for generating this information in Chapter 7. It's best to complete these worksheets **before** writing your resume.

14. **Keep each "Experience" section short and to the point:** Information for each job should be condensed into descriptions of five to eight lines. The language should be crisp, succinct, expressive, and direct. Keep editing – eliminate unnecessary words and phrases – until you have short, succinct, and powerful statements that grab the attention of the reader. Lengthy statements tend to lose the reader's attention and distract from your major points. The guiding principle here is to edit, edit, edit, and edit until you get it right! This will take some time, but it's time well worth taking once you see the compelling results.

15. Work experience should be presented in the language of skills and accomplishments rather than as a listing of formal duties and responsibilities: Employers are not really interested in learning about duties and responsibilities assigned to your previous jobs which are essentially a rehash of formal job descriptions rather than statements of what you actually accomplished on and beyond that job description. After all, assigned duties and responsibilities come with the position regardless of who occupies it. Instead, potential employers want to know how well you **performed** your assigned duties and responsibilities as well as any additional initiative you took that produced positive results.

What types of results do employers look for? Four big employee-generated outcomes managers look for are very simple and easy to measure and relate to on-the-job survival skills: (1) generate more profits (i.e., help grow the organization), (2) save the company more money (i.e., increase efficiency and effectiveness), (3) save your boss more time (i.e., take initiative and cooperate), and (4) help promote your boss in the eyes of his or her bosses (i.e., give your boss credits which may be undeserved but nonetheless demonstrates your understanding of organizational dynamics, such as loyalty, networking, mentoring, and politics). Other related positive outcomes are often outlined in evaluation criteria on annual performance appraisals.

Since employers are looking for indicators of your performance, it's to your advantage to describe your previous jobs in performance terms – what skills you used, what resulted from your work, and how your employer benefitted. These are usually termed your "accomplishments" or "achievements." An accomplishment or achievement is anything you did well that resulted in a positive outcome for the employer, the company/ organization, or clients. Accomplishments are what define your "patterns of performance." Examine the following statement:

> Responsibilities included conducting research projects assigned to office and coordinating projects with three research and development offices. Duties also involved evaluating new employees and chairing monthly review meetings.

Now, restate this "work experience" in terms of your actual accomplishments or achievements:

> Conducted research on transportation of hazardous wastes on interstate highways which provided the basis for new restrictive legislation (PL4921). Developed three proposals for studying the effects of toxic waste dumps on rural water supplies which received $1.75 million in funds. Chaired interdepartmental meetings that eliminated unnecessary redundancy and improved communications between technical professionals. Recommendations resulted in reorganizing R&D functions that saved the company $450,000 in annual overhead costs.

Accomplishment statements set you apart from so many other resumes that primarily list formal duties and responsibilities assigned to positions as "Experience." Keep focused on employers' needs by stressing your accomplishments in each of your experience statements and descriptions.

16. **Incorporate action verbs and use the active voice when describing your experience:** Some of the most powerful language you can use in a resume incorporates action or transitive verbs. It emphasizes taking action or initiative that goes beyond just formal assigned duties and responsibilities. If your grammar rules are a bit rusty, here are some examples of action or transitive verbs:

administered	conducted
analyzed	coordinated
assisted	created
communicated	designed
developed	planned
directed	proposed
established	recommended
evaluated	recruited
expanded	reduced
generated	reorganized
implemented	revised
increased	selected
initiated	streamlined
investigated	supervised
managed	trained
negotiated	trimmed
organized	wrote

When applied to the active voice, action or transitive verbs follow a particular grammatical pattern:

Subject	Transitive Verb	Direct Objective
I	increased	profits
I	initiated	studies
I	expanded	production

If written in the **passive voice**, these examples would appear in the "Experience" section of a resume in the following form – which you should avoid:

"Profits were increased by 32 percent."

"The studies resulted in new legislation."

"Production was expanded by 24 percent."

The passive voice implies the object was subjected to some type of action but the source of the action is unknown. If written in the **active voice**, these same examples would read as follows:

"Increased profits by 32 percent."

"Initiated studies that resulted in new legislation."

"Expanded production by 24 percent."

When using action verbs and the active voice, the action verb implies that you, the subject, performed the action. The active voice helps elevate you to a personal performance level that gets de-emphasized, if not lost, when using the passive voice.

17. **Use "keywords" appropriate for optical scanners and resume databases:** Since more and more employers use resume scanning software, automated applicant tracking systems, and resume databases on the Internet to initially sort resumes based on keywords, it would be wise to incorporate as many keywords in your resume as possible. Unlike the language of action or transitive verbs (Principle #16), keywords reflect the jargon of particular industries and employers – desired skills, interpersonal traits, duties, responsibilities, positions held, education attained, or equipment used. While many keywords are technical in nature, others can be more generic: "curriculum development," "customer service," "employee relations," "market research," "negotiations," "public speaking," "team building." An employer may select

> *Keywords reflect the jargon of particular employers – skills, responsibilities, positions held, and equipment used.*

a list of 30 keywords which will be used for searching and sorting resumes. If your resume includes many of the words identified in the employer's keyword profile, the higher the probability your resume will be selected for visual examination. For an excellent discussion, as well as a rich collection of resumes using keywords, see Wendy S. Enelow's *Best Keywords for Resumes, Cover Letters, and Interviews* (Impact Publications, 2003).

18. **Avoid using the personal pronoun "I":** When using the active voice, the assumption is that you are the one performing the action. As indicated in principle #16, there is no need to insert "I" when referring to your accomplishments. The use of "I" is awkward and inappropriate on a resume. It makes your resume too self-centered when you should be making it more employer-centered.

19. **Use numbers and percentages whenever possible to demonstrate your performance on previous jobs:** It's always best to state action and performance in some numerical fashion. Numbers command attention and communicate accomplishments. For example, take this "experience" statement:

    "Increased sales each year for five straight years."

    The same statement can be stated in more powerful numerical terms that are equally truthful:

    "Increased sales annually by 23% ($147,000) during the past five years."

    Which of these statements makes a more powerful impression on employers who are looking for evidence of performance patterns that might be transferred to their organization? To state you "increased" sales without stating by "how much" leaves a great deal to the imagination. Was it one percent or 100 percent? $5 or $500,000? If performance differences appear impressive, state them in numerical terms.

20. **Include quotes relevant to your performance:** Avoid including personal testimonials that are self-serving or are assumed to be solicited; they may appear dishonest to readers. But do include any special professional praise you have received from a company award or from a performance evaluation. Statements such as "Received the Employee of the Year Award for outstanding performance" or "Praised by employer for **exceptional performance** and consistently ranked in the upper 10 percent of the workforce" can be powerful additions to your resume.

21. **Eliminate any negative references, including reasons for leaving:** Keep your language focused on describing your accomplishments in positive terms. Never refer to your previous employers in negative terms and never volunteer information on why you left an employer, regardless of the reason. If you were terminated, volunteer this information only if asked to do so. This will usually occur during the job interview – not at the initial resume and letter writing stage. If an employer wants this information, he or she will ask for it during a telephone or face-to-face interview.

22. **Do not include names of supervisors:** Your experience and work history sections should only include job titles, organizations, inclusive employment dates, responsibilities, and accomplishments. Names of individuals other than yourself should be subjects you address in face-to-face interviews rather than volunteer on resumes.

23. **If you choose a chronological resume, begin with your most recent job and work backwards in reverse chronological order:** In a chronological resume, your present or last job should always be described first. The next job should be the one before that one and so on. However, it is not necessary to include or provide detailed information on all jobs you ever held. Keep in mind that hiring managers are looking for patterns of performance. The best evidence of such patterns is found by examining your most recent employment – not what you did 10, 20, or 30 years ago. Include your most recent employment during the past 10 years. If you held several part-time or short-term jobs or your employment record goes back for many years, you can summarize these jobs under a single heading. For example:

> **Part-time employment, 2002-2005.**
> Held several part-time positions – waitress, word processor,
> lab assistant – while attending college full-time.

> **Government employee, 1998-2005.**
> Served in several public works positions with both state and local government.
> Specialist on transportation policy in metropolitan areas with management-level
> experience.

24. **Be consistent in how you handle each description or summary:** The rule here is parallel construction. Each description or summary should have a similar structure and size. Use the same type of language, verb tense, grammatical structure, and punctuation in each section.

25. For each job or skill, put the most important information first:
Since most hiring managers want to know what you can do for them, put your most important performance-oriented information first. If you choose a chronological resume, begin with your job title and company and then stress your accomplishments. Your inclusive dates of employment should appear last, at the end of the description, rather than at the very beginning where it will tend to be the center of attention. If you choose a functional or combination resume format, put your most important accomplishments first in relation to your objective.

26. Be sure to account for major time gaps: If you use a chronological resume in which inclusive employment dates are prominent, check to see that you do not have major time gaps between jobs. You need to account for obvious time gaps. Were you in school, the military, unemployed, or incarcerated? If you were unemployed for a short time, you can easily handle this time gap by using years rather than exact months of a year when including dates of employment. For example, don't state your last four jobs began and ended on one of these dates,

> June 2003 to present
>
> July 2002 to April 2003
>
> December 2000 to February 2002
>
> June 1998 to July 2000

State they began and ended on these dates:

> 2003 to present
>
> 2002 to 2003
>
> 2000 to 2001
>
> 1998 to 2000

If you specify exact months you began and left jobs, you encourage the reader to look for obvious time gaps and thus raise negative questions about your employment history. If you only use years, you can cover most short-term time gaps.

27. If you are an obvious "job-hopper," you may want to choose a functional or combination resume rather than a chronological resume: The job descriptions associated with a chronological resume format will accentuate employment dates and make it easy for the reader to determine a pattern of career progression from one job to another. If you do not have a clear chronological pattern, you are well advised to choose another resume format that accentuates your patterns of skills.

Other Experience

28. Include "Other Experience" only if it further strengthens your objective in reference to the employer's needs or it helps account for employment time gaps: Standard categories include:

- **Military service:** Describe this experience as you would any other job – emphasize your skills and accomplishments. If none seem relevant to your resume objective and employers' needs, keep this section brief by including your rank, service, assignments, and inclusive service dates. However, most military personnel have numerous skills and accomplishments they can incorporate in their resumes. Most need to do a thorough self-assessment in order to uncover their skills and accomplishments. If you are a transitioning military veteran, see the resume writing advice outlined in Carl S. Savino and Ronald L. Krannich, *Military Resumes and Cover Letters* (Impact Publications, 2004).

- **Civic/Community/Volunteer:** You may have volunteer experience that demonstrates skills and accomplishments supporting your objective. For example, you may be involved in organizing community groups, raising funds, or operating a special youth program. These volunteer experiences demonstrate organization, leadership, and communication skills.

In each case, be sure to emphasize your accomplishments as they relate to both your objective and employers' needs.

Education and Training

29. State complete information on your formal education, including any highlights that emphasize your special skills, abilities, and motivation: Begin with your most recent education and provide the following details:

- Degree or diploma
- Graduation date

- Institution
- Special highlights, recognition, or achievements (optional)

The completed section might look like this:

B.A. in Sociology, 2004:
Ohio State University, Columbus, Ohio
Highlights:
    Graduated Magna Cum Laude
    Member, Phi Beta Kappa Honor Society

B.S. in Criminal Justice, 2005
Ithaca College, Ithaca, New York
- Major: Law Enforcement Administration
- Minor: Management Information Systems
G.P.A. in concentration 3.6/4.0

If your grade point and other achievements are not exceptional, do not highlight them here. Your educational achievements may appear mediocre to the reader and thus your education will become a negative.

30. **Recent graduates with little relevant work experience should emphasize their educational background more than their work experience:** Follow the principle that one's most important qualifications should be presented first. For recent graduates with little relevant work experience, education tends to be their most important qualification for entering the world of work. In such cases the "Education" category should immediately follow the "Objective." Include any part-time jobs, work-study programs, internships, extracurricular activities, or volunteer work under "Experience" to demonstrate your motivation, initiative, and leadership in lieu of progressive work experience.

31. **It's not necessary to include all education degrees or diplomas on your resume:** If high school is your highest level of education, include only high school. If you have a degree from both a community college and four-year college, include both under education, but eliminate reference to high school. Individuals with graduate degrees should only include undergraduate and graduate degrees.

32. **Include special training relevant to your objective and skills:** This may include specialized training courses or programs that led to certification or enhanced your knowledge, skills, and abilities. For example,

Additional training, 2003 to present
Completed several three-day workshops on written and oral communication skills: Making Formal Presentations, Briefing Techniques, Writing Memos, Audio-Visual Techniques.

When including additional education and training, include enough descriptive information so the reader will know what skills you acquired. Don't be surprised if your special training is viewed as more important to an employer than your educational degrees.

Professional Affiliations

33. **Include professional affiliations relevant to your objective and skills:** While you may belong to many groups, it is not necessary to include all of them on your resume. Select only those that appear to support your objective and skills and would be of interest to an employer. Include the name, inclusive dates of membership, offices held, projects, certifications, or licenses. Normally the name of the group would be sufficient. However, should your involvement go beyond a normal passive dues-paying membership role, briefly elaborate on your contributions. For example,

American Society for Training and Development: Served as President of Tidewater Virginia Chapter, 2002-2005. Developed first corporate training resource directory for Southeast Virginia.

Special Skills

34. **It's okay to include any special skills not covered in other sections of your resume:** These special skills might include an ability to communicate in foreign languages, handle specific computer software programs, operate special equipment, or demonstrate artistic talent. Again, if you have special skills relevant to your objective and skills and which should appeal to employers, include them in a separate section labeled "Special Skills" or "Other Relevant Skills."

Awards and Special Recognition

35. **Include any awards or special recognition that demonstrate your skills and abilities:** Receiving recognition for special knowledge, skills, or activities communicates positive images to employers: you are respected by your peers; you are a leader; you make contributions above and beyond what is expected as "normal." However, be selective in what you include here by relating awards or special recognition received to your

objective and skills. If you are seeking a computer programming position, including an award for "First Prize in Howard County's Annual Chili Cook Off" would distract from the main thrust of your resume! But receiving the "Employee of the Year" award in your last job or "Community Achievement Award" would be impressive; both awards would get the attention of employers who would be curious to learn more about the basis for receiving such awards – a good interview question.

Interests and Activities

36. You may want to include a personal statement on your resume: Normally we would not recommend including personal information on a resume, and many resume advisors recommend against doing so. However, there is one exception, though you should include such information sparingly. In addition to keeping your resume focused on your objective and skills as well as the employer's needs, you want to make you and your resume appear unique in comparison to other candidates. You may be able to achieve this in a "Personal Statement" or "Special Interests" section. This section might include hobbies or avocations. For example, if you are seeking a position you know requires a high energy level and the employer looks favorably on stable, married, family-oriented employees, you might include some personal information as well as interests and activities that address these silent issues. For example, your personal data could include the following:

> **PERSONAL:**   35 . . . excellent health . . . married . . . children . . .
> enjoy challenges . . . interested in results

Alternatively, you could write a personal statement about yourself so that the reader might remember you in particular. For example,

> **SPECIAL**   Love the challenge of solving problems, taking initiative and
> **INTERESTS:** achieving results . . . be it in developing new marketing
> strategies, programming a computer, climbing a mountain,
> white water rafting, or modifying a motorcycle.

Such statements can give hobbies and special talents and interests new meaning in reference to your objective. But again, be very careful about including such statements. More often than not, they can be a negative, distracting the reader from the most important information included on your resume. By all means avoid trite statements that may distract from the main thrust of your resume.

Salary History or Expectations

37. Never include salary information on your resume: While hiring officials are interested in your salary history and expectations, there is no good reason for including this information on your resume or even in your cover letter. Salary is something that needs to be negotiated, but only after you have had a chance to learn about the value of the position as well as communicate your value to the employer. This occurs at the end of the job interview. It should be the very last thing you talk about. Ideally it should be discussed only after you've received a job offer. If you include salary information on your resume or in your cover letter, you are likely to prematurely eliminate yourself from consideration – your expectations are either too high or too low.

References

38. Never include names, addresses, and phone numbers of references on your resume: You may want to include a final category on your resume:

> **REFERENCES:**   Available upon request

However, this is an empty category that does nothing to enhance your resume. Our recommendation is to eliminate it altogether or use it to fill out a short one-page resume. Remember, you want to control your references by providing the information upon request which usually occurs during the interview stage. If you volunteer your references on the resume, your references may be unprepared to talk about you to employers. It's best to list the names, addresses, and phone numbers of your professional references on a separate sheet of paper, but take that list with you to the job interview rather than volunteer the information on your résumé. Ask your references for permission to use their names and brief them on your interests in relation to the position. Make sure they have a copy of your resume for reference.

Other Information

39. You may want to include a few other categories of information on your resume, depending on your experience and the relevance of such information to employers: Consider including the following categories on your resume:

- Certificates
- Accreditations
- Licenses
- Publications
- Patents
- Foreign languages
- Government clearances

However, include them only if they strengthen your qualifications in reference to the needs of hiring officials. For example, if foreign languages are important to employers, include them on your resume. If you are in a professional field that requires certificates and licenses, include the appropriate information on your resume.

Language, Style, and Tone

40. Use an appropriate language to express your productivity and your understanding of the employer's needs: In addition to using action verbs and the active voice, try to use the language of the employer when describing your skills and experience. Use the jargon of the industry in demonstrating your understanding of the employer. Be especially sensitive to keywords that best represent the skills and experience desired by employers. As previously noted (Principle #17), this type of language will serve you well if your resume is electronically scanned using resume scanning software and automated applicant tracking systems or accessed from a resume database. Always stress your value in relation to the employer's needs – you will **add value** to the employer's operations!

41. Use crisp, succinct, expressive, and direct language: Avoid poetic, bureaucratic, vernacular, and academic terms that often tend to turn off readers. For example, instead of stating your objective as follows:

> I would like to work with a consulting firm where I can develop new programs and utilize my decision-making and system-engineering experience. I hope to improve your organization's business profits.

Re-word the objective so it reads like this:

> An increasingly responsible research and development position, where proven decision-making and system engineering abilities will be used for improving productivity.

Use the first person, but do not refer to yourself as "I" or "the author." The use of action verbs and the active voice implies you are the subject. Always use active verbs and parallel sentence structure. Avoid introductory and wind-up phrases like "My duties included . . ." or "Position description reads as follows . . ." Do not use jargon unless it is appropriate to the situation or enhances your keywords.

42. **Select an appropriate resume language that is particularly sensitive to today's resume scanning technology:** You should pay particular attention to the specific language you select for your resume. Indeed, the language component of resumes is now more important than ever in the history of resume writing. Given recent changes in employer resume screening techniques, there's a high probability your resume will be electronically scanned sometime during your job search. The key to getting your resume "read" in electronic screening systems is the specific language you incorporate in your resume. When scanning resumes electronically, employers select certain **keywords** which should appear on your resume. If you want to increase your probability of being "electronically acceptable" to employers, you must incorporate such keywords in your resume writing. For more information on the language requirements for electronically scanned resumes, see Susan Whitcomb and Pat Kendall, *e-Resumes* (McGraw-Hill, 2001); Rebecca Smith, *Electronic Resumes and Online Networking* (Career Press, 2000), and Pat Criscito, *Resumes in Cyberspace* (Barrons Educational Series, 2001).

Appearance and Visual Techniques

43. **Use appropriate highlighting and emphasizing techniques:** The most important information on a one- or two-page resume needs to be highlighted since many readers will only spend a few seconds skimming your resume. The most widely used highlighting and emphasizing techniques involve CAPITALIZING, <u>underlining</u>, *italicizing*, and **bolding** headings, words, and phrases or using bullets (●), boxes (■), dashes (–), or asterisks (*). However, use these techniques sparingly. Overuse of highlighting and emphasizing techniques can distract from your message. A major exception to this general rule relates to electronic resumes: avoid using italics, script, and underlining if your resume is likely to be electronically scanned.

44. **Follow the "less is more" rule when deciding on format and type style:** The fear of not getting all information onto one page leads some

resume writers to create crowded and cramped resumes that are most uninviting to read. Be sure to leave ample margins – at least 1" top to bottom and left to right – and "white space." Use a standard type style (Times Roman but not Helvetica) and size (10-11 point). Remember, the first thing a reader sees is layout, white space, and type style and size. Your resume should first be pleasing to the eye.

45. **Do not include special borders, graphics, or photos unless you are applying for a job in graphic arts or a related field:** Keep the design very basic and conservative. Special graphics effects are likely to distract from your central message. However, if you are in the graphics art or related art field, you may want to dress up your resume with graphics that demonstrate your creativity and style. Your photo does not belong on a resume. The rule of thumb for photos is this: Regardless of how great you or your mother may think you look in the photo, at least 50 percent of resume recipients will probably dislike your photo – and you. The photo gives them something to pick apart – your hairstyle, smile, eyes, color, dress. Why set yourself up by including a photo that will probably work against you? Your ego is best served with an invitation to an interview based solely on the content of your resume. Focus on your language rather than your photo. This principle is especially important for those who plan to do an online and/or video resume – see Principle #57 – which we do not recommend since such resumes mix critical face-to-face job interview elements with a resume.

Resume Length

46. **Keep sentences and sections short and succinct:** Keep in mind your readers will spend little time reading your resume. The shorter and more succinct you can write each section and sentence, the more powerful will be your message. Try to limit the length of each job description paragraph to five to eight lines – no more than ten.

47. **Limit your resume to one or two pages:** We agree with most resume advisors that the one- to two-page resume is the most appropriate, although one page is preferable. We prefer it because it focuses the busy reader's attention on a single field of vision. It's especially reader-friendly if designed with the use of highlighting and emphasizing techniques. The one-page resume is a definite asset considering the fact that many hiring officials must review hundreds of resumes each week. Research clearly demonstrates that retention rates decrease as one's eyes move down the

page and nearly vanish on a second or third page! At first the thought of writing a one- or two-page resume may pose problems for you, especially if you think your resume should be a presentation of your life history. However, many executives with 25 years of experience, who make $100,000 or more a year, manage to get all their major qualifications onto a one-page resume. If they can do it, so can you. When condensing information on yourself into a one-page format, keep in mind that your resume is an advertisement for a job interview. You only want to include enough information to grab the attention of the reader, who hopefully will contact you for a job interview. If you must present your qualifications in two pages rather than one, consider making the second page a "continuation page" that provides additional details on the qualifications outlined on the first page. Two resume examples using the continuation page strategy are presented in Chapters 5 (James C. Astor) and 6 (Michele R. Folger).

Production

Employers also want to see your best professional effort at the production stage of resume writing. This involves making the right choices on paper color, weight, and texture as well as production methods. Above all, the resume they receive must be error free, or they are likely to discard it as an example of incompetence.

48. **Carefully proofread and produce two or three drafts of your resume before producing the final copies:** Be sure to carefully proofread the resume for grammatical, spelling, and punctuation errors before producing the final camera-ready copy. Assuming you are word processing your resume, be sure to run the spell-check and grammar programs. Any spelling, grammatical, or punctuation errors will quickly disqualify you with employers. Read and reread the draft several times to see if you can improve various elements to make it more readable and eye appealing. Read for both form and content. Have someone else also review your resume and give you feedback on its form and content. Use the evaluation forms in Chapter 4 to conduct both internal and external evaluations.

49. **Choose white, off-white, ivory, or light grey 20 to 50 lb. bond paper with 100% cotton fiber ("rag content"):** Your choice of paper – color, weight, and texture – does make a difference to resume readers. It says something about your professional style. Choose a poor quality paper and inappropriate color and you communicate the wrong

messages to employers. There is nothing magical about ivory or off-white paper. As more and more people use these colors, off-white and ivory colors have probably lost their effectiveness. To be different, try a light grey or basic white. Indeed, white paper gives a nice bright look to what has become essentially a dull-colored process. Stay with black ink or use a dark navy ink for the light grey paper. If you are applying for a creative position, you may decide to use more daring colors to better express your creative style and personality. However, stay away form dark colored papers. Resumes should have a light bright look to them. The paper should also match your cover letter and envelope.

50. Produce your resume on 8½ x 11" paper: This is the standard business size that you should follow. Other sizes are too unconventional and thus communicate the wrong message to readers. Make sure the envelope matches the size of the paper (see Principle #62).

51. Print only on one side of the paper: Do not produce a two-sided resume. If your resume runs two pages, print it on two separate pages. Be sure to put your name at the top of the second page, similar to the following header:

Mary Smith   Page 2

52. Use a good quality machine and an appropriate typeface: It's best to produce your camera-ready copy (for reproduction) on a letter quality printer, preferably a laser printer. Avoid manual typewriters that produce uneven type and very amateurish documents. Never produce your resume on a dot matrix printer. Most such printers produce poor quality type that communicates a "mass production" quality. If you use a desktop publishing program, choose serif typefaces (Times Roman, Palatino, New Century). Avoid sans serif typefaces (Gothic, Helvetica, Avant Garde) which are difficult to read. Be sure you print dark crisp type.

Most individuals reproduce their resume on a copy machine. Indeed, given the high quality reproduction achieved on many copy machines available at local print shops, it's not necessary to go to the expense of having your resume professionally printed. However, if you need 2,000 or more copies – which is most unlikely unless you resort to a broadcast or "shotgun" marketing approach – it may be more cost effective to have them printed. Just take your camera-ready copy, along with your choice of paper, to a local printer and have them make as many copies as you need.

The cost per copy will run anywhere from 3¢ to 15¢, depending on the number of copies run. The larger the run, the cheaper will be your per unit cost.

Marketing and Distribution

Your resume is only as good as your marketing and distribution efforts. What, for example, will you do with your resume once you've completed it? How can you best get it into the hands of individuals who can make a difference in your job search? Are you planning to send it in response to vacancy announcements and want ads? Maybe you plan to broadcast it to hundreds of employers in the hope someone will call you for an interview? Should you include your resume in the resume databases of various Internet employment sites? Perhaps you only want to send it to a few people who can help you with your job search? Or maybe you really don't have a plan beyond getting it produced in a "correct" form.

53. **It's best to target your resume on specific employers rather than broadcast it to hundreds of names and addresses:** Broadcasting or "shotgunning" your resume to hundreds of potential employers will give you a false sense of making progress with your job search since you think you are actually making contact with numerous employers. However, you will be disappointed with the results. For every 100 resumes you mail, you will be lucky to get one positive response that leads to a job interview. Indeed, many individuals report no responses after mass mailing hundreds of resumes. It's always best to **target** your resume on specific employers through one or two methods:

   ■ **Respond to vacancy announcements or want ads:** Resumes sent in response to job listings also will give you a sense of making progress with your job search. Since competition is likely to be high for advertised positions, your chances of getting a job interview may not be good, although much better than if you broadcasted your resume to hundreds of employers who may not have openings.

   ■ **Target employers with information on your qualifications:** The most effective way of getting job interviews is to network for information, advice, and referrals. You do this by contacting friends, professional associates, acquaintances, and others who might have information on jobs related to your interests and skills. You, in effect, attempt to uncover job vacancies before they become publicized or meet an employment need not yet recognized by employers who may then create a position for you in line with your qualifications. The resume plays an important role in this networking process. In some cases, you will be referred to someone who is interested in seeing your resume; when that happens, send it along with a cover letter and follow up your mailing with a telephone call. In other cases, you will conduct informational interviews with individuals who can give you advice and referrals relevant to your career interests. You should take your resume to the informational interview and at the very end of your meeting ask your informant to critique your resume. In the process of examining your resume, your informant is likely to give you good feedback for further revising your resume as well as refer you and your resume to others. If you regularly repeat this networking and informational interviewing process, within a few weeks you should begin landing job interviews directly related to the qualifications you outlined in your dynamite resume!

54. **The best way to broadcast your resume is to enter it into resume databases, post it on online bulletin boards, or use resume blasting services:** We view the resume databases operated by various Internet employment sites as a new form of high-tech resume broadcasting. Resumes in these databases, which can be from 500 to 50,000 in number, are usually accessed by employers who search for candidates who have a particular mix of keywords on their resume. If you have the right combination of skills and experience and know how to write a dynamite resume with language sensitive to the search-and-retrieval software, you should be able to connect with employers through such electronic mediums. At the same time, you may want to use a more traditional direct-mail approach to broadcasting your resume via e-mail – spend from $19.95 to $49.95 on a service to have your resume sent to thousands of employment specialists (primarily headhunters) and websites with resume databases who wish to receive resumes. Dozens of groups, such as www.resumezapper.com and www.resumeagent.com, will broadcast you resume for a fee. However, we do not regard these services as effective ways to distribute a resume. At best, they will give you a false sense of making progress with your job search.

55. **Learn to properly send your resume by e-mail.** More and more employers request that resumes be sent to them by e-mail rather than by regular mail or by fax. The principles for producing and distributing (formatting, type style, etiquette, etc.) an e-mailed resume differ from those relevant for a paper resume sent by mail or faxed. If you communicate a

great deal with employers on the Internet, you will need to frequently transmit an e-mail version of your resume. Make sure you know how to write and distribute a first-class e-mailed resume.

56. Be prepared to complete online profile forms in lieu of a resume. Many of today's employers operate their own online career centers rather than advertise positions in newspapers or through employment websites. Indeed, you are well advised to visit employers' websites for details on employment opportunities, including vacancy announcements and online applications. Candidates complete online applications which often include a candidate profile form that substitutes for a resume. Much of the information requested for completing this form can be taken directly from your resume. You can clip and paste sections from your resume to complete this form.

57. Be careful in creating online and video resumes. We do not encourage job seekers to create online or video resumes. Online resumes often provide too much information to employers. They also assume busy employers will actually access your website to view your online creation. Video resumes include too many verbal and nonverbal elements that should be reserved for a job interview. Always remember the purpose of a resume – to persuade a hiring manager to invite you to a face-to-face interview. Online and video resumes are much less persuasive than traditional paper and electronic resumes.

58. Your resume should always be accompanied by a cover letter: A resume unaccompanied by a cover letter is a naked resume – like going to a job interview barefooted. The cover letter is very important in relation to the resume. After all, if sent through the mail, the letter is the first thing a hiring official reads before getting to the resume. If the letter is interesting enough, the person proceeds to read the resume. A well-crafted cover letter should complement rather than repeat the content of your resume. It should grab the reader's attention, communicate your purpose, and convince the reader to take action. See our *Nail Your Cover Letter, 201 Dynamite Job Search Letters,* and *Haldane's Best Cover Letters for Professionals* books for an extensive discussion of the principles of effective cover letter writing, production, distribution, and follow-up. If you neglect the cover letter, you may effectively kill your resume! In many cases, your cover letter may be more important than your resume in landing an interview and getting the job. Your cover letter should command as much attention as your resume.

59. **Never enclose letters of recommendation, transcripts, or other information with your resume unless requested to do so:** Unsolicited letters of recommendation are negatives. Readers know they have been specially produced to impress them and thus they may question your integrity. Like personal photos, unsolicited transcripts may communicate negative messages, unless you have perfect grades. Such information merely distracts from your resume and cover letter. It does not contribute to getting a job interview. It indicates you do not know what you are doing by including such information with your resume and letter.

60. **Address your resume to a specific person:** Always try to get the correct name and position of the person who should receive your resume. Unless you are specifically instructed to do so, addressing your correspondence to "Dear Sir," "Director of Personnel," or "To Whom It May Concern" is likely to result in lost correspondence; the mail room may treat it as junk mail. If you later follow up your correspondence with a phone call, you have no one to communicate with. A couple of phone calls should quickly result in the proper name. Just call the switchboard or a receptionist and ask the following:

    "I need to send some correspondence to the person in charge of _____. Whom might that be? And what is the correct address?"

    Keep in mind that the people who have the power to hire are usually not in the Personnel Office; they tend to be the heads of operating units or hiring managers. So target your resume accordingly!

61. **Don't limit the distribution of your resume only to vacancy announcements.** Your goal should be to get your resume in as many hands as possible. Send it to individuals in your network – your relatives, friends, former colleagues and employers, and anyone else who might be helpful in uncovering job leads. Remember, you want to cast a big net. Let your resume do the fishing by casting it on as many waters as possible.

62. **Enclose your resume and letter in a matching No. 10 business envelope or in a 9 x 12" envelope:** We prefer the 9 x 12" envelope because it keeps your correspondence flat and has greater presence than the No. 10 business envelope. Keep all your stationery matching, including the 9 x 12" envelope. If, however, it's difficult to find a matching 9 x 12" envelope, go with a white or buff-colored envelope or use a U.S. Postal Service "Priority Mail" envelope.

63. Type the envelope or mailing label rather than handwrite the address: Handwritten addresses look too personal and amateurish, give off mixed messages, and suggest a subtle form of manipulation on your part. This is a dumb thing to do after having enclosed a professional looking resume. Contrary to what others may tell you, in a job search handwritten addresses – and even handwritten letters or notes – do not gain more attention nor generate more positive responses; they may actually have the opposite effect – label you as being unprofessional or someone who is trying to manipulate the employer with the old handwritten technique. Typed addresses look more professional; they are consistent with the enclosed resume. After all, this is business correspondence, not a social invitation to invite yourself to an interview. Don't confuse communicating your qualifications to employers with selling real estate, automobiles, or insurance – fields that teach salespeople to routinely "personalize" relationships with handwritten addresses and notes to potential customers. Such a sales analogy is inappropriate for your job search.

64. Send your correspondence by first-class or priority mail or special next-day services, and use stamps: If you want to get the recipient's immediate attention, send your correspondence in one of those colorful next-day air service envelopes provided by the U.S. Postal Service, Federal Express, UPS, or other carriers or couriers. However, first-class or priority mail will usually get your correspondence delivered within two to three days. It's best to affix a nice commemorative stamp rather than use a postage meter. A stamp helps personalize your mailing piece and does not raise questions about whose postage meter you used!

65. Never fax or e-mail your resume unless asked to do so by your recipient: It is presumptuous for anyone to fax or e-mail their resume to an employer without express permission to do so. Such faxes are treated as junk mail and e-mails are viewed as spam; they may be seen as an unwarranted invasion of private channels of communication. If asked to fax or e-mail your correspondence, be sure to follow up by mailing a copy of the original and indicating you sent materials by fax or e-mail on a specific date as requested. The poor quality transmission of many fax machines and the bland look of most e-mail will not do justice to the overall visual quality of your resume. You need a paper follow-up which will also remind the individual of your continuing interest in the position.

Follow-Up

Follow-up remains the least understood but most important step in any job search. Whatever you do, make sure you follow up **all** of your job search activities. If you fail to follow up, you are likely to get little or no response to your job search initiatives. Follow-up means taking action that gets results.

66. **Follow up your resume within seven days of mailing it:** Do not let too much time lapse between when you mailed your resume and when you contact the resume recipient. Seven days should give the recipient sufficient time to examine your communication and decide on your future status. If a decision has not been made, your follow-up action may help accelerate a decision.

67. **The best follow-up for a mailed resume is a telephone call:** Don't expect your resume recipient to take the initiative in calling you for an interview. State in your cover letter that you will call the recipient at a particular time to discuss your resume. For example,

    > I will call your office on the morning of March 17 to see if a meeting can be scheduled at a convenient time.

    And be sure you indeed follow up with a phone call at the designated time. If you have difficulty contacting the individual, try three times to get through. After the third try, leave a message as well as write a letter as an alternative to the telephone follow-up. In this letter, inquire about the status of your resume, mention your continued interest in the position, and thank the individual for his or her consideration.

68. **Follow-up your follow up with a nice thank-you letter:** Regardless of the outcome of your follow-up phone call, send a nice thank-you letter based upon your conversation. You thank the letter recipient for taking the time to speak with you and to reiterate your interest in the position. While some career counselors recommend sending a handwritten thank-you note to personalize communication between you and the employer, we caution against doing so. Remember, you are engaged in a business transaction rather than in social communications. We feel a handwritten letter is inappropriate for such situations. Such a letter should be produced in a typed form and follow the principles of good business correspondence. You can be warm and friendly in what you say. The business letter form keeps you on stage – you are putting your best business foot forward.

The examples found in the remainder of this book are based upon many of these resume writing and production principles. Examine those examples for ideas on how to develop each section of your resume. But be sure **you write your own resume** based upon the above principles rather than merely plug in your own information in the subsequent examples.

4

Evaluate and Improve Your Resume Competence

ONCE YOU COMPLETE YOUR RESUME, be sure to evaluate it according to the principles outlined in Chapter 3. You should conduct two evaluations: internal and external. With an internal evaluation, you assess your resume in reference to specific self-evaluation criteria. An external evaluation involves having someone else critique your resume for its overall effectiveness.

Conduct an Internal Evaluation

The first evaluation should take place immediately upon completing the first draft of your resume. Examine your resume in reference to the following evaluation criteria. Using the numerical ratings at the right, respond to each statement by circling the appropriate number that most accurately describes your new dynamite resume:

1 = Strongly Agree
2 = Agree
3 = So-So
4 = Disagree
5 = Strongly Disagree

The numbers in parenthesis at the end of each statement correspond to each principle previously outlined in Chapter 3. Refer to these principles for further clarification.

Writing

1. Wrote the resume myself – no creative plagiarizing from others' resume examples. (#1)

   1   2   3   4   5

2. Conducted a thorough self-assessment which became the basis for writing each resume section. (#1)

   1   2   3   4   5

3. Have a plan of action that relates my resume to other job search activities. (#2)

   1   2   3   4   5

4. Selected an appropriate resume format that best presents my interests, skills, and experience. (#3)

   1   2   3   4   5

5. Included all essential information categories in the proper order. (#4-5)

   1   2   3   4   5

6. Eliminated all extraneous information unrelated to my objective and employers' needs (date, picture, race, religion, political affiliation, age, sex, height, weight, marital status, health, hobbies) or better saved for discussion in the job interview – salary history and references. (#6)

   1   2   3   4   5

7. Put the most important information first. (#5)

   1   2   3   4   5

8. Resume is oriented to the future rather than to the past. (#4)

   1   2   3   4   5

9. Contact information is complete – name, address, and phone number. No P.O. Box numbers or nicknames. (#7-8)

   1   2   3   4   5

10. Limited abbreviations to a few accepted words. (#8)

    1   2   3   4   5

11. Contact information attractively
formatted to introduce the resume. (#8)   1   2   3   4   5

12. Included a thoughtful employer-oriented
objective that incorporates both skills
and benefits. (#9)   1   2   3   4   5

13. Objective clearly communicates to
employers what I want to do, can do,
and will do for them. (#9)   1   2   3   4   5

14. Objective is neither too general nor
too specific. (#10)   1   2   3   4   5

15. Objective serves as the central organizing
element for all other sections of the
resume. (#11)   1   2   3   4   5

16. Considered including a "Summary
of Qualifications" section. (#12)   1   2   3   4   5

17. Elaborated work experience in detail,
emphasizing my skills, abilities, and
achievements. (#13 and #15)   1   2   3   4   5

18. Each "Experience" section is short and
to the point. (#14)   1   2   3   4   5

19. Consistently used action verbs and
the active voice. (#15-16)   1   2   3   4   5

20. Incorporates language appropriate
for the keywords of electronic resume
scanners. (#17)   1   2   3   4   5

21. Did not refer to myself as "I." (#18)   1   2   3   4   5

22. Used specifics – numbers and percentages –
to highlight my performance. (#19)   1   2   3   4   5

23. Included positive quotations about
my performance from previous
employers. (#20)   1   2   3   4   5

24. Eliminated any negative references,
    including reasons for leaving. (#21) 1 2 3 4 5

25. Does not include names of supervisors. (#22) 1 2 3 4 5

26. Summarized my most recent job and
    then included other jobs in reverse
    chronological order. (#23) 1 2 3 4 5

27. Descriptions of "Experience" are
    consistent. (#24) 1 2 3 4 5

28. Put the most important information
    about my skills first when summarizing
    my "Experience." (#25) 1 2 3 4 5

29. No time gaps nor "job hopping"
    apparent to reader. (#26-27) 1 2 3 4 5

30. Documented "other experience" that
    might strengthen my objective and
    decided to either include or exclude
    it on the resume. (#28) 1 2 3 4 5

31. Included complete information on
    my educational background, including
    important highlights. (#29) 1 2 3 4 5

32. If a recent graduate with little
    relevant work experience, emphasized
    educational background more than
    work experience. (#30) 1 2 3 4 5

33. Put education in reverse chronological
    order and eliminated high school
    if a college graduate. (#31) 1 2 3 4 5

34. Included special education and training
    relevant to my major interests and
    skills. (#32) 1 2 3 4 5

35. Included professional affiliations and
    memberships relevant to my objective
    and skills; highlighted any major
    contributions. (#33) 1 2 3 4 5

36. Documented any special skills not
    included elsewhere on resume
    and included those that appear
    relevant to employers' needs. (#34)   1   2   3   4   5

37. Included awards or special recognitions
    that further document my skills and
    achievements. (#35)   1   2   3   4   5

38. Weighed pros and cons of including a
    personal statement on my resume. (#36)   1   2   3   4   5

39. Did not mention salary history
    or expectations. (#37)   1   2   3   4   5

40. Did not include names, addresses,
    and phone number of references. (#38)   1   2   3   4   5

41. Included additional information to
    enhance the interest of employers. (#39)   1   2   3   4   5

42. Used a language appropriate for the
    employer, including terms that associate
    me with the industry. (#17 & #40)   1   2   3   4   5

43. My language is crisp, succinct, expressive,
    and direct. (#41)   1   2   3   4   5

44. Used emphasizing techniques to make
    the resume most readable. (#42)   1   2   3   4   5

45. Selected language that is appropriate for
    being "read" by today's resume scanning
    technology. (#43)   1   2   3   4   5

46. Resume has an inviting, uncluttered look,
    incorporating sufficient white space and
    using a standard type style and size. (#44)   1   2   3   4   5

47. Kept the design very basic and
    conservative. (#45)   1   2   3   4   5

48. Kept sentences and sections short and
    succinct. (#46)   1   2   3   4   5

49. Resume runs one or two pages. (#47)   1   2   3   4   5

Production

50. Carefully proofread and produced two or
    three drafts which were subjected to both
    internal and external evaluations before
    producing the final copies. (#48)   1   2   3   4   5

51. Chose a standard color and quality of
    paper. (#49)   1   2   3   4   5

52. Used 8½ x 11" paper. (#50)   1   2   3   4   5

53. Printed resume on only one side of
    paper. (#51)   1   2   3   4   5

54. Used a good quality machine and an
    easy-to-read typeface. (#52)   1   2   3   4   5

Marketing and Distribution

55. Targeted resume toward specific
    employers. (#53)   1   2   3   4   5

56. Used resume properly for networking
    and informational interviewing
    activities. (#53 and #61)   1   2   3   4   5

57. Posted an electronic version of my
    resume to several resume databases
    operated by Internet employment sites
    as well as explored numerous bulletin
    boards, discussion groups, and employer
    sites on the Internet. (#54)   1   2   3   4   5

58. Know how to properly send my resume
    by e-mail. (#55)   1   2   3   4   5

59. Prepared to complete online profile forms
    in lieu of my resume. (#56)   1   2   3   4   5

60. Considered the pros and cons of creating
    online and video resumes. (#57)   1   2   3   4   5

61. Resume accompanied by a dynamite
    cover letter. (#58)   1   2   3   4   5

62. Only enclosed a cover letter with my
    resume – nothing else. (#59)   1   2   3   4   5

63. Addressed to a specific name and
    position. (#60)   1   2   3   4   5

64. Mailed resume and cover letter in
    a matching No. 10 business envelope
    or in a 9 x 12" envelope. (#62)   1   2   3   4   5

65. Typed address on envelope. (#63)   1   2   3   4   5

66. Sent correspondence by first-class or
    priority mail or special next-day services;
    affixed attractive commemorative
    stamps. (#64)   1   2   3   4   5

67. Considered pros and cons of faxing and/or
    e-mailing resume to prospective employers
    (#65)   1   2   3   4   5

Follow-Up

68. Followed up the mailed resume within
    seven days. (#66)   1   2   3   4   5

69. Used the telephone for following up. (#67)   1   2   3   4   5

70. Followed up the follow-up with a nice
    thank-you letter. (#68)   1   2   3   4   5

TOTAL

Add the numbers you circled to the right of each statement to get a cumulative score. If your score is higher than 100, you need to work on improving your resume. Go back and institute the necessary changes to create a truly dynamite resume.

Finalize With an External Evaluation

In many respects the external resume evaluation plays the most crucial role in your overall job search. It helps you get remembered which, in turn, leads to referrals and job leads.

The best way to conduct an external evaluation is to circulate your resume to two or more individuals. Choose people whose opinions you value for being objective, frank, and thoughtful. Do not select friends and relatives who might flatter you with positive comments. Professional acquaintances or people you don't know personally but whom you admire may be good candidates for this type of evaluation.

An ideal evaluator has experience in hiring people in your area of expertise. In addition to sharing their experience with you, they may refer you to other individuals who would be interested in your qualifications. You will encounter many of these individuals in the process of networking and conducting informational interviews. You, in effect, conduct an external evaluation of your resume with this individual during the informational interview. At the very end of the informational interview you should ask the person to examine your resume; you want to elicit comments on how you can better strengthen the resume. Ask him or her the following questions:

"If you don't mind, would you look over my resume? Perhaps you could comment on its clarity or make suggestions for improving it?"

"How would you react to this resume if you received it from a candidate? Does it grab your attention and interest you enough to talk with me?"

"If you were writing this resume, what changes would you make? Any additions, deletions, or modifications?"

Answers to these questions should give you invaluable feedback for improving both the form and content of your resume. You will be eliciting advice from people whose opinions count. However, it is not necessary to incorporate all such advice. Some evaluators, while well-meaning, will not provide you with sound advice. Instead, they may reinforce many of the pitfalls found in weak resumes.

Another way to conduct an external evaluation is to develop a checklist of evaluation criteria and give it, along with your resume, to individuals whose opinions and expertise you value. Unlike the evaluation criteria used for the internal evaluation, the evaluation criteria for the external evaluation should be more general. Examine your resume in relation to these criteria:

Circle the number that best characterizes various aspects of my resume as well as include any recommendations on how to best improve the resume:

> 1 = Excellent
> 2 = Okay
> 3 = Weak

**Recommendations for
improvement**

1. Overall appearance   1   2   3 _____

2. Layout   1   2   3 _____

3. Clarity   1   2   3 _____

4. Consistency   1   2   3 _____

5. Readability   1   2   3 _____

6. Language   1   2   3 _____

7. Organization   1   2   3 _____

8. Content/completeness   1   2   3 _____

9. Length   1   2   3 _____

10. Contact information/header 1   2   3 _____

11. Objective   1   2   3 _____

12. Experience   1   2   3 _____

13. Skills   1   2   3 _____

14. Achievements   1   2   3 _____

15. Education   1   2   3 _____

16. Other information   1   2   3 _____

17. Paper color   1   2   3 _____

18. Paper size and stock   1   2   3 _____

19. Overall production quality 1   2   3 _____

20. Potential effectiveness   1   2   3 _____

Summary Evaluation: _____

_____

_____

_____

After completing these external evaluations and incorporating useful suggestions for further improving the quality of your resume, it's a good idea to send a copy of your revised resume to those individuals who were helpful in giving you advice. Thank them for their time and thoughtful comments. Ask them to keep you in mind should they hear of anyone who might be interested in your experience and skills. In so doing, you will be demonstrating your appreciation and thoughtfulness as well as reminding them to remember you for further information, advice, and referrals.

In the end, **being remembered in reference to your resume** is one of the most important goals you want to repeatedly achieve during your job search. As you will quickly discover, your most effective job search strategy involves networking with your resume. You want to share information, by way of the informational interview, about your interests and qualifications with those who can give advice, know about job vacancies, or can refer you to individuals who have the power to hire. Your resume, and especially this external evaluation, plays a critical role in furthering this process.

> *As you'll quickly discover, your most effective job search strategy involves networking with your resume.*

5

Transform an Ordinary Resume Into a Dynamite Resume

OST RESUMES CAN BE IMPROVED by following several basic rules as outlined in Chapter 3. If you already have a completed resume, you should review it in reference to the evaluation criteria outlined in Chapter 4.

Better still, let's look at four sets of examples that incorporate many of our principles of effective resume writing. These are actual examples from individuals who started with weak resume writing skills and, with a little help, managed to transform an ordinary resume into a dynamite resume that led to interviews and job offers.

Purposeful Employer-Centered Resumes

Transforming an ordinary resume into a dynamite resume is not difficult if you keep focused on your purpose and incorporate a few basic principles of effective resume writing. Indeed, after 25 years of resume writing, the single most important problem we have encountered with clients has been their inability to keep their writing, as well as their job search, **focused** on clear goals and purposes. They often wander aimlessly. The most important guiding principle is that your resume should be **employer-centered** rather than self-centered. It should respond to the **needs of employers** rather than merely catalog your work history and express some interests. Everything you decide to put in your resume, including each sentence and phrase you craft, must be done in reference to this principle. Keep everything focused around your purpose. You must separate information that belong in a resume from matters that are best discussed in a job interview, such as salary, references, reasons for leaving previous jobs, names of supervisors, or employment gaps. The resume should be designed to generate positive responses about you as both a professional and an individual rather than raise and/or answer questions in a negative manner.

Always keep your resume simple and focused on its purpose – **to elicit action on the part of the reader**. Like good advertising copy, your resume should provide just enough interesting information to motivate your reader to take action. If you fail to keep this purpose in mind, you are likely to produce anything but a dynamite resume.

Keep everything on your resume focused around your purpose.

If written properly, your resume will begin taking on a life of its own. It will capsulize in one page what exactly you:

- **Want to do:** A statement of your goals and objectives.

- **Can do:** Statements of your actual performance in previous jobs.

- **Will do in the future:** A probability conclusion drawn by the reader based upon a summary analysis of your resume content.

It should clearly address the **needs of employers**. You do this by answering the key questions employers ask concerning you in reference to your resume:

- What can this person do for me?

- How will this person fit into our organization?

- Will this person be able to solve our problems and grow within our company or organization?

- Should I contact this person for an interview to answer several other equally important questions?

The following resume transformations speak to these principles. Primarily focusing on the needs of employers rather than the interests of the resume writer, each resume should be viewed as a concerted effort to **motivate employers** to take action – invite the resume writer to a job interview.

Gail Topper

The first case, Gail Topper (page 85), is an actual case study of one of our first clients whom we assisted in making a significant career change. While somewhat dated, including her use of technology, nonetheless, this example illustrates important points that are relevant to anyone offering a variety of skill sets in different occupational fields. This is not a typical case, but it does emphasize how to handle important employment problems with different types of resumes.

The individual had held several full-time positions as a typist, secretary, receptionist, and sales clerk while working her way through college. After graduation, she continued in her former occupation as a secretary. Wanting to break out of the "once a secretary, always a secretary" pattern, she has several resume options for changing careers. Everything appearing here is true except for names and addresses which have been altered to protect her identity. One of the major differences is the truth is better communicated to her advantage in some of her resumes than in others.

The story of Gail Topper is not unusual. Indeed, Gail Topper is the poster child of all that is bad and good in a job search. In fact, over the years we have encountered many similar situations – individuals who possess marketable skills but who lack a clear understanding of both their major accomplishments and goals for communicating those accomplishments to prospective employers. The result is often a deadly resume that communicates all the wrong messages to employers – the individual stresses many negatives as well as gives little indication of what he or she will do for the employer. Through a process of self-assessment, in which they identify their motivated abilities and skills (see our *I Want to Do Something Else, But I'm Not Sure What It Is*, Impact Publications, 2005), such individuals can identify their accomplishments, formulate a powerful objective, and develop an employer-centered resume that motivates hiring managers to invite them to job interviews. Their dynamite resume also helps focus the job interview around their relevant experiences. With such a resume, these candidates are able to go on and land a job they do well and enjoy doing – the ultimate goal of any smart job search.

Traditional Chronological Resume

Résumé

Gail S. Topper	Weight: 122 lbs.
136 W. Davis St.	Height: 5'4"
Washington, DC 20030	Born: 8/4/54
202-465-9821	Health: Good
	Marital Status: Married

Education

1980-1983 George Mason University, Fairfax, Virginia. I received my B.A. in Comunications.

1977-1979 Northern Virginia Community College, Annandale, Virginia. I completed my A.A. degree.

1972-1976 Harrisonburg High School, Harrisonburg, Virginia.

Work Experience

2/14/86 to present: Secretary, MCT Coporation, 2381 Rhode Island Ave., Philadelphia, Pennsylvania 19322.

2/30/84 to 2/9/86: Secretary, Martin Computer Services, 391 Old Main Rd., Charleston, South Carolina 37891.

4/21/83 to 2/20/84: Secretary, STR Systems, Inc., 442 Virginia Ave., Rm. 21, Washington, D.C. 20011.

9/28/82 to 1/4/83: Typist, NTC Corporation, 992 Fairy Avenue, Springfield, Virginia 22451.

1/9/82 to 7/30/92: Secretary, Foreign Language Department, George Mason University, Fairfax, Virginia 22819

3/1/80 to 9/14/81: Salesclerk, Sears Reobuck & Co., 294 Wisconsin Avenue, Boston, Massachusetts 08233

5/3/77 to 2/1/79: Salesclerk, JT's, 332 Monroe St., New Orleans, Louisiana 70014.

1972-1976: Held several jobs as cook, counter help, salesclerk, typist, and secretarial assistant.

Community Involvement

1987 to prsent: Sunday school teacher. Grace Methodist Church.
        Falls Church, Virginia.

1983: Volunteer. Red Cross. Falls Church, Virginia.

1979: Stage crew member. Community Theatre Group.
        New Orleans, Louisiana

1978: Extra. Community Theatre Group. Annandale, Virginia.

Hobbies

I like to swim, cook, garden, bicycle, and listen to rock music.

Personal Statement

I have good mannual dexterity developed by working back stage in theatrical productions and working with various office machines. I can operate IBM Mag Card A and II typeriters, dictaphones, IBM 6640 (ink jet printer), various duplicating machines, and several copying machines. Familiar with addressograph. I am willing to relocate nad travel.

References

John R. Teems, Manager, Martin Computer Services, 391 Old
        Main Rd., Charleston, South Caroline 37891

James Stevens, Secretary, STR Systems, Inc., 442 Virginia Ave.,
        Rm. 21, Washington, D.C. 20011.

Alice Bears, Assistant Personnel Director, MCT Corporation,
        2381 Rhode Island Ave., Philadelphia, Pennsylvania 19322

Also contact the Office of Career Planning and Placement at
        George Mason University.

This is Gail Topper's first resume, which represents the **traditional chronological or "obituary" resume**. It stresses dates and positions rather than skills and accomplishments in relationship to an objective. The writer presents a chronology of different jobs and employers that says nothing about what she has done, can do, and will do in the future. The reader must interpret what this jumble of dates, jobs, employers, community activities, and hobbies means in terms of future performance. In other words, what skills and accomplishments does Gail Topper bring to any job?

Alternative Formats and Transformations

The **improved chronological resume** on page 91 presents a totally different picture of Gail Topper. It stresses skills and accomplishments in relationship to an objective. She presents jobs with supports that strengthen her objective.

The **functional resume** on page 92 presents another picture of her qualifications. Here, employment dates and job titles are eliminated in favor of presenting transferable skills and accomplishments. While this resume is ideal for someone entering the job market with little job related experience, this resume does not take advantage of this individual's work experience with specific employers.

The **combination resume** on page 93 is ideal for this particular person. It minimizes employment dates and job titles, stresses transferable skills and accomplishments, and includes work history. Here, the individual appears purposeful, skilled, and experienced.

The resume letter on page 94 also is a good alternative for this person in lieu of the traditional resume. The individual can present a resume – preferably the combination resume – to the employer at some later date.

Notice the secretarial experience does not appear on the improved chronological, functional, or combination resumes. If it did, it would tend to stereotype this individual prior to being invited to an interview. It is important, however, that this individual be able to explain the secretarial experience during the interview, especially how it will make her a particularly good salesperson – familiarity with the particular equipment and problems from the perspective of those who will use it on a day-to-day basis.

Critical Analysis

This individual was pleased with her chronological resume on pages 84-85 – she thought it outlined a great deal of education and work experience that would "appeal" to prospective employers. However, if you examine this resume carefully, you will notice the writer violated several principles of good resume writing. First, she includes a great deal of **extraneous information**, beginning with weight, height, age, health, and marital status in the header, and including irrelevant hobbies as well as names and addresses of references. None of this information relates to any bona fide hiring criteria. It distracts from the resume as well as raises possible negative questions.

This resume also clearly **lacks a focus**. Worst of all, it **raises many negative questions and conclusions** about the individual's goals, interests, and employment history. Remember, employers look for **patterns of work behavior** that will provide clues about the individual's **probable future performance**. Since the reader is left to "interpret" such an open-ended resume, three unflattering patterns immediately come to mind from just a cursory 30-second analysis of this dreadful resume:

- She appears to be a job-hopper.

- She's someone with an unfocused career.

- She's an educated secretary/typist with a communication major who makes spelling mistakes!

Based on previous experience, the employer also might conclude this is possibly someone with low self-esteem who lacks goals.

An employer reading this resume is likely to raise these negative questions and draw several negative conclusions:

- What is it she wants to do?

- What useful skills will she bring to our organization?

- Why has she changed jobs so often?

- Maybe she's a secretary, but she could be a salesclerk, a typist, or a computer operator. Her occupational profile is unclear.

- Can't spell! I wonder what else she can't do.

- I think she'll leave her next job within a few months. I wouldn't give her more than a year in our organization.

- My intuition or gut feeling tells me that this will be a bad hire – the person will need lots of direction and supervision.

- I don't want to waste my time on this one. She spells trouble!

You should never have such negative questions raised nor conclusions drawn about you based on your resume. After all, you are trying to persuade the reader to invite you to a job interview where you will have a chance to tell your whole story about what you will do for the employer. This is truly an obituary resume, destined to join the graveyard of so many other ineffective resumes.

This resume has numerous problems, but the most serious problem is found in the **choice of resume format**. Remember, resume format helps structure one's thinking about an individual's qualifications. Moreover, you always want to put your most important information first. If you present dates first, you invite the reader to analyze your resume chronologically and thus ask chronological questions. The reader will begin looking for time gaps as well as average length of employment with each employer.

Gail Topper obviously has a checkered employment history when she presents her experience in chronological terms. Unfortunately, employment dates were her weakest point, but she presented them initially and thus did just the opposite of what she should have done – presented her weakest points first! In fact, the reason for making so many job changes was her family situation – her husband was in the U.S. Navy and was transferred often – something employers would not know except in a job interview after asking *"Why did you leave your job at companies A, B, C, D, and E?"* Since she will never get to the interview stage with most employers, she let the reader raise a negative question mentally, then intuitively answer it:

"Why did she change jobs so often? She's probably an unstable employee who may lack good work habits. We don't need to hire this problem!"

The reality is that she took sales, typing, and secretarial jobs because she was unable to build a career in such a mobile family situation. These jobs actually accentuated her weaknesses – regardless of all her education and training, she couldn't spell! She was dyslexic. She had excellent skills, many unrelated to secretarial work, and was an outstanding worker. But Uncle Sam called her husband to often pack up and move to another military installation. When looking for new employment, she managed to always shoot herself in the foot with this type of resume. Her biggest problem was in putting all her experience into a traditional chronological format that further accentuated her unstable work history and communicated low value to potential employers.

There were other ways she could have presented her qualifications to employers, but she didn't know how to do it. In fact, she thought she already had a good resume – she had used other examples as the basis for writing her own resume rather than generate important job and career information on herself. The first thing she needed to do was to undergo a complete self-assessment for identifying her major interests, skills, and abilities. She needed this information in order to focus her resume around an objective and her major strengths and to develop an appropriate language – using action verbs and the active voice – for writing each resume section. Since her employment dates were her weakest points, she had to abandon the traditional chronological resume in favor of other resume formats that could better present her strongest qualifications first.

The process of transforming this resume in reality also became a process of self-discovery. It was a personal journey into the world of career planning, which involves such issues as self-esteem, identifying interests and values, charting goals, specifying achievements, and planning for the next 10 years of her worklife. She went through both a personal and professional transformation as she learned a great deal about herself – her goals, interests, skills, and abilities, which were previously buried under the irrelevant baggage of the traditional chronological resume. Above all, she discovered she was pursuing her career weaknesses (remember, she can't spell!) rather than her strengths which she had yet to systematically identify. In other words, she had been in all the wrong jobs most of her adult working life.

In the process of creating a new resume, she literally transformed her whole job and career orientation. Indeed, the resume writing exercise became an important transformation in her life. The good news is that she has found terrific jobs ever since! Her husband, who retired from the U.S. Navy not long ago, has also applied the same principles in writing his own dynamite resume, which has resulted in similar career success.

After much soul searching centered on identifying her major strengths – motivated abilities and skills (MAS) – we were able to point her in more fruitful career directions that emphasized what was **right** about her. She developed a new resume with a new career objective, which was supported by patterns of skills and accomplishments. Moving away from the traditional chronological resume that had been inappropriate given her background and career interests, we developed four different types of resumes using other resume formats: Improved Chronological, Functional, Combination, and Resume Letter. Examine each of these examples carefully on pages 91-94. Keep in mind that everything in these resumes is true, but we've been able to refocus this person's life around clear goals, patterns of accomplishments, and the needs of employers. You will quickly see that Gail had many **strengths** that were not apparent from reading her Traditional Chronological Resume.

Improved Chronological Resume

GAIL S. TOPPER
136 West Davis Street
Washington, DC 20030　　202-465-9821

OBJECTIVE: A professional sales position. . . leading to management. . . in information processing where administrative and technical experience, initiative, and interpersonal skills will be used for maximizing sales and promoting good customer relations.

EDUCATION: <u>B.A. in Communication, 1983</u>
George Mason University, Fairfax, Virginia.
- Courses in interpersonal communication, psychology, and public speaking.
- Worked full-time in earning 100% of educational and personal expenses.

TECHNICAL EXPERIENCE: <u>MCT Corporation, 2381 Rhode Island Avenue, Philadelphia, PA 19322</u>: Office management and materials production responsibilities. Planned and re-organized word processing center. Initiated time and cost studies, which saved company $30,000 in additional labor costs. Improved efficiency of personnel. 1986 to present.

<u>Martin Computer Services, 391 Old Main Road, Charleston, SC 37891</u>: Communication and materials production responsibilities. Handled customer complaints. Created new tracking and filing system for Mag cards. Improved turnaround time for documents production. Operated Savin word processor. 1984 to 1986.

<u>STR Systems, 442 Virginia Avenue, Rm. 21, Washington, DC 20011</u>: Equipment operation and production responsibilities. Operated Mag card and high speed printers: IBM 6240, Mag A, I, II, IBM 6640. Developed and organized technical reference room for more effective use of equipment. 1983-1984.

SALES EXPERIENCE: <u>Sears Roebuck & Co., 294 Wisconsin Avenue, Boston, MA 08233</u>: Promoted improved community relations with company. Solved customer complaints. Reorganized product displays. Handled orders. 1980 to 1981.

<u>JT's, 332 Monroe St., New Orleans, LA 70014</u>: Recruited new clients. Maintained inventory. Developed direct sales approach. 1977 to 1979.

Functional Resume

GAIL S. TOPPER

136 West Davis St.   Washington, DC 20030   202-465-9821

OBJECTIVE: A professional sales position . . . leading to management . . . in information processing where administrative and technical experience, initiative, and interpersonal skills will be used for maximizing sales and promoting good customer relations.

EDUCATION: B.A. in Communication, 1983
George Mason University, Fairfax, Virginia.
- Courses in interpersonal communication, psychology, and public speaking.
- Worked full-time in earning 100% of educational and personal expenses.

AREAS OF EFFECTIVENESS

SALES/ CUSTOMER RELATIONS: Promoted improved community relations with business. Solved customer complaints. Recruited new clients. Re-organized product displays. Maintained inventory. Received and filled orders.

PLANNING/ ORGANIZING: Planned and re-organized word processing center. Initiated time and cost studies, which saved company additional labor costs and improved efficiency of personnel. Developed and organized technical reference room for more effective utilization of equipment. Created new tracking and filing system for Mag cards which resulted in eliminating redundancy and improving turnaround time.

TECHNICAL: Eight years of experience in operating Mag card and high speed printers: IBM 6240, Mag A, I, II, IBM 6640, and Savin word processor.

PERSONAL: Excellent health . . . enjoy challenges . . . interested in productivity . . . willing to relocate and travel.

REFERENCES: Available upon request.

Combination Resume

GAIL S. TOPPER

---

136 West Davis St.　　　Washington, DC 20030　　　202-465-9821

OBJECTIVE: A professional sales position. . .leading to management. . . in information processing where administrative and technical experience, initiative, and interpersonal skills will be used for maximizing sales and promoting good customer relations.

AREAS OF EFFECTIVENESS

SALES/ CUSTOMER RELATIONS: Promoted improved community relations with business. Solved customer complaints. Recruited new clients. Re-organized product displays. Maintained inventory. Received and filled orders.

PLANNING/ ORGANIZING: Planned and re-organized word processing center. Initiated time and cost studies, which saved company additional labor costs and improved efficiency of personnel. Developed and organized technical reference room for more effective utilization of equipment. Created new tracking and filing system for Mag cards which resulted in eliminating redundancy and improving turnaround time.

TECHNICAL: Eight years of experience in operating Mag card and high speed printers: IBM 6240, Mag A, I, II, IBM 6640, and Savin word processor.

EMPLOYMENT EXPERIENCE: MCT Corporation, Philadelphia, PA
Martin Computer Services, Charleston, SC
STR Systems, Inc., Washington, DC
NTC Corporation, Springfield, VA

EDUCATION: <u>B.A. in Communication, 1998</u>
George Mason University, Fairfax, Virginia.
- Courses in interpersonal communication, psychology, and public speaking.
- Worked full-time in earning 100% of educational and personal expenses.

PERSONAL: Excellent health . . . enjoy challenges . . . interested in productivity . . . willing to relocate and travel.

REFERENCES: Available upon request.

Resume Letter

> 136 W. Davis Street
> Washington, DC 20030
> January 7, _____

James C. Thomas, President
Advanced Technology Corporation
721 West Stevens Road
Bethesda, MD 20110

Dear Mr. Thomas:

Advanced Technology's word processing equipment is the finest on the market today. I know because I have used different systems over the past eight years. Your company is the type of organization I would like to be associated with.

Over the next few months I will be seeking a sales position with an information processing company. My technical, sales, and administrative experience include:

- Technical: eight years operating Mag card and high speed printers: IBM 6240, MAG A, I, II, IBM 6640, and Savin word processor.

- Sales: recruited clients; maintained inventory; received and filled orders; improved business-community relations.

- Administrative: planned and re-organized word processing center; created new tracking and filing systems; initiated time and cost studies which reduced labor costs by $30,000 and improved efficiency of operations.

In addition, I have a bachelor's degree in communications with emphasis on public speaking, interpersonal communication, and psychology.

Your company interests me very much. I would appreciate an opportunity to meet with you to discuss how my qualifications can best meet your needs. I will call your office next Monday, January 18, to arrange a meeting with you at a convenient time.

Thank you for your consideration.

> Sincerely yours,
>
> *Gail S. Topper*
>
> Gail S. Topper

Karen Jones

The second set of examples (pages 96-101) relates to a situation faced by thousands of educators each year – making a career transition from education to some other occupational field. These resumes also are relevant to millions of other individuals who decide to make career changes at some point in their work lives. The question facing them is how to best present their past work history which is not directly related to jobs held in another career field. How can you appear qualified when you don't have direct work experience in the other field? The secret is to focus on **transferable skills** – those skills which are common in many different occupational fields – and then present them in an appropriate resume format that will stress the particular talents of the career changer. We apply this strategy in this set of examples.

In these examples, our subject, Karen Jones, begins with the Traditional Chronological Resume and transforms it into an Improved Chronological, Functional, and Combination resume as well as a Resume Letter. Each resume format tends to emphasize different aspects of her qualifications. For example, the Traditional Chronological Resume on pages 96-97 basically tells prospective employers that she is a teacher without career goals. It lacks an objective, includes extraneous information, and lists work history by dates. Accentuating her negatives, this is an inappropriate resume for such a career changer.

The Improved Chronological Resume on page 98 gives us a clearer picture of what she wants to do as well as what she has done in the past. However, it still emphasizes the fact that she is a former teacher. This format does not enable her to emphasize those skills that are most relevant to her objective. Nonetheless, this is a great improvement over her Traditional Chronological Resume.

The Functional, Combination, and Letter resumes on pages 99-101 enable Karen Jones to better demonstrate her transferable skills in relation to a desired non-teaching position. Any of these resume formats would be most appropriate for someone making a significant career change.

Traditional Chronological Resume

Karen Jones

Address: 1234 Main Street
                 Norfolk, VA 23508

Telephone: Area Code 804, Number 440-4321

Marital Status: Divorced; 2 children; ages 10 and 12
Date of Birth: April 1, 1958
Health: Excellent
Height: 5 feet, 4 inches
Weight: 125 lbs.

Educational Background:

University of Virginia, Charlottesville, Virginia. Bachelor of Arts
Degree in English Literature with Certification in Secondary
Education, June 1980.

Old Dominion University, Norfolk, Virginia. Master of Science
Degree in Secondary Education, June 1985.

Work History:

1986 to Present—Norfolk Public Schools, Norfolk, VA.
English Teacher—I teach 11th and 12th grade English composition and creative writing classes. I have also served as co-
director of the senior class play, coordinated student fund
raising activities, and chaired the school committee which
developed recruiting and public relations materials. I have given
speeches at student events and helped write speeches for the
school administration.

1981-1986—Full-time Homemaker.

1979-1981—Chesapeake Public Schools, Chesapeake, Virginia.
English Teacher—I taught 10th and 11th grade composition
classes.

Community Involvements:

Toastmaster's International. Since 1985, I have been very active
and have held a variety of chapter offices. During the past three
years I have served as a district representative and officer.

Hobbies and Interests:

I enjoy physical exercise (running and racquetball), sailing, piano, theater, gardening, and gourmet cooking.

References:

Dr. James Smith, Superintendent of Norfolk Public Schools.
Mr. Robert Sinclair, Principal, Norfolk High School.
Mr. Paul Amos, Governor, Tidewater District, Toastmasters International.

Improved Chronological Resume

KAREN JONES
1234 Main Street
Norfolk, VA 23508
804-440-4321

OBJECTIVE: A public relations position involving program planning and coordination which requires an ability to work with diverse populations, develop publicity and promotional campaigns, market services and benefits, and meet deadlines.

WORK EXPERIENCE:

English Teacher: Norfolk Public Schools, Norfolk, VA.
Taught creative writing and composition. Organized and supervised numerous fund-raising projects which involved local businesses, media, parents, and students. Co-directed senior class plays. Wrote and gave several "keynote" speeches at special student programs. Served as school liaison to Parent-Teachers Association; designed a plan to increase membership and involve parents in school activities. Chaired city-wide public relations committee; coordinated development and production of promotional materials. Served as speech "ghost-writer" and editor for administrators. (1986 to present)

English Teacher: Chesapeake Public Schools, Chesapeake, VA.
Taught English composition. Wrote, designed, and developed multi-media instructional programs to interest students in writing. Served as advisor to student newspaper. (1979-1981)

ADDITIONAL EXPERIENCE:

Toastmasters International, Tidewater Chapter, VA.

District Representative: Elected to governing board of Southeast Virginia District. Served in liaison capacity between district officers and local chapter. Planned, organized, and publicized training workshops and regional competition. (1992 to present).

Chapter Officer (President, Treasurer, Sergeant-at-Arms):
Developed a publicity plan which increased membership by 20 percent. Kept financial records and prepared budget reports. Acquired extensive public speaking experience and training. (1988-1995)

EDUCATION:

M.S.Ed. in Secondary Education, 1985: Old Dominion University, Norfolk, VA

B.A. in English Literature, 1980: University of Virginia, Charlottesville, VA

REFERENCES: Available upon request.

Functional Resume

KAREN JONES
1234 Main Street
Norfolk, VA 23508
804-440-4321

OBJECTIVE: A public relations position involving program planning and coordination which requires an ability to work with diverse populations, develop publicity and promotional campaigns, market services and benefits, and meet deadlines.

AREAS OF EFFECTIVENESS

PLANNING AND COORDINATING   Organized and supervised several fund-raising projects. Designed and implemented membership campaigns. Chaired public relations committee for school system; coordinated development and production of promotional materials. Publicized special events and pro grams to constituent groups. Developed multimedia instructional package to facilitate learning and involve students. Taught creative writing.

PROMOTING PUBLICIZING, MARKETING, AND WRITING   Developed promotional plan to attract new members to organizations. Coordinated publicity of special events and media. Wrote and edited speeches for self and school administrators. Helped design and produce promotional materials. Publicized special events and programs to constituent groups. Developed multimedia instructional package to facilitate learning and involve students. Taught creative writing.

COMMUNICATING AND INSTRUCTING   Gave numerous speeches over a seven-year period to a variety of audiences. Conducted meetings and chaired committees. Coached administrators in writing and presenting speeches. Taught English for ten years in public schools.

EDUCATION: M.S.Ed., Old Dominion University, Norfolk, VA, 1985. B.A., University of Virginia, Charlottesville, VA, 1980.

REFERENCES: Available upon request.

Combination Resume

KAREN JONES
1234 Main Street
Norfolk, VA 23508
804/440-4321

OBJECTIVE: A public relations position involving program planning and coordination which requires an ability to work with diverse populations, develop publicity and promotional campaigns, market services and benefits, and meet deadlines.

AREAS OF EFFECTIVENESS

PLANNING COORDINATING Organized and supervised several fund-raising projects. Designed and implemented membership campaigns. Chaired public relations committee for school system; coordinated development and production of promotional materials. Publicized special events and programs to constituent groups. Developed multimedia instructional package to facilitate learning and involve students. Taught creative writing.

PROMOTING PUBLICIZING, MARKETING, AND WRITING Developed promotional plan to attract new members to organizations. Coordinated publicity of special events and media. Wrote and edited speeches for self and school administrators. Helped design and produce promotional materials. Publicized special events and programs to constituent groups. Developed multimedia instructional package to facilitate learning and involve students. Taught creative writing.

COMMUNICATING AND INSTRUCTING Gave numerous speeches over a seven-year period to a variety of audiences. Conducted meetings and chaired committees. Coached administrators in writing and presenting speeches. Taught English for ten years.

WORK EXPERIENCE:

English Teacher: Norfolk Public Schools, Norfolk, VA.
11th and 12th grade creative writing and composition. (1986-present)

English Teacher: Chesapeake Public Schools, Chesapeake, VA.
10th and 11th grade composition. Advisor to student newspaper. (1979-1981).

EDUCATION:

M.S.Ed., Old Dominion University, Norfolk, VA, 1985.
B.A., University of Virginia, Charlottesville, VA, 1980.

REFERENCES: Available upon request.

Resume Letter

1234 Main Street
Norfolk, VA 23508
April 30, _____

Mr. Dale Roberts
Business Manager
Virginia Beach Convention Center
Virginia Beach, VA 23519

Dear Mr. Roberts:

A mutual acquaintance of ours, Paul Amos, suggested that I contact you about the new Virginia Beach Convention Center. He remarked that you are developing a comprehensive public relations and marketing plan to attract convention business.

As an officer of my local chapter and regional division of Toastmasters International, I have acquired a substantial amount of public relations, special events planning, and program coordination experience. Along with my professional work, my background includes working with diverse audiences, developing publicity campaign and promotional materials, marketing services and benefits, recruiting new members, handling financial records, and meeting important deadlines. Furthermore, I have experience in writing and giving speeches, chairing work groups, representing organizations, creative writing, and teaching.

Since I have a strong interest in public relations-type activities and have a thorough knowledge of our region and its resources, I was quite interested to hear that your new marketing plan may use conference coordinators to work with your sales staff. I would be very interested in learning more about your plans and exploring future possibilities.

I plan to be near your office next week and wonder if we could have a brief meeting? I'll give your office a call in the next few days to see if a mutually convenient time could be arranged.

Sincerely,

Karen Jones

Karen Jones

James C. Astor

Our third set of examples follows a similar pattern – transforming a Traditional Chronological Resume into Improved Chronological, Functional, Combination, and Letter resumes. In this case, the individual has a background in counseling and training. He seeks to move from public sector employment to a private firm. He was actually terminated from his last government job due to budgetary cutbacks that eliminated his position. This is the first time he has had to write a one-page resume appropriate for the private sector – and he manages to incorporate numerous errors associated with resume writing.

Notice, again, how we take what is essentially a weak self-centered resume filled with potential negatives and transform it into a coherent resume. The new resumes incorporate the individual's major skills and accomplishments as well as target them toward the needs of employers. Take special note of the Combination Resume example. Here we extend the basic one-page resume to a second "Supplemental Information" page. This is a good alternative to writing a two-page resume. The "Supplemental Information" page summarizes major achievements that are best pulled together in this format rather than incorporated into the "Experience" section of the first page.

Traditional Chronological Resume

Résumé

James C. Astor	Weight: 190 lbs.
4921 Taylor Drive	Height: 6'0"
Washington, D.C. 20011	Born: June 2, 1960
	Health: Good
	Marital Status: Divorced

EDUCATION

1989-1990: M.A., Vocational Counseling, Virginia Commonwealth University, Richmond, Virginia.

1978-1982: B.A., Psychology, Roanoke College, Salem, Virginia.

1974-1978: High School Diploma, Richmond Community High School, Richmond, Virginia.

WORK EXPERIENCE

6/13/90 to 8/22/97: Supervisory Trainer, GS-12, U.S. Department of Labor, Washington, D.C. Responsible for all aspects of training. Terminated because of budget cuts.

9/10/88 to 11/21/89: Bartender, Johnnie's Disco, Richmond, Virginia. Part-time while attending college.

4/3/86 to 6/2/88; Counselor, Virginia Employment Commission, Richmond, Virginia. Responsible for interviewing unemployed for jobs. Resigned to work full-time on Master's degree.

8/15/83 to 6/15/85: Guidance counselor and teacher, Petersburg Junior High School, Petersburg, Virginia.

2/11/81 to 10/6/81: Cook and Waiter, Big Mama's Pizza Parlor, Roanoke, Virginia. Part-time while attending college.

PROFESSIONAL AFFILIATIONS

American Personnel and Guidance Association
American Society for Training and Development
Personnel Management Association
Phi Delta Pi

HOBBIES

I like to play tennis, bicycle, and hike.

REFERENCES

David Ryan, Chief, Training Division, U.S. Department of Labor, Washington, D.C. 20012, (202) 735-0121.

Dr. Sara Thomas, Professor, Department of Psychology, George Washington University, Washington, D.C. 20030, (201) 621-4545.

Thomas V. Grant, Area Manager, Virginia Employment Commission, Richmond, Virginia 26412, (804) 261-4089

Improved Chronological Resume

JAMES C. ASTOR
4921 Tyler Drive
Washington, DC 20011   212-422-8764

OBJECTIVE: A training and counseling position with a computer firm,
where strong administrative, communication, and planning
abilities will be used for improving the work performance
and job satisfaction of employees.

EXPERIENCE: <u>U.S. Department of Labor, Washington, DC</u>
Planned and organized counseling programs for 5,000
employees. Developed training manuals and conducted
workshops on interpersonal skills, stress management, and
career planning; resulted in a 50 percent decrease in absen-
teeism. Supervised team of five instructors and counselors.
Conducted individual counseling and referrals to community
organizations. Advised government agencies and private
firms on establishing in-house employee counseling and
career development programs. Consistently evaluated as
outstanding by supervisors and workshop participants. 1990
to 1997.

<u>Virginia Employment Commission, Richmond, VA</u>
Conducted all aspects of employment counseling. Interviewed, screened, and counseled 2,500 job seekers. Referred
clients to employers and other agencies. Coordinated job
vacancy and training information for businesses, industries,
and schools. Reorganized interviewing and screening processes which improved the efficiency of operations by 50
percent. Cited in annual evaluation for "outstanding contributions to improving relations with employers and clients."
1986-1988.

<u>Petersburg Junior High School, Petersburg, VA</u>
Guidance counselor for 800 students. Developed program of
individualized and group counseling. Taught special social
science classes for socially maladjusted and slow learners.
1983-1985.

EDUCATION: M.A., Vocational Counseling, Virginia Commonwealth
University, Richmond, VA, 1990.

B.A., Psychology, Roanoke College, Salem, VA, 1982.

REFERENCES: Available upon request.

Functional Resume

JAMES C. ASTOR

4921 Tyler Drive   Washington, DC 20011   212-422-8764

OBJECTIVE: A training and counseling position with a computer firm, where strong administrative, communication, and planning abilities will be used for improving the work performance and job satisfaction of employees.

EDUCATION: Ph.D. in process, Industrial Psychology, George Washington University, Washington, DC

M.A., Vocational Counseling, Virginia Commonwealth University, Richmond, VA, 1990.

B.A., Psychology, Roanoke College, Salem, VA, 1982.

AREAS OF EFFECTIVENESS:

Administration

Supervised instructors and counselors. Coordinated job vacancy and training information for businesses, industries, and schools.

Communication

Conducted over 100 workshops on interpersonal skills, stress management, and career planning. Frequent guest speaker to various agencies and private firms. Experienced writer of training manuals and public relations materials.

Planning

Planned and developed counseling programs for 5,000 employees. Reorganized interviewing and screening processes for public employment agency. Developed program of individualized and group counseling for community school.

PERSONAL: Enjoy challenges and working with people . . . interested in productivity . . . willing to relocate and travel.

REFERENCES: Available upon request.

Combination Resume

JAMES C. ASTOR

4921 Tyler Drive
Washington, DC 20011   212-422-8764

OBJECTIVE:	A training and counseling position with a computer firm, where strong administrative, communication, and planning abilities will be used for improving the work performance and job satisfaction of employees.

AREAS OF EFFECTIVENESS

ADMINISTRATION:	Supervised instructors and counselors. Coordinated job vacancy and training information for businesses, industries, and schools.
COMMUNICATION:	Conducted over 100 workshops on interpersonal skills, stress management, and career planning. Frequent guest speaker to various agencies and private firms. Experienced writer of training manuals and public relations materials.
PLANNING:	Planned and developed counseling programs for 5,000 employees. Reorganized interviewing and screening processes for public employment agency. Developed program of individualized and group counseling for community school.
WORK HISTORY:	Supervisory Trainer, U.S. Department of Labor, Washington, DC, 1994-1999.
	Counselor, Virginia Employment Commission, Richmond, VA, 1989-1993.
	Guidance counselor and teacher, Petersburg Junior High School, Petersburg, VA, 1983-1988.
EDUCATION:	M.A., Vocational Counseling, Virginia Commonwealth University, Richmond, VA, 1990.
	B.A., Psychology, Roanoke College, Salem, VA, 1982.
PERSONAL:	Enjoy challenges and working with people . . . interested in productivity . . . willing to relocate and travel.

SUPPLEMENTAL INFORMATION   **JAMES C. ASTOR**

Continuing Education and Training

- Completed 12 semester hours of computer science courses.
- Attended several workshops during past three years on employee counseling and administrative methods:

  "Career Development for Technical Personnel," Professional Management Association, 3 days, 1999.

  "Effective Supervisory Methods for Training Directors," National Training Associates, 3 days, 1998.

  "Training the Trainer," American Society for Training and Development, 3 days, 1997.

  "Time Management," U.S. Department of Labor, 3 days, 1996.

  "Counseling the Substance Abuse Employee," American Management Association, 3 days, 1995.

Training Manuals Developed

- "Managing Employee Stress," U.S. Department of Labor, 1997.
- "Effective Interpersonal Communication in the Workplace," U.S. Department of Labor, 1996.
- "Planning Careers Within the Organization," U.S. Department of Labor, 1995.

Research Projects Completed

- "Employment Counseling Programs for Technical Personnel," U.S. Development of Labor, 1997. Incorporated into agency report on "New Directions in Employee Counseling."
- "Developing Training Programs for Problem Employees," M.A. thesis, Virginia Commonwealth University, 1990.

Professional Affiliations

- American Personnel and Guidance Association
- American Society for Training and Development
- Personnel Management Association

Educational Highlights

- Completing Ph.D. in Industrial Psychology, George Washington University, Washington, D.C.
- Earned 4.0/4.0 grade point average as graduate student.
- Organized the Graduate Student Counseling Association for George Washington University, 1996.

Resume Letter

4921 Taylor Drive
Washington, DC 20011

March 15, _____

Doris Stevens
STR Corporation
179 South Trail
Rockville, MD 21101

Dear Ms. Stevens:

STR Corporation is one of the most dynamic computer companies in the nation. In addition to being a leader in the field of small business computers, STR has a progressive employee training and development program which could very well become a model for other organizations. This is the type of organization I am interested in joining.

I am seeking a training position with a computer firm which would use my administrative, communication, and planning abilities to develop effective training and counseling programs. My experience includes:

Administration: Supervised instructors and counselors. Coordinated job vacancy and training information for businesses, industries, and schools.

Communication: Conducted over 100 workshops on interpersonal skills, stress management, and career planning. Frequent guest speaker to various agencies and private firms. Experienced writer of training manuals and public relations materials.

Planning: Planned and developed counseling programs for 5,000 employees. Reorganized interviewing and screening processes for public employment agency. Developed program of individualized and group counseling for community school.

In addition, I am completing my Ph.D. in industrial psychology with emphasis on developing training and counseling programs for technical personnel.

Could we meet to discuss your program as well as how my experience might relate to your needs? I will call your office on Tuesday morning, March 23, to arrange a convenient time to meet with you.

I especially want to share with you a model employee counseling and career development program I recently developed. Perhaps you may find it useful for your work with STR.

Sincerely,

James Astor

James Astor

George Willington

Because of our international work, we receive numerous inquiries from individuals who seek international employment. Some individuals have many years of experience working abroad. Others wish to re-enter the international job market after a lengthy absence. And still others wish to break into this job market with little or no experience nor marketable international skills. Unfortunately, we hear from a disproportionate number of individuals who are high on motivation to work abroad but very low on international skills and experience and knowledge of international employers and jobs. Many are construction workers who have unrealistic expectations about the marketability of their skills abroad. Indeed, this is the job market for many dreamers who see themselves making tons of money working in some exotic location. It is also a job market for individuals who seriously pursue international careers based upon a sound understanding of the realities of the international job market. In either case, they need a resume that best communicates their qualifications to international employers.

The final set of resume transformation examples are different from the previous examples. Here we show how to change an objective for two different employment arenas – international and domestic – as well as how to move from a self-employed situation to that of an employee in someone else's organization. It incorporates the interests of a talented individual who is interested in pursuing many different professional and personal interests which cannot be accommodated in a single job. While he may appear to lack a clear focus – doesn't seem to know what he wants to do – he really wants to do many different things, all of which present new career challenges. So he takes it one job at a time. Whichever job falls in line will be the one he will enjoy.

This individual has a strong professional background in both architecture and construction as well as a personal interest in international travel and work. He also has an interesting personal/professional background that includes technical and writing skills and travel/relocation interests – interesting enough to be included in "Additional Skills and Experience" and "Personal" sections. These additional skills and interests give his resume "personality." They set him apart from many other applicants. In the end, they may be the real reason employers invite him to interviews.

Most of George Willington's experience is as an independent contractor rather than as an employee working for someone else. He's interested in using his professional skills in either the United States or abroad. However, if he is to appear qualified for an international position, he needs to develop an international objective and then relate his international experience and patterns of achievement to that objective. Notice how we attempt to make this international linkage in the case of an individual with little international work experience.

In the second example, this same individual seeks a building inspection position in a very tight job market related to his architecture and construction skills. This is the first resume he has ever written. The resume represents a significant career change – from an independent contractor to a salaried employee. In making this career change, George Willington presents his skills as **patterns of accomplishments** related to his architectural and construction experience.

The third example could be used for either a domestic or international position. Here the objective is generic enough to be used with a variety of different employers. We've also elaborated more on the "Project Management" experience section since this is his strongest skill and it reinforces the objective.

The outcome of these three different resumes is that George Willington acquired an exciting and flexible building inspection position which could eventually lead to some international work. It also allows him to pursue several other professional and personal interests. The job represents an excellent "fit" with his ongoing and evolving professional skills and personal interests. He's using the skills he most enjoys using as well as acquiring new knowledge and experience in both the architectural and construction fields.

GEORGE WILLINGTON
1131 N. Bridge Road
Baltimore, MD 21027
301-111-0000
Willingtong@aol.com

OBJECTIVE: An overseas construction management/supervision position with an international design/build firm.

AREAS OF EFFECTIVENESS

MANAGEMENT: Owner and President for 12 years of a design/build firm with annual revenues between $1 and $2 million.

CONSTRUCTION: Direct experience with most methodologies of construction including wood frame, masonry, and light metal.

SUPERVISION: Responsible for 15 full-time employees. Concurrently supervised several hundred sub-contractors/crews. Many crews were non-English speaking.

ARCHITECTURAL DESIGN:
- Residential experience with custom and tract family homes ranging from 1,000 to 10,000 square feet.
- Commercial experience with retail, office, office/warehouse, warehouse, restaurants, and marinas.

OVERSEAS:
- Fluent in German, written and spoken.
- Experienced working, researching, and residing abroad – 11 years in northern Europe and several Third World countries.

COMMUNITY: President of Western Maryland Building Industries Association, an affiliate of the National Association of Home Builders.

ADDITIONAL SKILLS AND EXPERIENCE:
- Computer Proficient (including Acad)
- P-IFR Pilot
- U.S. Coast Guard Commercial Captain's License
- Ham Radio Operator
- Co-author of 3 books

EDUCATION: New York Institute of Technology
Albany, New York
Bachelor's in Architecture, 1992

Technische Universitat Hannover, Doctoral Program
Hannover, Germany
World Student Fund Fellowship, 1995

PERSONAL: Single, excellent health, enthusiastic to travel and/or relocate for the appropriate challenge.

REFERENCES: Available upon request.

GEORGE WILLINGTON
1131 N. Bridge Road
Baltimore, MD 21027
301-111-0000
Willingtong@aol.com

OBJECTIVE:	A building inspection position involving all phases of both residential and commercial construction.

AREAS OF EFFECTIVENESS

MANAGEMENT:	Owner and President for 12 years of a design/build firm with annual revenues between $1 and $2 million.
CONSTRUCTION:	Direct experience with most methodologies of construction including wood frame, masonry, and light metal.
SUPERVISION:	Responsible for 15 full-time employees. Concurrently supervised several hundred sub-contractors/crews.
ARCHITECTURAL DESIGN:	▪ Residential experience with custom and tract family homes, ranging from 1,000 to 10,000 square feet. ▪ Commercial experience with retail, office, office/warehouse, warehouse, restaurants, and marinas.
COMMUNITY:	President of Western Maryland Building Industries Association, an affiliate of the National Association of Home Builders.
ADDITIONAL SKILLS AND EXPERIENCE:	▪ Computer Proficient (including Acad) ▪ P-IFR Pilot ▪ U.S. Coast Guard Commercial Captain's License ▪ Ham Radio Operator ▪ Co-author of 3 books
EDUCATION:	New York Institute of Technology Albany, New York Bachelor's in Architecture, 1992 Technische Universitat Hannover, Doctoral Program Hannover, Germany World Student Fund Fellowship, 1995
PERSONAL:	Willing to travel and/or relocate for the appropriate challenge.
REFERENCES:	Available upon request.

GEORGE WILLINGTON
1131 N. Bridge Road
Baltimore, MD 21027
301-111-0000
Willingtong@aol.com

OBJECTIVE:	A construction/contract management position on a multi-faceted project requiring strong managerial, scheduling, and supervisory skills.

AREAS OF EFFECTIVENESS

PROJECT MANAGEMENT:	Owner and President for 12 years of a multi-million dollar design/build firm. Involved in all phases of project management, including contract negotiations, change order administration, scheduling, and personnel.
CONSTRUCTION:	Direct experience with most methodologies of construction including wood frame, masonry, and light metal.
SUPERVISION:	Responsible for 15 full-time employees. Concurrently supervised several hundred sub-contractors/crews.
ARCHITECTURAL DESIGN:	▪ Residential experience with custom and tract family homes, ranging from 1,000 to 10,000 square feet. ▪ Commercial experience with retail, office, office/warehouse, warehouse, restaurants, and marinas.
OVERSEAS:	▪ Fluent in German, written and spoken. ▪ Experienced working, researching, and residing abroad – 11 years in northern Europe and several Third World countries.
COMMUNITY:	President of Western Maryland Building Industries Association, an affiliate of the National Association of Home Builders.
ADDITIONAL SKILLS AND EXPERIENCE:	▪ Computer Proficient (including Acad) ▪ P-IFR Pilot ▪ U.S. Coast Guard Commercial Captain's License ▪ Ham Radio Operator ▪ Co-author of 3 books
EDUCATION:	New York Institute of Technology Albany, New York Bachelor's in Architecture, 1992 Technische Universitat Hannover, Doctoral Program Hannover, Germany World Student Fund Fellowship, 1995
PERSONAL:	Willing to travel and/or relocate for the appropriate challenge.
REFERENCES:	Available upon request.

Before and After Resumes for Professionals

In our final set of resume transformations, we examine "before" and "after" resumes for professionals who seek jobs paying between $75,000 and $300,000 a year. Drawn from our work with Bernard Haldane Associates, a leading career coaching firm that has pioneered many of today's major career planning and job search approaches, these resumes emphasize the importance of presenting **objectives** and **achievements** on resumes.

Representing a variety of occupational fields, many of our examples of "before" resumes may strike readers as good resumes. However, once you examine the content of the "before" resumes and compare them to the transformed "after" resumes, you'll clearly see how our principles of resume writing outlined in Chapter 3 come together and play a central role in creating a dynamite resume – one that clearly communicates a candidate's major strengths centered around an objective and key achievements.

The newly transformed resumes represented in this final section give prospective employers a complete picture of performance and thus minimize the amount of interpretation by their reader. These are good examples of how candidates also can set the agenda for focusing job interviews around their major skills and accomplishments. All of our candidates showcased in the "after" examples went on to find excellent jobs that were perfect fits for their particular mix of interests, skills, and achievements.

The following resume examples represent some of the very best resumes you can write in today's job market. Examine them carefully since they may well become model resumes directing your own resume writing activities. For an extended discussion of these resumes, including many more examples of such achievement-oriented resumes, see our companion *Haldane's Best Resumes for Professionals (Impact Publications*, 1999).

BEFORE

Barry Thomas
181 Queens Street
Albany, New York 11111
(555) 555-5555

****

EDUCATION: New York State University. Buffalo, New York.
                   B.S. Economics. June, 1990.
                   Emphasis: Finance.

EXPERIENCE:

11/92-Present   TILTON MANUFACTURING, Albany, New York. (555) 555-5555.
                   Management Quality Assurance:
                   Set daily production goals.   Ensure performance standards.
                   Performance appraisals.   Compile reports.
                   Train/supervise staff.   Train Staff.
                   Compile reports.   Assist member services as needed.
                   Control costs. Safety Committee.

8/92-9/92   WILLIAMS RENT-TO-OWN, Buffalo, New York. (444) 444-4444.
                   Retail:
                   Open and close store.
                   Cashier.
                   Compile reports.
                   Customer service.

11/91-7/92   BARRETT TEMPORARY SERVICES, Albany, New York. (333) 333-3333.
and   **Production:**
10/92-11/92   Sanitation.
                   Manage production rooms.
                   Train/supervise staff.
                   Line production.

8/91-10/91   VOLUME DISCOUNTERS, Albany, New York. (111) 111-1111.
                   Store Manager Trainee:
                   Train/supervise staff.
                   Performance appraisals.
                   Compile reports.
                   Control costs.
                   Cashier.
                   Customer service.

REFERENCES: Available upon request.

****

BARRY THOMAS

181 Queens Street
Albany, New York 11111   **(555) 555-5555**

OBJECTIVE

An entry level position in human resource administration involving skills in communication, project management and training.

QUALIFICATIONS

Ten years of progressively increasing responsibility and expertise in:

- Managing
- Supervising
- Communicating
- Negotiating
- Conceptualizing
- Motivating
- Evaluating

ACHIEVEMENTS

Streamlined a production department for manufacturing company. Reorganized; established and implemented new procedures. *Results:* Erased a production deficit and produced a surplus in two months.

Conceptualized a new process for a sawmill. Ascertained the problem; perceived the solution; researched the feasibility; presented findings to management. *Results:* Dramatic improvement in effectiveness and time efficiency.

Negotiated own schedule for a manufacturing company. Perceived the need; orchestrated the schedule; monitored the results. *Results:* Increased productivity; reduced employee turnover.

Motivated Boy Scouts to attain requirements. Coached; counseled; educated them. *Results:* Scouts generally achieved requirements ahead of schedule.

PROFESSIONAL EXPERIENCE

Tilton Manufacturing
Quality Assurance Lead Person   1992-1996
Analyzed and inspected production units to verify conformance to specifications; diagnosed technical problems; oral and written communication; compiled production reports; trained and supervised employees in work methods and procedures; initiated action on safety committee.

Department Supervisor   1994
Supervised and coordinated activities of employees; trained employees in work methods and procedures; troubleshot; planned production operations; developed operational procedures; initiated personnel actions; compiled, sorted and retrieved production data using computer.

Barrett Temporary Services
Production   1991-1992
Supervised and coordinated activities of employees; trained employees in work methods and procedures; compiled production reports.

Great Investor's Inc.
Registered Representative   1990
Identified, solicited, and interviewed clients; provided information and advice, initiated action on developing and implementing financial plans.

Thomas
Page Two

Zebra Lumber   1987-1990
Assistant Supervisor
Supervised and coordinated activities of employees; trained employees in work methods
and procedures; troubleshot; served on safety committee.

EDUCATION

B.S., Economics   New York State University   Buffalo, NY

AFFILIATIONS

Toastmasters International

BEFORE

Charles G. Phillips   *1852 Chutney Road*   *(937) 555-1212*
Beaver, PA 56432   *(937) 555-1234*

Background: 41 year old retired Air Force officer.
Married and have one son, Spencer (13).
Active in the Beaver community, Boy Scouts of America, and
St. Peter's Orthodox Church

Objective: A middle level or senior level management position in a security
related field within the Beaver, Pittsburgh, or Philadelphia area.

Experience: Seventeen years of experience in a multifaceted security environment
with increasing responsibility and documented success in the United
States Air Force.

Education: West Virginia University   Wheeling, WV
Forensic Studies   1978

Central State University   Baldwin AFB, PA
Masters in Administration   1998

WORK EXPERIENCE:

June 1993 – June 1995	Chief, B-2 Security Management Division
July 1992 – June 1993	System Security Engineering Manager
June 1990 – July 1992	Director, Space Systems Security Engineering Management
January 1988 – June 1990	System Security Engineer and Acquisition Plans Manager
October 1985 – January 1988	Chief of Security Police
February 1984 – October 1985	Squadron Section Commander
June 1983 – February 1984	Security Staff Officer
October 1982 – June 1983	Director, Security Police Operations
January 1979 – October 1982	Shift Supervisor

Charles G. Phillips

1852 Chutney Road, Beaver, PA 56432 • (937) 555-1212

OBJECTIVE   Operations Management

Lead a team of operations support professionals to develop and implement strategic plans, improve process flows, and enhance revenues – utilizing proven abilities to:

- Work with diverse groups of people to assess individual strengths, listen closely to innovative recommendations, and encourage open team communications.
- Identify problem areas, seek out expert advice, develop alternative solutions, follow-up implementation efforts and deliver results above expectations.

QUALIFICATIONS

- Team Building
- Process Improvement
- Project Management
- Policy/Procedures Development

- Consulting Expertise
- Strategic Planning
- Problem Solving/Innovation
- Interpersonal Communications

SELECTED ACHIEVEMENTS

Created new security discipline applied to an engineering process. Reviewed physical, personnel, electronic, industrial, and computer issues related to manufacturing. The process became an effective model, which was emulated throughout the Department of Defense.

Developed policy and planned a major public relations effort to manage crowds of 700,000. Coordinated with local, state, and government officials for 200 additional personnel and equipment to support this three day event. Widespread public approval was a key success factor and the event came off without incident.

Reorganized security office responsible for 300 people, five manufacturing plants, and over $900 million in equipment. Identified staffing shortfalls, developed new mission statement, and created implementation plan. This model system saved $25 million over a two year period.

Organized junior high athletic competition involving 12 schools, 75 student athletes, 20 parents, and city facilities. Developed implementation schedule, established deadlines, and ensured each event was properly staffed. Program was a tremendous boost for the school's public image, and the athletic department raised additional revenues.

Managed five individuals responsible for 120 employees, and $2 billion of resources. Initiated incentive programs which improved morale, and increased productivity. Instilled a high degree of professionalism which led to winning a quarterly achievement award ten times in four years.

Charles G. Phillips   Page 2

EXPERIENCE

Director, Security Management Division, BAFB, Baldwin, Pennsylvania 1993 – 1995

Manager, System Security Engineering, BAFB, Baldwin, Pennsylvania 1992 – 1993

Director, Space Systems Security Engineering Management, **Lenning AFB,** Chilton, KY 1990 – 1992

System Security Engineer and Acquisition Plans Manager, **Lenning AFB,** Chilton, KY 1988 – 1990

Chief of Security Police, **Main AB,** Germany 1985 – 1988

EDUCATION

MS *Administration*, Central State University, BAFB, Baldwin, Pennsylvania 1998

BA *Forensic Studies*, West Virginia University, Wheeling, West Virginia 1978

GARY L. CALHOUN

1250 Vancouver Ave, #123
Victoria, UT 88888-8888

Home Phone: 555-555-1212
E-mail: gary@anywhere.net

SUMMARY

I bring quantitative and analytical skills, an excellent education (PhD, MBA, CFP), business knowledge and extensive IS experience to my next position. I can program and design databases, manage a website, write, instruct, supervise salespeople and technical personnel, and make platform presentations. I can apply quantitative data-base marketing techniques (segmentation, Lifetime Customer Value, modeling etc.). And I have particularly strong and recent experience doing that in the financial services industry. I understand management's perspective because I have been both sales manager and marketing manager. I have worked in teams, conducted business overseas and participated in three start-ups. I particularly enjoy solving complex business problems in ambiguous settings.

MARKETING/DATABASE MARKETING

8/96 -present

Senior Consultant, ***Data Matrix Technologies***
Project leader of three-person team to troubleshoot and redirect database marketing effort of women's clothing direct marketer in Germany. Designed, using *FrontPage 97* and provided content for 1:1 Marketing website on DataMatrix*'s* intranet. Developed database and 1:1 marketing strategies for DataMatrix ventures into the insurance industry. Performed market research, using Internet sources for banking, insurance, telephone and utility industries. Presented 1-hour slide lecture, summarizing database and 1:1 marketing opportunities and pitfalls at company-wide seminar. Marketing analyst for Project applying database and 1:1 Marketing strategies to an electrical utility's efforts to penetrate the corporate and residential retail energy market.

6/94-8/96

Consultant, Hyleton & Company, Inc.
Completely redesigned their consulting firm's database marketing program for the financial services industry. Applied SAS tools (Base SAS, proc SQL, and SAS/Assist) on a *Sun* SPARCstation to import our clients' data and restructure it into a relational format. Scrubbed, parsed and corrected the names and addresses, using a 900-line program I wrote in the SAS data step language. Householded the records, and overlaid individual-specific demographics imported from *InfoBase* (Acxiom). Using techniques that I developed specifically for the mutual fund, banking and insurance industries, I perfected formulas for Lifetime Customer Value, then applied proprietary segmentation strategies and account growth and attrition models to identify and prioritize those sales and customer service programs likely to be most effective.

8/93-5/94

Manager of Sales Administration, ***Big Money Investor Services***
As inside support for the field sales staff, recognized that the DBMS the Sales Department was using was inadequate, identified a distributed, relational database called *Commence* and adapted it to the department's needs. So successful were my efforts that the use of *Commence* spread to other departments.

11/91-12/92   *Director of Marketing, **Bronson, Hardig & Morris***
                  Identified, contacted and followed up on potential clients among moderate-size Manhattan businesses for this 20-professional CPA firm, utilizing a computerized method I developed of identifying, importing electronically from *D&B*, contacting, and following up on sales leads.

4/78-4/81   *Marketing Manager, **Magma Steel Corporation***
                  Prepared sales and marketing plans for this US subsidiary of a French multinational steel firm, designed and implemented a computerized sales reporting system, developed econometrics forecasts and set up a competition for and selected an advertising agency. Supervised a staff of 3 outside and 4 inside salespersons; sales increased 22% during my tenure.

SALES

11/81-11/87   *Sales Engineer, **Chadwick Associates, Inc.***
                  In my spare time, I developed a spreadsheet/database program that reduced the time needed by the clerical staff to calculate salespersons' monthly commissions from days to hours while also providing management with more meaningful reports. My primary responsibility was sales of metalworking services, however and within 4 years, I had tripled sales in my territory to $4.55 million, taking the territory from worst to best in the firm.

1982-1983   *Certified Instructor, **Rockefeller Sales Course***
                  After being top student, taught the course to three successive classes in my spare time.

FINANCIAL SERVICES

12/92-7/93   *Investment Advisor, **Secure Insurance Services***
4/90-12/90   *Financial Planner, **The Peterson Group***
6/89-4/90   *Insurance Agent/Registered Representative, **Smithson Financial Group***
8/88-5/89   *Insurance Agent, **American Insurance Company***
                  Sold individual and group life and health insurance, fixed and variable annuities, limited partnerships and mutual funds for all four firms.

1989-1990   *Instructor, **Financial Management Seminar***
                  Taught at *Riverdale Junior College* in Riverdale to successively larger classes.

PROFESSIONAL

- **MBA**, The University of Virginia
- **BS**, **MS** and **Ph.D.** in Metallurgy, Boston Institute of Technology
- Certified Financial Planner (**CPF**).
- Attended first semester of New York University Computer Technology & applications program, Relational Database option.
- Able to speak, read and write German fluently.
- Proficient in SAS, MS Front Page, and MS Office 97, including Access 7.0.

GARY L. CALHOUN

9834 152nd Avenue
Victoria, UT 88888

Tel: (555) 555-1212
E-mail: gary@anywhere.net

AFTER

BUSINESS PROCESS ARCHITECT

Decision Support. . . Activity-Based Management. . . Demographics. . . Data Warehousing
Balanced Scorecard. . . Business Process Mapping. . . Customer Relationship Management

Preoccupied with turning <u>outside</u> data into information, information into knowledge.

STRATEGY

According to Peter Drucker (Forbes, August 24, 1998), "collecting and analyzing <u>outside</u> information is the next frontier in information systems for top management." Analyzing and restructuring business processes with an eye on applying such <u>out-side</u> information as customer demographics to calculation of Lifetime Customer Value for past five years. Over that span, I have changed the way insurers, mutual funds, and utilities look at their customers and the effectiveness of the sales, customer service and marketing processes that serve them*.

EXAMPLES

In the course of creating a database marketing program for a Wall Street consultant, perfected Lifetime Customer Value parameters for firms in the insurance, banking and mutual fund industries. RESULT: A quantitative approach to planning, executing and evaluating their respective marketing campaigns.

For a soon-to-be deregulated electrical utility, developed a technique for segmenting the customer database in terms of business and individual demographics. RESULT: Utility had a basis for comparing customer segments in terms of the value each brought to the bottom line.

Reorganized product data from legacy system silos belonging to a large southern life insurance company into a customer-centric data warehouse. Identified and corrected data inconsistencies and omissions, restructured data into a relational database architecture, calculated Lifetime Customer Value and ran statistical analyses. RESULT: An analysis which Gary Desalt, co-inventor of *Multi-part Marketing* liked so much, he plans to use it in his next book.

EDUCATION/ADVANCED TRAINING

Ph.D. in Metallurgy	*Boston Institute of Technology*	Boston, MA
M.B.A. in R&D Management	*University of Virginia*	Charlottesville, VA
Computer Applications classes	*New York University*	New York, NY

---

* MANAGEMENT BOOKS
   THAT INFLUENCED ME

- WORKING KNOWLEDGE
- THE ONE-TO-ONE FUTURE
- CUSTOMER INTIMACY

- THE LOYALTY EFFECT
- BUILT TO LAST
- COST & EFFECT

- STRATEGIC DATABASE MARKETING
- COMPETING FOR THE FUTURE

EXPERIENCE

Sequence Computer Systems, Inc.   *(Salt Lake City, UT)*   1998
<u>Product Marketing Manager, Worldwide Decision Support Marketing</u>. Responsible for "vertical" industry marketing plans, integrating company's computer hardware, partner software and professional services. Gave 90-minute illustrated talk on One-to-One Marketing as part of call center training for sales force in the UK. Oversaw production of multimedia CD-ROM on customer relationship management.

DataMatrix Technologies, Inc.   *(Park City, UT)*   1997
<u>Senior Consultant</u>. Led and participated in consulting projects to implement database marketing at a retailer, an electrical utility and an insurance company. Designed and provided content for company's One-to-One Marketing intranet site. Performed market research on banking, insurance and electrical utility industries, using Internet resources. Presented one-hour slide lecture on the opportunities and pitfalls of database marketing.

Hyleton & Company, Inc.   *(Jersey City, NJ)*   1994-96
<u>Consultant</u>. Designed *NylRoad*, this consulting firm's database marketing program for the financial services industry. Applied SAS tools (*Base SAS, proc SQL, and SAS/Assist*) on a Unix workstation to import our clients' data and restructure it into a relational format. Scrubbed, parsed and corrected the names and addresses, using a 900-line program I wrote in the SAS data step language. Householded the records and overlaid individual-specific demographic information imported from *Acxiom*. Perfected formulas for Lifetime Customer Value, then applied proprietary segmentation strategies and account growth and attrition models to identify and prioritize those sales and customer service programs likely to be most effective.

Big Money Investor Services, Inc.   *(Jersey City, NJ)*   1993
<u>Manager of Sales Administration</u>. Maintained database of customers and prospects on a distributed, relational database, called *Commence*, which I adapted to the Sales Department's needs, then overlaid commercially available data *(Sheshunoff)* on banking industry prospects. Prepared proposals, contracts, follow-up letters. Participated in design of sales materials.

Bronson, Hardig & Morris   *(Jersey City, NJ)*   1992
<u>Marketing Manager</u>. Organized and maintained database of prospective customers for this 30-person accounting firm, using sales automation software. Contacted prospects for sales presentations by firm's principals.

American Life, New Jersey Mutual, State Mutual   *(Jersey City, NJ)*   1992
Financial Insurance Services   *(Essex County, NJ)*   1989-91
<u>Insurance Agent/Investment Advisor/Certified Financial Planner</u>. Sold life/health insurance, annuities and mutual funds to individuals and small businesses. Used sales automation software *(Act!)* to facilitate efforts.

Magna-Empire, Inc.   *(Garden City, NJ)*   1988
<u>Sales & Purchasing Manager</u>. For this 125-person manufacturer of jet engine components, coordinated sales activities of two field representatives and purchase of over $3 million in Mil-spec parts.

Chadwick Associates   *(Brooklyn, NY)*   1982-87
<u>Sales Engineer</u>. Sold metalworking services for this manufacturer's representative, mostly to aerospace firms on Long Island.

Hy-Core, Inc.   *(Queens, NY)*   1981
<u>Sales & Marketing Manager</u>. Created a business plan for this foundry start-up, covering production, pricing, projected sales and marketing. Identified and then surveyed national market; rank-ordered and contacted prospects. Identified tooling costs as major barrier to sale; reduced those costs by 60% through CAD/CAM.

Magma Steel Corporation   *(Queens, NY)*   1978-81
<u>Marketing Manager</u>. Prepared marketing plan, designed and implemented computerized sales reporting system, developed econometrics forecasts, set up and ran competition between 8 advertising agencies and worked with successful agency to draw up and implement an advertising plan. <u>Sales Manager</u>, Bar Department. Supervised eight employees, including three field salespersons; sales rose 22% during my tenure. <u>Sales Manager</u>. Foundry Department. Represented five foundries of *Magma SA* in the U.S., identifying and calling on US customers in the nuclear, hydroelectric and pump industries.

GARY D. PETERSON
1531 Plymouth Way
Vancouver, Washington 98685
(360) 555-1212

EDUCATION

University of Nevada, 1976; Bachelor of Science in Business Administration, emphasis in Accounting

West State University. Entered MBA program September 1992. Aspiration currently on hold.

Hundreds of hours of specialized training in areas such as Management and Supervision, How to Work with People, Equal Employment Opportunity, Interviewing, Dealing with Unions, Leadership, Managing for Results, Leading a Diverse Workforce, Team Building. Attend University Research Administration Association (URAA) annual meetings and training sessions.

SPECIAL ACHIEVEMENT

Successfully completed CPA exam.

EXPERIENCE

August 1984-Present
Manager, Sponsored Projects Administration - Washington Health Science University
Responsible for the cash management and financial administration of $101 million, ($17 million when hired), which is 650 projects, (137 when hired), of grants and contracts from outside public and private sponsors; prepare external and internal reports; interpret various rules, regulations and guidelines applicable to each reward.

Responsible for 12 individuals, including 1 Manager. Despite tremendous growth, coupled with rapid changes which are inherent in this type of operation, have successfully kept staff morale to the point of that my average employee has been with me 8+ years.

The University has only incurred a cumulative $34.00 audit disallowance during my tenure. Identified $1,600,000 of annual indirect cost billings that had been overlooked. Oversee office budget. Member of multiple committees. Brought PC's into office and oversaw conversion. Assisted in the conversion from the State's General Ledger to an internal system (Oracle), and in the conversion from a State agency to a Public Corporation.

May 1983 - August 1984
President and Owner - Peterson Family Enterprises.
Developed and manufactured games and novelty items. Product development, engineering, manufacturing, art work, advertising, marketing and sales.

April 1979 - May 1983
Chief Accountant - Vancouver Wire and Iron Works/Central Products.
General ledger through financial statements, investment analysis, banking and cash management, leases and contracts, shareholder reports, fleet manager, insurance administration, credit and collections, review all payable vouchers, Profit Sharing Committee Chairman. Participated with all levels of management, including written and oral presentations.

PETERSON   **Page Two**

PROFESSIONAL EXPERIENCE

Manager, Sponsored Projects Administration
Washington Health Sciences University   1984 - Present
Managed the financial administration of $101 million annually ($17 million when hired) of grants and contracts from outside public and private sponsors; supervised 12 individuals, including one manager in multiple support services; controlled office budget; negotiated with principal investigators as necessary; developed departmental plans, set goals and deadlines; dismissed employees; formulated internal personnel policy; identified hostile researchers/sponsors and defused the situation; coordinated the members of multiple departments on various projects; interpreted rules and regulations applicable to each award; converted office to PCS; participated in the conversion of an internal accounting system (Oracle); contributed to the transformation from a State Agency to a Public Corporation.

General Manager
Peterson Family Enterprises   1983-1984
Developed and manufactured games and novelty items, product development, engineering, manufacturing, artwork, advertising, marketing, sales.

Chief Accountant
Vancouver Wire and Iron Works/Central Products   1979-1983
Oversaw the general ledger through financial statements; coordinated investment analysis; presided over banking and cash management; negotiated leases and contracts; prepared shareholder reports; managed the automotive fleet; administered insurance requirements; supervised credit collections; Chairman of the Profit Sharing committee.

Accountant I and Auditor II
State of Washington   1976-1979
Hired as an Accountant I for the Washington Department of Fish and Wildlife. Promoted to Auditor II with the Washington Department of Transportation, Fuels Tax Division. As an accountant, managed the general journal through financial statements; analyzed budgets; implemented/coordinated statewide financial reporting; internal auditor for the department. At the Fuels Tax Division, audited records of licensed motor fuel dealers; prepared audit reports; worked independently in client offices.

EDUCATION/ADVANCED TRAINING

(M.B.A.)	West State University	Portland, OR	(2000)
B.S. - Business	University of Nevada	Reno, NV	1976

AFFILIATIONS

University Research Administration Association (URAA)

GARY D. PETERSON
1531 Plymouth Way
Vancouver, Washington 98685
(360) 555-1212

EDUCATION

University of Nevada, 1976; Bachelor of Science in Business Administration, emphasis in Accounting

West State University. Entered MBA program September 1992. Aspiration currently on hold.

Hundreds of hours of specialized training in areas such as Management and Supervision, How to Work with People, Equal Employment Opportunity, Interviewing, Dealing with Unions, Leadership, Managing for Results, Leading a Diverse Workforce, Team Building. Attend University Research Administration Association (URAA) annual meetings and training sessions.

SPECIAL ACHIEVEMENT

Successfully completed CPA exam.

EXPERIENCE

August 1984-Present
<u>Manager, Sponsored Projects Administration</u> - Washington Health Science University
Responsible for the cash management and financial administration of $101 million, ($17 million when hired), which is 650 projects, (137 when hired), of grants and contracts from outside public and private sponsors; prepare external and internal reports; interpret various rules, regulations and guidelines applicable to each reward.

Responsible for 12 individuals, including 1 Manager. Despite tremendous growth, coupled with rapid changes which are inherent in this type of operation, have successfully kept staff morale to the point of that my average employee has been with me 8+ years.

The University has only incurred a cumulative $34.00 audit disallowance during my tenure. Identified $1,600,000 of annual indirect cost billings that had been overlooked. Oversee office budget. Member of multiple committees. Brought PC's into office and oversaw conversion. Assisted in the conversion from the State's General Ledger to an internal system (Oracle), and in the conversion from a State agency to a Public Corporation.

May 1983 - August 1984
<u>President and Owner</u> - Peterson Family Enterprises.
Developed and manufactured games and novelty items. Product development, engineering, manufacturing, art work, advertising, marketing and sales.

April 1979 - May 1983
<u>Chief Accountant</u> - Vancouver Wire and Iron Works/Central Products.
General ledger through financial statements, investment analysis, banking and cash management, leases and contracts, shareholder reports, fleet manager, insurance administration, credit and collections, review all payable vouchers, Profit Sharing Committee Chairman. Participated with all levels of management, including written and oral presentations.

PROFESSIONAL EXPERIENCE

Manager, Sponsored Projects Administration

Washington Health Sciences University   1984 - Present

Managed the financial administration of $101 million annually ($17 million when hired) of grants and contracts from outside public and private sponsors; supervised 12 individuals, including one manager in multiple support services; controlled office budget; negotiated with principal investigators as necessary; developed departmental plans, set goals and deadlines; dismissed employees; formulated internal personnel policy; identified hostile researchers/sponsors and defused the situation; coordinated the members of multiple departments on various projects; interpreted rules and regulations applicable to each award; converted office to PCS; participated in the conversion of an internal accounting system (Oracle); contributed to the transformation from a State Agency to a Public Corporation.

General Manager

Peterson Family Enterprises   1983-1984

Developed and manufactured games and novelty items, product development, engineering, manufacturing, artwork, advertising, marketing, sales.

Chief Accountant

Vancouver Wire and Iron Works/Central Products   1979-1983

Oversaw the general ledger through financial statements; coordinated investment analysis; presided over banking and cash management; negotiated leases and contracts; prepared shareholder reports; managed the automotive fleet; administered insurance requirements; supervised credit collections; Chairman of the Profit Sharing committee.

Accountant I and Auditor II

State of Washington   1976-1979

Hired as an Accountant I for the Washington Department of Fish and Wildlife. Promoted to Auditor II with the Washington Department of Transportation, Fuels Tax Division. As an accountant, managed the general journal through financial statements; analyzed budgets; implemented/coordinated statewide financial reporting; internal auditor for the department. At the Fuels Tax Division, audited records of licensed motor fuel dealers; prepared audit reports; worked independently in client offices.

EDUCATION/ADVANCED TRAINING

(M.B.A.)	West State University	Portland, OR	(2000)
B.S. - Business	University of Nevada	Reno, NV	1976

AFFILIATIONS

University Research Administration Association (URAA)

Martha Ralston Miller
1234 Sunset Way, San Francisco, CA 91111
555-555-1212

EXPERIENCE	**The Charleton Grains Company, Foodservice Division, Chicago, IL**
June, 1990- September, 1997	*Assistant Marketing Manager*. April 1996 - September, 1997

Assistant Marketing Manager. April 1996 - September, 1997
- Developed and executed Foodservice operator and distributor marketing plans, programs, and promotional events for the Western Zone.
- Developed in-house creative production, market research, and direct mail capabilities and managed outside production of POS literature, premiums, and promotional items.
- Analyzed and quantified trends and opportunities to support marketing plan development, financially rationalized field programs, performed pricing and mix analysis, and assisted in the development of the marketing portion of the annual financial plan for the Foodservice Division. Created a new process for managing and tracking marketing development funds.

Financial/Planning Analyst: June, 1990 - March, 1996
- Responsible for the development of the annual financial plan for the Western Zone including sales forecasting and product mix and margin analysis. Participated in negotiation of final plan accountabilities with Eastern Zone and Food Service Division management.
- Developed standards and quarterly business review processes for the Western Zone and tracked performance versus plan in order to identify key issues and trends in support of management and logistics decision making.
- Monitored and tracked cost management savings and developed reporting and audit-trail processes to support internal financial and legal audit.
- Provided ad hoc cost/benefit financial analysis to Division management, Product Managers, Regional Sales Managers, and Field Marketing Managers.

Ad Hoc Project Management. 1992-1997.
- **Operator Chain Management Project:** conceptualized and developed a new process for managing chain account business which won Team Charleton and Charleton Golden Oat awards for outstanding achievement and developed the information technology that is its foundation. Led the team that implemented the new process nationwide in 1994.
- **Customer Payment/Pricing Project:** project leader for a team assigned to develop a new process for managing and controlling customer payments associated with chain account programs including financial rationalization of program rebates and pricing to Division plan margin targets.
- **Work Process Improvement and Database Development:** Developed new work processes and related custom software applications with user interfaces to : manage budgeting and tracking of market development funds; audit and control distributor spending; customize operator call reporting using a third-party database; manage a new distributor marketing fund allocation process; and automate monthly financial reporting for the field. These applications are all now used nation-wide by Field Sales, Marketing, and Finance.
- **Training and Development:** Developed computer skills training curriculum and materials and conducted training sessions in computer literacy, Windows, Excel, Word, e-mail, and Charleton mainframe programs for field laptop computer recipients.

September, 1983 - July, 1989	**Marston Communications, West Coast office, Palo Alto, California.**

Show Operations Manager: Exposition Division, 1988 - 1989. Managed the marketing, promotion and operations functions for 10 annual trade and consumer shows. Accountable for P&L performance of the portfolio.

Director of Human Resources, West Coast, 1985 - 1988. Managed all HR/Personnel activities including recruiting, training and development, employee relations, compensation, etc. Supervised the Administrative Services function and was accountable for all budget activities related to staffing, training, purchasing, and operations.

Administrative Services Manager, 1983 -1985. Managed personnel and office services activities including office equipment purchasing and maintenance, mailroom, liaison with building management, communications services, and in-house fulfillment activities. Accountable for developing and managing the departmental budget.

April - August, 1983

American Radio Service, Washington, D.C.

Consultant: Directed marketing and research activities for an adult education project involving a consortium of colleges and universities and public radio stations including the co-writing of a $2,000,000 grant proposal to the Broadcasting Corporation of America.

September, 1980- December, 1982

Sunnydale University, Sunnydale. Full-time student, Bachelor's Degree program.

August 1976 - June 1980

Bernadino Community College, Bernadino Valley, California.

Telecourse Development Associate: Coordinated projects related to development of college-level television courses for credit including curriculum research, course evaluation, writing funding proposals, and planning related national meetings.

EDUCATION

June, 1994

MBA, Marketing Emphasis. *University of the Nation, San Jose, California.* Graduated With Distinction.

August, 1989- May, 1990

Juris Doctor. *Western University, College of Law, Santa Barbara, California.* Completed first year courses: Contracts, Torts, Property, Civil Procedure, and Legal Writing.

April, 1988

BBA, Human Resources Emphasis. *University of the Nation, San Jose, California.* Graduated Magna Cum Laude.

TECHNICAL SKILLS:

- Advanced project management and work process re-engineering skills including team leadership, critical path analysis, process mapping, stakeholder consensus building, and management presentation.
- Advanced information management expertise, particularly decision support systems and relational database design and application.
- Advanced user of Microsoft Access, Excel, PowerPoint, Word, and Project and various custom mainframe applications used by Miller.
- Skilled user of e-mail and Internet services.

MARTHA MILLER

AFTER

1234 Sunset Way
San Francisco, CA 91111

(555) 555-1212
email: martham@anywhere.net

OBJECTIVE

An organizational development position for a company that is changing functions and processes to meet competitive challenges in its marketplace.

QUALIFICATIONS

More than fourteen years experience creating and developing job functions and processes to improve organizational performance and profit. Demonstrated proficiency in project leadership, change management and process implementation.

RELATED SKILLS

- Broad business function knowledge
- Team building and leadership
- Training and staff development
- Project management

- Human resources management
- Process innovation and improvement
- Performance measurement
- Program development and implementation

TECHNICAL SKILLS

Advanced user of Microsoft spreadsheet, project, word processing, presentation and Internet software. Advanced database design and development skills with MS Access.

KEY ACCOMPLISHMENTS

Charleton Grains Company
- **Created** and **developed** new sales, marketing and finance job functions and related processes and technology resulting in improved analysis, performance tracking and strategic decision making.
- **Proposed** and **led** a series of projects to re-engineer the processes for managing and controlling customer-related sales and marketing programs. The cumulative impact from improved strategic management and elimination of program abuses and poor financial controls was $1 million annually.
- **Designed** and **managed** training programs for the implementation phase of a re-engineering projects resulting in successful national roll-out of the new processes and technology.

Marston Communications
- **Developed** a full-service human resources organization that reduced turnover, improved performance planning and development of internal human resources and reduced legal exposure resulting from poor employment practices.
- **Restructured** and **streamlined** the administrative services function supporting two company divisions that reduced the cost of administrative overhead by 25%.
- **Restaffed** and **restructured** the show operations function after a mass resignation and led the new team in the production of ten trade and consumer shows, which were produced on time and within budget.

EXPERIENCE

Project Manager	The Charleton Grains Company	1992 - 1997
Assistant Marketing Manager	The Charleton Grains Company	1996 - 1997
Financial/Planning Analyst	The Charleton Grains Company	1990 - 1995
Director for Show Services	Marston Communications	1988 - 1989
Director of Human Resources	Marston Communications	1985 - 1988
Administrative Services Manager	Marston Communications	1983 - 1985

EDUCATION

MBA - Marketing Emphasis	University of the Nation	San Jose, CA
BA - Human Resource Emphasis	University of the Nation	San Jose, CA
Juris Doctor	Western University College of Law	Santa Barbara, CA

STEVEN R. JACKSON, JD, MBA
3140 SW Door Road
Salt Lake City, UT 93359
405-555-1212

SUMMARY STATEMENT

I have a combination of legal and financial experience including ten years in law as a transaction negotiator and business attorney, four years in finance as a business appraisal expert, and three years as a mediator and arbitrator.

FINANCIAL EXPERIENCE

- **BUSINESS APPRAISAL** - Four years of experience appraising closely-held corporations and intangible assets for companies with equity ranging from $100,000 to $50,000,000.

  - Appraisals performed in variety of industries including: professional practices, retail clothing, trucking, automobile parts retailing, equipment leasing, garbage collection, manufacturing, steel and rubber industries, hard rock minerals, oil & gas, natural resources.

  - Expert witness testimony offered before the Utah Department of Revenue and civil divorce courts concerning business valuation issues.

- **DAMAGE ASSESSMENTS** - Financial analysis and research for damage assessment of the Universal Tanker Express oil spill, including the development of database using 10,000 interrelated pieces of information and financial calculations to evaluate $300 million in claimed damages.

- **BUDGETING/FINANCIAL ANALYSIS** - Developed annual operating budgets and five year plans for companies earning $10-$20 million per year. Designed, modeled, and administered a corporate overhead cost allocation program for Fortune 500 company, resulting in better profitability analysis and restructuring of job functions to the subsidiary level.

LEGAL EXPERIENCE

- **NEGOTIATION** - Ten years of experience in contract negotiation for a Fortune 500 corporation.

  - Drafted and negotiated over $500 million in financing facilities with 20 major financial institutions like New York Mutual, American Data Exchange, Flocassa, & Carmichael, Inc. The arrangements allowed the company to avoid approximately $2 million in interest expense.

  - Negotiated hundreds of business transactions in a wide variety of areas including more than $20 million in engineering and construction contracts, $5 million in office leasing, $10 million in real estate transactions, $10 million in joint venture agreements, $750,000 in loan workouts, and a variety of equipment leases, joint operating agreements, and royalties.

  - Successfully negotiated a variety of major contract disputes which directly resulted in more than $4 million improved profit.

STEVEN R. JACKSON
3140 SW Door Road
Salt Lake City, UT 93359
405-555-1212

- **LEGAL ADMINISTRATION**

  - Designed and implemented a company wide contract system covering the acquisition of more than $50 million of goods and services annually from 500 contractors in four states. The system included computerized monitoring of contractual data and performance. Indemnity shifting provisions allowed the company to avoid about $5 million in damages.

  - Worked with Risk Management Department to review insurance coverage in due diligence review of $500 million acquisition candidates. Managed program to enforce insurance coverage provided by outside contractors.

  - Managed the liquidation and buy-out of five publicly held and financially distressed limited partnerships. Program was accomplished without incurring any legal consequences from the 600 limited partners, reduced overhead by over 5,000 hours per year, and cleared title to properties.

  - Designed internal procedure and computerized system to manage 30-40 active lawsuits, directed outside counsel, and acted as an intermediary to Risk Management department.

- **MEDIATION & ARBITRATION -** Three years of experience mediating and arbitrating disputes on a variety of matters including debt collection, breach of contract, warranty, real estate transactions, business transactions, and consumer law. Conducted more than 140 mediations and 35 arbitrations.

EDUCATION

- **MASTERS OF BUSINESS ADMINISTRATION**
  - University of California
  - California Executive MBA

- **JURIS DOCTORATE**
  - University of Oregon School of Law
  - Top 20% of Class

- **BACHELORS OF SCIENCE IN FINANCE**
  - University of Utah
  - Top 10% of Class

ORGANIZATIONS

- California Bar Association, Membership number 3142
- Cyranda Bar Association - Alternative Dispute Resolution Committee
- California Mediation Association

STEVEN R. JACKSON

3140 S.W. Door Road
Salt Lake City, UT 93359   **(405) 555-1212**

OBJECTIVE

A member of a strategic planning team using proven skills in legal and financial analysis, organization and negotiation to solve complex business problems for a values-driven organization.

QUALIFICATIONS AND BACKGROUND

Eighteen years of progressively increasing responsibility and expertise in:

Appraising Businesses	Negotiating	Planning
Problem solving	Organizing	Analysis

ACHIEVEMENTS

Organized a calculation of damages caused by the Universal Tanker Express for the North America Pipeline Liability Fund which resulted in awards of $40 million on over $450 million in claims.

Negotiated $500 million of trading lines for a commodities producer which protected them from market fluctuations and saved $2 million in interest.

Planned and **implemented** a standardized contract system for a Fortune 500 company resulting in the purchase of over $50 million in goods and services annually.

Conceptualized and **negotiated** a buy-out program to eliminate the legal liability created by 500 individual minority working interest holders for an oil and gas company which saved about $1 million in reduced administrative time and potential litigation costs.

Analyzed the financial impact of a buy out provision in the sales contract of plastics manufacturer for the attorneys representing the seller. The $5.4 million value of the provision brought the estimated total sales price to $32.5 million.

Appraised a steel manufacturing facility for property tax hearing; the taxpayer received a refund of $1.8 million in past property taxes.

PROFESSIONAL EXPERIENCE

Self-Employed
Business Valuation   1991 - Present
Research and appraisal of businesses and business interest; expert testimony; project management; report writing; marketing; client consultation. Clients include the North America Pipeline Liability Fund, Sugar Sweet Corporation, Panzer Steel, Superseek, California Steel Corporation, Sweet Roll-Ups.

Contract Compliance Administrator
STENI Oil & Gas, Inc.   1990 - 1991
Managed company contracts; reviewed and negotiated sales, transportation, construction, land purchases and sales, joint operating agreements and other contracts; supervised insurance documentation; conducted due diligence reviews; monitored outside litigation.

Director of Legal Services
STENI Minerals Company   1986 - 1990
Reviewed and negotiated company contracts prior to execution; coordinated with outside counsel on conflicts and litigation; managed relationships with gold brokers/dealers, royalty holders, joint venture partners; performed other projects as assigned.

EDUCATION

Juris Doctorate   University of Oregon
Master of Business Administration   University of California
Bachelor of Science - Finance   University of Utah

AFFILIATIONS

California State Bar Association
Cyranda Bar Association
Alternative Dispute Resolution Committee

6

Dynamite Resume Sampler

THE RESUME EXAMPLES SHOWCASED in this chapter illustrate different educational, experience, and occupational levels. Each resume follows the principles outlined in previous chapters. All of these resumes are more or less scannable. Individuals with technical backgrounds, such as Suzanne Russell on pages 157-158, have a much richer mix of keywords than individuals who are looking for jobs as police officers (page 156) or flight attendants (page 161).

The resumes on pages 138-141 and 161 reflect different educational and experience levels. The resume on page 138, for example, is for a high school graduate with vocational skills and experience. The resume on page 139 is for a junior college graduate with a non-traditional background. The resume on page 140 is appropriate for a recent B.A. graduate. The resume on page 161 is actually from a high school graduate, but we decided to omit educational background altogether since it might be a negative for this individual. In fact, no one noticed this missing category, and she did get several interviews for flight attendant positions.

The example on pages 141-142 differs from all others. Especially appropriate for individuals with an M.A. or Ph.D. degree, or for those with specialized research, publication, and other production experience, this example includes an add-on supplemental sheet which lists relevant qualifications. The main resume is still one page. The add-on sheet is designed to reinforce the major thrust of the resume without distracting from it. This is an ideal resume for those who need to include examples of their work within the framework of the one- to two-page resume.

The remaining resumes in this chapter represent different occupations and positions such as accounting, attorney, bookkeeping, computers, construction, financial analyst, international development, paralegal, publishing, sales, police officer, telecommunications, industrial engineering, financial services, and travel. Several examples use a "Summary of Qualifications" and a two-page resume. The resumes on pages 150-158 are appropriate for transitioning military personnel. The resume on page 159 is for an immigrant from Ghana and the former Soviet Union who is seeking an international job.

> *Stressing skills and productivity, these are both employer-centered and value-added resumes. They clearly illustrate key resume principles.*

The resumes on pages 162-177 represent some of the best resumes drawn from the files of Bernard Haldane Associates, whose clients generally earn more than $75,000 a year in professional- and executive-level positions. These resumes are very achievement-oriented, with several showcasing their strongest accomplishments in separate achievement sections.

The resumes on pages 178-195 represent some of the best international resumes produced by professional resume writers. Most of the individuals profiled in these resumes are experienced professionals and executives who earn in excess of $100,000 a year.

The final five examples on pages 196-206 include resumes of experienced professionals seeking a variety of high-level positions in both the nonprofit and private sectors. It includes one three-page resume that stresses a powerful chronology of achievements.

While the resumes presented in this chapter are from individuals with different occupational, skill, experience, and educational backgrounds, they in no way represent resumes in general. That's not our purpose. Rather, our purpose in presenting this particular set of resumes is to clearly illustrate the major resume writing principles outlined throughout this book. Individual resume elements relate to a carefully stated job objective, a summary of qualifications, or a summary profile. Stressing skills and productivity, these are value-added resumes; they are employer-centered rather than self-centered. Several of the examples are appropriate for career changers.

ARCHITECTURAL DRAFTER

JOHN ALBERT
1099 Seventh Avenue
Akron, OH 44522
322-645-8271
albertj@aol.com

OBJECTIVE: **A position as architectural drafter** with a firm specializing in commercial construction where technical knowledge and practical experience will enhance construction design and building operations.

EXPERIENCE: <u>Draftsman</u>: Akron Construction Company, Akron, OH. Helped develop construction plans for $14 million of residential and commercial construction. (2003 to present).

<u>Cabinet Maker</u>: Jason's Linoleum and Carpet Company, Akron, OH. Designed and constructed kitchen counter tops and cabinets; installed the material in homes; cut and laid linoleum flooring in apartment complexes. (1998 to 2000).

<u>Carpenter's Assistant</u>: Kennison Associates, Akron, OH. Assisted carpenter in the reconstruction of a restaurant and in building of forms for pouring concrete. (Summer 1997).

<u>Materials Control Auditor</u>: Taylor Machine and Foundry, Akron, OH. Collected data on the amount of material being utilized daily in the operation of the foundry. Evaluated the information to determine the amount of materials being wasted. Submitted reports to production supervisor on the analysis of weekly and monthly production. (Summer 1996)

TRAINING: <u>Drafting School, Akron Vocational and Technical Center</u>, 2000. Completed 15 months of training in drafting night school.

EDUCATION: <u>Akron Community High School</u>, Akron, OH. Graduated in 1997.

PERSONAL: Single...willing to relocate...prefer working both indoors and outdoors...strive for perfection...hard worker...enjoy photography, landscaping, furniture design and construction.

REFERENCES: Available upon request.

SYSTEMS ANALYSIS/
MANAGEMENT INFORMATION SYSTEMS

GARY S. PLATT
2238 South Olby Road, Sacramento, CA 97342
712-564-3981
plattg@aol.com

OBJECTIVE

A position in the areas of systems analysis and implementation of Management Information Systems which will utilize a demonstrated ability to improve systems performance. Willing to relocate.

RELATED EXPERIENCE

Engineering Technician, U.S. Navy.
Reviewed technical publications to improve operational and technical descriptions and maintenance procedures. Developed system operation training course for high-level, nontechnical managers. Developed PERT charts for scheduling 18-month overhauls. Installed and checked out digital computer equipment with engineers. Devised and implemented a planned maintenance program and schedule for computer complex to reduce equipment down-time and increase utilization by user departments. (2002 to present)

Assistant Manager/System Technician, U.S. Navy, 37 person division.
Established and coordinated preventive/corrective maintenance system for four missile guidance systems (9 work centers) resulting in increased reliability. Advised management on system operation and utilization for maximum effectiveness. Performed system test analysis and directed corrective maintenance actions. Interfaced with other managers to coordinate interaction of equipment and personnel. Conducted maintenance and safety inspections of various types of work centers. (1998 to 2001)

Assistant Manager/System Technician, U.S. Navy, 25 person division.
Supervised system tests, analyzed results, and directed maintenance actions on two missile guidance systems. Overhauled and adjusted within factory specifications two special purpose computers, reducing down-time over 50%. Established and coordinated system and computer training program. During this period, both systems received the "Battle Efficiency E For Excellence" award in competition with others units. (1995 to 1997)

EDUCATION

U.S. Navy Schools, 2000-2004:
Digital System Fundamentals, Analog/Digital Digital/Analog Conversion Techniques, UNIVAC 1219B Computer Programming, and Technical Writing.

A.S. in Education, June 1998:
San Diego Community College, San Diego, CA
Highlight:
Graduated Magna Cum Laude
Member, Phi Beta Kappa Honor Society

RESEARCH/LAW ENFORCEMENT ADMINISTRATION

CHERYL AYERS
2589 Jason Drive   202-467-8735
Ithaca, NY 14850   Ayersc@aol.com

OBJECTIVE: A research, data analysis, and planning position in law
                        enforcement administration which will use leadership,
                        responsibility, and organizational skills for improving the
                        efficiency of operations.

EDUCATION: <u>B.S. in Criminal Justice</u>, 2005
                        Ithaca College, Ithaca, NY
                        ▪ Major: Law Enforcement Administration
                        ▪ Minor: Management Information Systems
                          G.P.A. in concentration 3.6/4.0

AREAS OF   <u>Leadership</u>
EFFECTIVENESS: Head secretary while working at State Police.
                        Served as Rush Chair and Social Chair for Chi Phi Sorority.
                        Elected Captain and Co-Captain three times during ten years
                        of cheerleading.

                        <u>Responsibility</u>
                        Handled highly confidential information, material, and files for
                            State Police.
                        Aided in the implementation of on-line banking system.
                        In charge of receiving and dispersing cash funds for drive-in
                            restaurant.

                        <u>Organization</u>
                        Revised ticket system for investigators' reports at State Police.
                        Planning schedules and budget, developed party themes and
                            skits, obtained prop material, and delegated and coordinated
                            work of others during sorority rush.

                        <u>Data Analysis</u>
                        Proficient in dBase, Excel, and Access.
                        Analyzed State Police data on apprehensions; wrote report.

PERSONAL: Excellent health...single...enjoy all sports and challenges...willing
                        to relocate.

REFERENCES: Available upon request from the Office of Career Planning and
                        Placement, Ithaca College, Ithaca, NY

PUBLIC RELATIONS

MICHELE R. FOLGER
733 Main Street
Williamsburg, VA 23572
804-376-9932
folgerm@aol.com

OBJECTIVE: A manager/practitioner position in public relations which will use research, writing, and program experience. Willing to relocate.

EXPERIENCE: <u>Program Development</u>
Conducted research on the representation of minority students in medical colleges. Developed proposal for a major study in the field. Secured funding for $945,000 project. Coordinated and administered the program which had major effect on medical education.

Initiated and developed a national minority student recruitment program for 20 medical colleges.

<u>Writing</u>
Compiled and published reports in a variety of educational areas. Produced several booklets on urban problems for general distribution. Published articles in professional journals. Wrote and presented conference papers.

<u>Research</u>
Gathered and analyzed information concerning higher education in a variety of specialized fields. Familiar with data collection and statistics. Good knowledge of computers.

<u>**Administration and Management**</u>
Hired and trained research assistants. Managed medium-sized office and supervised 30 employees.

<u>Public Relations</u>
Prepared press releases and conducted press conferences. Organized and hosted receptions and social events. Spoke to various civic, business, and professional organizations.

WORK HISTORY: ATS Research Associates, Washington, DC
Virginia Education Foundation, Richmond, VA
Eaton's Advertising Agency, Cincinnati, OH

EDUCATION: M.A., Journalism, College of William and Mary, 2002.
B.A., English Literature, University of Cincinnati, 1996.

REFERENCES: Available upon request.

SUPPLEMENTAL INFORMATION   **MICHELE R. FOLGER**

Public Speaking

- "The New Public Relations," New York Public Relations Society, New York City, April 8, 2005.
- "How to Prepare an Effective Press Conference," Virginia Department of Public Relations, Richmond, Virginia, November 21, 2004.
- "New Approaches to Public Relations," United States Chamber of Commerce, Washington, D.C., February 26, 2003.

Professional Activities

- Delegate, State Writer's Conference, Roanoke, VA, 2004.
- Chair, Journalism Club, College of William and Mary, 2003.
- Secretary, Creative Writing Society, University of Cincinnati, 2002.
- Co-Chair, Public Relations in the United States Conference, College of William and Mary, 2001.
- Chair, Women's Conference, Junior League of Cincinnati, 2000.

Publications

- "The Creative Writer Today," Times Literary, Vol. 6, No. 3 (September 2004), pp. 34-51.
- "Representation of Minority Medical Students," Medical Education, Vol. 32, No. 1 (January 2003), pp. 206-218.
- "Recruiting Minority Students to Medical Colleges in the Northeast," Medical College Bulletin, Vol. 23, No. 4 (March 2002), pp. 21-29.

Reports

- "Increasing Representation of Minority Students in 50 Medical Colleges," submitted to the Foundation for Medical Education, Washington, DC, May 2004, 288 pages.
- "Urban Education as a Problem of Urban Decay," submitted to the Urban Education Foundation, New York City, September 2003, 421 pages.

Continuing Education

- "Grantsmanship Workshop," Williamsburg, Virginia, 2004.
- "Developing Public Relations Writing Skills," workshop, Washington, DC, 2002.
- "New Program Development Approaches for the 21st Century," Virginia Beach, Virginia, 2001.
- "Research Design and Data Analysis in the Humanities," University of Michigan, 2000.

Educational Highlights

- Assistant Editor of the Literary Times, University of Cincinnati, 1997-1998.
- Earned 3.8/4.0 grade point average as undergraduate and 4.0/4.0 as graduate student while working full time.
- M.A. Thesis: "Creating Writing Approaches to Public Relations."

PUBLISHING/COMPUTERS

MARY FURNISS

7812 W. 24th Street   821-879-1124
Dallas, TX 71234   furnissm@aol.com

OBJECTIVE: **A management position** involving the application of computer technology for improving the efficiency of publishing operations.

EXPERIENCE: <u>**Computer Applications Manager, 2003 to present**</u>
Stevens Publishing Company, Fort Worth, TX

Managed all computer-related projects for publishing firm with annual sales of $40 million. Presented yearly capital expenditure and general systems budget, negotiated computer service contracts, evaluated and recommended new equipment and software purchases, and trained staff to use software and hardware. Replaced ATEX typesetting with desktop publishing system that immediately saved the company $650,000 in operational costs.

<u>**Editorial/Production Supervisor, 2000-2002**</u>
Benton Publishing Company, San Francisco, CA

Supervised all computer-related projects. Trained staff of 27 to use WordPerfect and other software applications. Devised an innovative system that transformed traditional galley editing into an efficient electronic editing system. New computerized system eliminated the need for two additional employees to handle the traditional galley editing system. Reduced errors by 70 percent.

<u>**Editorial Assistant, 1998-1999**</u>
Benton Publishing Company, San Francisco, CA

Prepared annual *Encyclopedia of International Forestry* materials for editing and production. Supervised freelancers for special editorial projects. Proofread and copy-edited materials for 18 books produced annually. Received "Employee of the Year" award for initiating a new computerized editing system that saved the company $70,000 in annual freelance editing fees.

EDUCATION: <u>University of Washington</u>
B.A., Journalism, 1998.

SPECIAL
SKILLS: Familiar with the ATEX typesetting system and the application of Ventura desktop publishing software. Attended two advanced training programs in the use of computerized editing systems.

PERSONAL: Enjoy developing innovative and cost-saving approaches to traditional publishing tasks that involve the application of computer technology. Work well in team settings and with training groups. Willing to relocate for the appropriate challenge.

CONSTRUCTION/PROJECT MANAGER

JAMES BARSTOW

7781 West Gate Road   421-827-0841

Cincinnati, OH 44411   barstowj@aol.com

OBJECTIVE

A challenging project manager position involving all phases of construction where a demonstrated record of timely and cost-effective completion of projects is important to both the company and its clients.

SUMMARY OF QUALIFICATIONS

- 28 years of progressively responsible construction management experience involving all facets of construction, from start-up to final inspection.
- Experienced in supervising all aspects of construction including masonry, concrete work, carpentry, electrical, mechanical, and plumbing.
- Communicate and work well with individuals at all levels from client to architect to subcontractors.

EXPERIENCE

Independent Contractor, Barstow & Thomas, Cincinnati, OH

Owned and managed a general contracting company doing $8 million in commercial construction each year. Performed all estimating, established contacts with subcontractors, purchased specialty items and materials, and handled shop drawings. Managed all time scheduling, monthly and submonthly draws, and guaranties. Hired all superintendents. Completed most jobs within 30 days of projected completion dates and managed to keep costs 5 percent under estimates. 1990 to present.

Job Superintendent, J.P. Snow, Columbus, OH

Supervised all work from start-up to final inspection as well as established all time schedules from start to finish. Handled shop drawings, lab testing, job testing, change orders, daily reports, job progress reports, payroll, and hiring. Worked with client, architect, and city, state, and federal inspectors. Responsible for all concrete and carpentry work including piers, beams, slabs, paving, walls, curbs, and walkways. Initiated an innovative scheduling system that saved the employer more than $60,000 in projected down-time. Consistently praised for taking initiative, providing exceptional leadership, and communicating well with clients, architects, and subcontactors. 1983-1989.

Subcontractor, Smith & Company, Columbus, OH

Conducted all bidding, estimating, and purchasing for more than 50 commercial masonry projects. Worked with both union and open shop help. Managed payroll for 75 employees during different project phases. Projects included hospitals, churches, schools, office buildings, and retail shops. 1977-1982.

ACCOU

JANET SOUTHERN
721 James Court
Chicago, IL 60029

OBJECTIVE: An accou
skills wil
corporat

146

CHARLES DAV
771 Anderson Str
Knoxville, TN

OBJE

EXPERIENCE: <u>Accountant, J.S.</u>
Analyzed accounting sys
for over 30 corporate accounts. C
attended by more than 500 accountants w
Developed proposals, presented demonstration pr
prepared reports for corporate clients. Increased new acc
42% over a four year period. 2001 to present.

<u>**Junior Accountant, Simon Electrical Co., Chicago, IL**</u>
Acquired extensive experience in all aspects of corporate
accounting while assigned to the Controller's Office. Prepared
detailed financial records for corporate meetings as well as
performed basic accounting tasks such as journal entries,
reconciling discrepancies, and checking records for accuracy and
consistency. Assisted office in converting to a new computerized
accounting system that eliminated the need for additional personnel
and significantly improved the accuracy and responsiveness. 1997to
2000.

<u>**Accounting Clerk, Johnson Supplies, Chicago, IL**</u>
Acquired working knowledge of basic accounting functions for a
200+ employee organization with annual revenues of $45 million.
Prepared journal vouchers, posted entries, and completed standard
reports. Proposed a backup accounting system that was
implemented by the Senior Accountant. 1994 to 1996.

EDUCATION: <u>**Roosevelt University, Chicago, IL**</u>
B.S., Accounting, 1993.
Highlights:
  Minor in Computer Science. Worked as a summer intern with
  Ballston Accounting Company. Honors graduate with a 3.7/4.0
  GPA in all course work.

REFERENCES: Available upon request.

PARALEGAL

IS
eet   421-789-5677
7921   davisc@aol.com

TIVE: **A paralegal position** with a firm specializing in criminal law where research and writing skills and an attention to detail will be used for completing timely assignments.

EDUCATION: **University of Illinois, Champaign, IL**
B.A., Criminal Justice, 2005.
Highlights:
  Minor, English
  President, Paralegal Student Association, 2004.
  3.7/4.0 GPA

Rock Island Junior College, Rock Island, IL
A.A., English, 1995.

AREAS OF EFFECTIVENESS

LAW: Completed 36 semester hours of criminal justice course work with special emphasis on criminal law. Served as an intern with law firm specializing in criminal law. Interviewed clients, drafted documents, conducted legal research, assisted lawyers in preparing court briefs. Participated in criminal justice forums sponsored by the Department of Criminal Justice at the University of Illinois.

RESEARCH: Conducted research on several criminal cases as both a student and a paralegal intern. Experienced in examining court cases, interviewing lawyers and judges, and observing court proceedings. Proficient in using microfiche and computerized data bases for conducting legal research.

COMMUNICATION: Prepared research papers, legal summaries, and memos and briefed attorneys on criminal cases relevant to assignments. Used telephone extensively for interviewing clients and conducting legal research.

WORK EXPERIENCE: **Paralegal Intern, Stanford and Rollins, Peoria, IL.**
Summer Intern, 1996. Assigned to numerous research projects relevant to pending criminal cases.

Part-time employment.
Held several part-time positions while attending school full-time. These included student assistant in the Department of Criminal Justice, University of Illinois.

BOOKKEEPER

JANE BARROWS
997 Mountain Road
Denver, CO 80222

717-349-0137
barrowsj@aol.com

OBJECTIVE: **A manager or assistant manager position** with an Accounting Department requiring strong supervisory and communication skills.

EXPERIENCE: **Manager, Accounts Payable, T.L. Dutton, Denver, CO.**
Supervised 18 employees who routinely processed 200 invoices a day. Handled vendor inquiries and adjustments. Conducted quarterly accruals and reconciliations. Screened candidates and conducted annual performance evaluations. Reduced the number of billing errors by 30 percent and vendor inquiries by 25% within the first year. 2003 to present.

Supervisor, Accounts Payable, AAA Pest Control, Denver, CO.
Supervised 10 employees who processed nearly 140 invoices a day. Audited vendor invoices, authorized payments, and balanced daily disbursements. Introduced automated accounts receivable system for improving the efficiency and accuracy of receivables. 2000 to 2002.

Bookkeeper, Davis Nursery, Ft. Collins, CO.
Processed accounts payable and receivable, reconciled accounts, balanced daily disbursements, and managed payroll for a 20-employee organization with annual revenues of $1.8 million. 1996 to 1999.

Bookkeeper, Jamison's Lumber, Ft Collins, CO.
Assisted accountant in processing accounts payable and receivable and managing payroll for 40-employee organization with annual revenues of $3.2 million. 1992 to 1995.

EDUCATION: **Colorado Junior College, Denver, CO.**
Currently taking advanced courses in accounting, computer science, and management.

Terrance Vo-Tech School, Terrance, CO.
Completed commercial courses, 1991.

REFERENCES: Available upon request.

FINANCIAL ANALYST

SUSAN ALLEN
325 West End Street   402-378-9771
Atlanta, GA 30019   allens@aol.com

OBJECTIVE: **A financial analyst position** with a bank where
                        experience with investment portfolios will be used
                        for attracting new clientele.

EXPERIENCE: **Investment Analyst, First City Bank, Atlanta, GA.**
                        Managed $650 million in diverse portfolios for bank's
                        major clients which averaged 12 percent annual return on
                        investment. Regularly met with clients, reviewed current
                        investments, and presented new investment options for
                        further diversifying portfolios. Introduced biweekly news-
                        letter for communicating investment strategies with clients
                        and bank officers. 2003 to present.

                        Research Analyst, Georgia Bank, Atlanta, GA.
                        Conducted research, wrote reports, and briefed supervisor
                        on stock market trends and individual companies which
                        affected the bank's $1.2 billion securities portfolio. Worked
                        closely with Investment Analyst in developing new ap-
                        proaches to communicating research findings and summary
                        reports to clients and bank officers. 1999 to 2002

                        **Research Assistant/Intern, Columbia Savings Bank,
                        Columbia, SC.**
                        Served as a Summer Intern while completing undergraduate
                        degree. Assigned as Research Assistant to Chief Analyst.
                        Followed stock market trends and conducted research on
                        selected investment banks. 1996 to 1997.

EDUCATION: **University of Miami, Miami, FL.**
                        MBA, Business Administration, 1998.
                        Focused course work on finance and management.
                        Thesis: "Successful Investment Strategies of Florida's
                                  Ten Major Banks."

                        University of South Carolina, Columbia, SC.
                        B.S., Finance, Department of Commerce, 1996.
                        Summer Intern with Columbia Savings Bank.
                        Secretary/Treasurer of the Student Business Association.

REFERENCES: Available upon request.

SALES MANAGER

MARK ABLE
7723 Stevens Avenue
Phoenix, AZ 80023

802-461-0921
ablem@aol.com

OBJECTIVE:

A retail management position where demonstrated skills in sales and marketing and enthusiasm for innovation will be used for improving customer service and expanding department profitability.

SUMMARY OF QUALIFICATIONS:

Twelve years of progressively responsible experience in all phases of retail sales and marketing with major discount stores in culturally diverse metropolitan areas. Annually improved profitability by 15 percent and consistently rated in top 10 percent of workforce.

EXPERIENCE:

Sales Manager, K-Mart, Memphis, TN
Managed four departments with annual sales of nearly $8 million. Hired, trained, and supervised a culturally diverse workforce of 14 full-time and 6 part-time employees. Reorganized displays, developed new marketing approaches, coordinated customer feedback with buyers in upgrading quality of merchandise, and improved customer service that resulted in 25 percent increase in annual sales. Received "Outstanding" performance evaluation and "Employee of the Year" award. 2003 to present.

Assistant Buyer, Wal-Mart, Memphis, TN
Maintained inventory levels for three departments with annual sales of $5 million. Developed more competitive system of vendor relations that reduced product costs by 5 percent. Incorporated latest product and merchandising trends into purchasing decisions. Worked closely with department managers in maintaining adequate inventory levels for best-selling items. 1999 to 2002.

Salesperson, Zayres, Knoxville, TN
Responsible for improving sales in four departments with annual sales of $3.5 million. Reorganized displays and instituted new "Ask An Expert" system for improved customer relations. Sales initiatives resulted in a 20 percent increase in annual sales. Cited for "Excellent customer relations" in annual performance evaluation. Worked part-time while completing education. 1996-1998.

EDUCATION:

University of Tennessee, Knoxville, TN
B.S., Marketing, 1996.
Earned 80 percent of educational expenses while working part-time and maintaining full course loads.

ATTORNEY

STEVEN MARSH   Home: 501-789-4321
2001 West James Ct.   Work: 501-789-5539
Seattle, WA 98322   marshs@aol.com

OBJECTIVE

A position in aviation law where proven management, organization, and supervisory skills and an exceptional record of success in investigating, adjudicating, settling, defending, and prosecuting cases will be used in settling cases to the benefit of employer and clients.

EXPERIENCE

Chief Circuit Defense Counsel, Davis Air Force Base, Ogden, UT
Personally defended all Flying Evaluation Boards (4), winning every one. Successfully defended felony trials covering offenses of drug use, distribution, assault, DUI, and perjury. Supervised, trained, and directed 22 attorneys and 17 paralegals responsible for total defense services across 16 Air Force installations located in 12 states. Included oversight of over 500 trials with every offense up to and including premeditated murder. 2002-present

Chief, Aviation Settlement Branch, U.S. Air Force, Washington, DC
Directed the investigation, adjudication, and either settlement or litigation of all aviation, environmental, medical malpractice, and other tort claims filed against the Air Force. In 2000, this topped a $40 billion dollar exposure with the percentage of payout to claimed amount the lowest in over a decade. Supervised staff of 13 attorneys and 5 paralegals. Re-formulated U.S. Air Force policy on tort claim and litigation matters in conjunction with the Department of Justice leading to a better concept and application of paying the losers and spending time and resources to win-the-winners. 2000-2001

Chief, Tort Section, U.S. Air Force, Washington, DC
Supervised the investigation and recommended adjudication or litigation of all aviation tort claims against the Air Force, including the last of the Agent Orange cases and the KAL 007 Korean airliner shoot-down by the Soviet Union. Supervised staff of 3 attorneys and 1 paralegal. Recommended U.S. Air Force policy change on aviation tort claims that directly resulted in greater Agency latitude for meritorious claims independent of the previously required GAO Office requirements. 1999

Staff Judge Advocate, Stevens Air Force Base, Miami, FL
Advised top management of all legal issues to include the convening of Aircraft Accident Boards and Flying Evaluation Boards. Directed tort, labor, environmental, procurement, and criminal law procedures. During this period, defended two state environmental Notice of Violations successfully, and over 40 criminal cases were prosecuted without a single acquittal. Served as management's Chief Labor Resolution Negotiator securing settlements at 60 percent of the previously approved maximums. Supervised staff of 4 attorneys and 5 paralegals. 1996-1998

STEVE MARSH

Assistant Staff Judge Advocate, Lowry Air Force Base, CO
Served as government prosecutor for over 35 trials with no acquittals. Served as government representative in over 20 administrative hearings with no losses. Counseled clients on rights/duties under state and federal law. 1992-1995

Area Defense Counsel, Marshall Air Force Base, Austin, TX
Defended over 300 clients in criminal trials, administrative hearings, or minor disciplinary concerns. 1991

Assistant Staff Judge Advocate, Myrtle Beach Air Force Base, SC
Investigated and adjudicated all claims arising from a major B-52 bomber aircraft accident, supervising team of paralegals. Government prosecutor for 12 trials and boards, with zero losses. 1990.

EDUCATION

J.D., Boston University College of Law, Boston, MA, 1990
B.A. (Political Science), University of North Carolina, Chapel Hill, NC, 1982

TRAINING

Armed Forces Staff College, Joint Service Program, Residence, 2000
Air War College, USAF, Seminar Program, 1999
Air Command and Staff College, USAF, Seminar Program, 1995
Squadron Officers School, USAF, Residence Program (Dist. Grad.), 1992
Officer Training School, USAF, Residence Program (Dist. Grad.), 1985

AWARDS

Stuart Reichart Award, Senior Attorney, HQ USAF, 2003
Ramirez Award, Outstanding Attorney Tactical Air Command, 1999
Outstanding Attorney, U.S. Air Forces Colorado, 1995

OTHER EXPERIENCE

U.S. Parole Board Hearing Member, USAF, 2003
Joint Services Consolidation Committee, 1999-2000
Navigator and Weapons Officer, U.S. Air Force, F-4 Phantom Aircraft, 100+ sorties, 1987-1989
Police Officer, U.S. Air Force, 1985-1986

BAR MEMBERSHIPS

U.S. Supreme Court, 2003
U.S. Court of Appeals, 4th Circuit, 1999
U.S. Court of Military Appeals, 1993
Supreme Court of Massachusetts, 1990

FINANCIAL SERVICES

DONALD TERRENCE
1193 Daniel Road
St. Louis, MO 60000
512-888-1121 (H) / 512-888-1112 (W)
terrenced@aol.com

OBJECTIVE: A financial services position where strong communication and leadership skills will result in increased sales.

ACCOMPLISHMENTS:

Financial Management   Assisted in developing a $12 million annual budget for a department of 180 employees. Introduced new cost-cutting measures that resulted in saving $500,000 in a single year.

Leadership   Held various leadership and staff positions (Platoon Leader, Company Commander, Executive Officer, Personnel Staff Officer) while serving in the U.S. Army. Received three commendations for quality of performance.

Communication   Coordinated aviation training for the Third Armored Division, Frankfurt, Germany (17,000 soldiers, 360 armored vehicles, and 120 helicopters). Implemented a new unit training system for the division. System rated the best and most innovative in Germany.

Training   Raised training ratings from the worst to the best for six helicopter attack companies on two evaluations. Received a Zero Aircraft Accident Safety Award, and raised aircraft readiness rate to 85% which was 15% above the standard.

WORK HISTORY: **Assistant Athletic Director, Administration**, U.S. Military Academy, 2002-2005.

Division Aviation Staff Officer, Third Armored Division, Germany, 1999-2001.

Aviation Company Commander, 111th Helicopter Company, Fort Rucker, AL, 1997-1998

Infantry and Aviation Officer, Fort Benning, GA, 1993-1996.

EDUCATION: **University of Michigan, Ann Arbor, MI**
M.S. in Business Administration, 2001

United States Military Academy, West Point, NY
B.S. in General Engineering, 1993

INDUSTRIAL ENGINEERING

JEFFREY THOMPSON
391 Taylor Avenue
Denver, CO 80808

Home: 499-217-3219
Work: 499-217-9123
Thompsonj@aol.com

OBJECTIVE: An industrial engineering position with a broad-based manufacturing firm.

EXPERIENCE:

Systems Analysis
- Developed mainframe-based computer forecasting models to predict an individual's risk for selection by a separation board.
- Designed computer programs that resulted in removing 2,000 erroneous records.
- Created and implemented a system acceptance testing plan for a $3 million out-sourced optimization model resulting in four critical design enhancements and an 8.2% reporting accuracy increase.

Data Automation
- Developed a PC-based pavement management decision support systems; saved $200,000 in first six months through quantitative decision analysis.
- Automated typewriter-based office environment reducing administrative processing time by 35%

Personnel Management
- Managing human resource matters for a 750 employee organization including compensation and benefits, education, legal support, performance appraisals, reassignments, and personnel strength.

Management
- Supervised 180 employees with 34 different specialty skills performing maintenance and supply operations.
- Managed a 24-hour repair and warehouse facility servicing 13 retail customers' vehicles, missile, and communications equipment valued at $2.1 million.

WORK HISTORY:

- **Operations Research and Systems Analyst**, US Total Army Personnel Command, Alexandria, VA, 2004-present.

- **Consultant**, Massachusetts Department of Public Works, Wellesley, 2002-2003.

- **Personnel Officer**, US Army, 3rd Support Command, Giessen, Germany, 2000-2001.

- **General Manager**, US Army, 32d Army Air Defense Commands, Sweinfurt, Germany, 1997-1999.

EDUCATION: **University of Massachusetts**, Amherst, MA.
M.S. in Industrial Engineering and Operations Research, 2004.

Louisiana State University, Baton Rouge, LA.
B.S. in Industrial Engineering, 1995, Deans List.

PRODUCT MANAGEMENT/TELECOMMUNICATIONS

CHRIS JACKSON
1922 American Way
Cincinnati, OH 45556

Home: 413-658-9877
Work: 413-658-8993
Jacksonc@aol.com

OBJECTIVE: A product management position in a fast growing cellular communication company where organization, leadership, and communication experience will be used for improving product quality and innovation.

EXPERIENCE:

Organization Designed and coordinated communications for Pacific Command Joint Training Exercises. Organized and chaired engineering conferences. Presented decision briefings and prepared staff action papers for a variety of communication-related issues of considerable importance to the command. Served as Watch Officer during operations and exercises.

Leadership Installed, operated, and maintained satellite, switching, cable, and message communications in support of numerous U.S. Army units distributed throughout central Germany. Led 110 soldiers in performing all assigned communications missions. Total responsibility for the training, morale, welfare and discipline of all the soldiers under my command.

Communication Planned and supervised installation of telecommunication systems of V Corps exercises. Maintained and accounted for vehicle and communications equipment valued at approximately $1.5 million. Planned and conducted individual and collective training in technical skills and general military subjects. Supervised, trained, and led 23 personnel.

WORK HISTORY: Communication Staff Officer, 12th Signal Brigade, Fort Lewis, Washington, 2004-2005.

Communications Company Commander, C Company, 430th Signal Battalion, Mainz, West Germany, 2002-2003.

Platoon Leader, B Company, 17th Signal Battalion, Hoechst, West Germany, 1999-2001.

EDUCATION & TRAINING:
- U.S. Army Directory of Information Management Course, Fort Gordon, GA, 2002

- B.A., Psychology, Brigham Young University, Salt Lake City, UT, 1993-1997

ORGANIZATIONAL DEVELOPMENT

CHRIS MASON
4810 Grant Circle
Louisville, KY 41016
(999) 752-4832
masonc@infinet.com

OBJECTIVE

An organizational development position with a security company requiring leadership and management expertise.

SUMMARY OF EXPERIENCE

Fourteen years of leadership and training experience. Responsible for organizing, motivating, and directing soldiers in accomplishing assigned missions.

WORK HISTORY

Platoon Sergeant, 24th Division, Fort Stewart, GA (2003-present).
Responsible for the well-being, discipline, morale, and readiness of a 30-member unit. Set and enforced high standards in the areas of personal appearance, physical fitness, and weapons qualifications. Demonstrated essential leadership, supervision, management, and team building skills for accomplishing the platoon's mission.

Training NCO, 5th Infantry Division, Fort Polk, LA (1999-2002).
Assisted in developing weekly training plans for the company. Helped establish and conduct training programs in the areas of nuclear biological and chemical protection, physical fitness, land navigation, weapons qualifications, and equipment maintenance.

Infantry Squad Leader, 3rd US Infantry, Fort Myer, VA (1995-1997).
Organized and led a 10-member team through numerous missions. Planned team work schedules and training for accomplishing mission objectives. Set and enforced high standards of performance.

Team Leader, 197th Infantry Brigade, Fort Benning, GA (1993-1994).
First line supervisor responsible for the productivity of a four-man team. Organized training, planned daily activities, and supervised team members.

EDUCATION AND TRAINING

- Infantry Advanced Noncommissioned Officers Course, 1998
- Infantry Basic Noncommissioned Officers Course, 1996
- Leadership Development Course, Noncommissioned Officers Academy, 1994
- Infantry Basic Training, 1992

POLICE OFFICER

ALLEN STRONG   Home: 139-287-2256
59 Watergate Road, Apt. 1   Work: 139-287-7667
New Orleans, LA 77777   Stronga@aol.com

OBJECTIVE

Become a police officer in a diversified, bilingual community where leadership
and communication skills will be used for improving community relations.

EXPERIENCE

Training: Provided the Battalion's soldiers with training in Infantry tactics, land
navigation, physical fitness, marksmanship, weaponry, leadership, and drill and
ceremonies. Raised overall proficiency level from 75% to 90%.

Leadership: Served as an Infantry squad leader responsible for the discipline,
morale, and training of ten soldiers. Counseled and motivated soldiers in all aspects
of military training.

Weapons Proficiency: Developed proficiency in light weapon systems. Became
the recognized expert in land navigation. Received award for Best Soldier of the
Quarter.

WORK HISTORY

Training NCO, 75th Infantry Battalion, 82nd Airborne Division, Fort Bragg, NC,
2003-present.

Squad Leader, 82nd Airborne Division, Fort Bragg, NC, 2002.

Infantry Scout, 82nd Airborne Division, Fort Bragg, NC, 1999-2001.

EDUCATION

- Air Assault School, 2004
- Primary Leadership Development Course, Fort Benning, GA, 2002
- Airborne School, 2000
- Basic Infantry Course, 1999
- High School Diploma, Freedom High, Tallahassee, FL, 1998

PERSONAL

Secret security clearance

TELECOMMUNICATIONS/NETWORKING

SUZANNE RUSSELL
891 Galveston Drive
Las Vegas, NV 89321

Home: (277) 975-1467   russells@aol.com   Work: (277) 975-1988

OBJECTIVE

A technical position with a dynamite telecommunication firm specializing in the design, development, and fielding of local area networks.

HIGHLIGHTS OF QUALIFICATIONS

- Five years experience with microcomputers, desktop applications, and local area networks (LANs).
- Installed cable and connected associated LAN/WAN hardware.
- Skilled in recognizing and troubleshooting problems with network and computer systems.
- Committed to patient, observant, and personable interaction with users and their problems.

RELEVANT EXPERIENCE

Network Administrator

- Loaded software for 100 terminals.
- Skilled in troubleshooting Ethernet networks.
- Added, deleted, and updated users and mail groups for a 100 terminal, 200 user 3Com Network.
- Analyzed networks using Network General's Sniffer protocol analyzer.
- Tested new software for LAN compatibility.
- Coordinated System Trouble Reports.

Software Instructor

- Trained users to be self-sufficient on a 100 terminal, 200 user LAN:
  — Introduced the Macintosh operating system;
  — Introduced the 3+Share network operating system;
  — Taught the 3+Mail E-mail program;
  — Taught the application, Microsoft Works.
- Taught advanced word processing and desktop publishing using Microsoft Word, version 4.0 for the Macintosh.
- Received an Army Achievement medal for exceptional computer training while stationed in Fort Lewis, WA.

Computer Operator

- Developed and maintained a large tape and disk library.
- Made RS-232 connectors for twisted pair cables and installed cabling.
- Installed Etherlink cards.
- Installed math co-processors in 40 PCs.
- Prepared color graphics and color slide presentations.
- Designed and edited the unit newsletter.

ADDITIONAL TECHNICAL EXPERIENCE

- Knowledge and experience with Unix and DEC VAX VMS operating systems.
- Knowledge and experience with Wiudows and Macintosh operating systems.
- Knowledge and experience with the following IBM PC applications: MS Works, MS Word, MacDraw II, MacDraw Pro, MacPaint, SuperPaint, MS Excel, and Aldus Pagemaker.

WORK HISTORY

Served in the U.S. Army from 1999 to the present. Held positions of increasing responsibility in the areas of local area networks and microcomputer-based systems. Trained military personnel in a variety of desktop software applications. Assigned to bases in Panama and at Ft. Sill, Oklahoma and Fort Lewis, Washington. Acquired experience in the following positions:

- **Network Administrator**, Fort Stewart, GA, 2003-present
- **Instructor, Fort Lee**, VA, 2002
- **Computer Operator**, Fort Lee, VA, 2001

EDUCATION AND TRAINING

Education

- Completing a B.S. in Computer Information Systems, University of Washington, Seattle, WA.

Training

- 3Com 3+Network Installation and Administration.
- 3Com Network Architectures, Standards, and Protocols.
- Network General's Introduction to LAN Technology and Analysis.
- Network General's Ethernet Network Analysis and Troubleshooting.
- U.S. Army Ultrix/Unix Systems Operations.

INTERNATIONAL RURAL DEVELOPMENT

MARCIA TAYLOR
1305 Jefferson Street
Boston, MA 02311

Home: 817-568-7311
Work: 817-568-1111
taylorm@aol.com

OBJECTIVE

A position with an NGO specializing in rural development, where experience in proposal development, policy analysis, and project planning, monitoring, and evaluation relevant to agricultural economics and women in development in Africa and the Ukraine will be used for successful project implementation.

PROFESSIONAL EXPERIENCE

Administrative Officer: Collins Training Group, 9614 Lightning Road, Boston, MA 02182. Responsible for organizing administrative packages for training programs conducted by a major government contractor and private training organization. Responsibilities include scheduling and evaluating training sites, coordinating logistics, communicating with sales and instructional staff, and monitoring the implementation of contracts. 2003 to present.

Planning and Monitoring Officer: Department of Agricultural Extension Services, Ministry of Agriculture, Accra, Ghana. Major responsibility for planning, coordinating, and monitoring Ghana's decentralized planning process.

Planning

- Worked with 10 regions (including 118 administrative districts) in collecting and compiling plans for developing the national extension program. Assessed regional objectives. Coordinated technical, health, nutrition, and research staffs to implement the national extension program.

- Managed the review and evaluation of the Extension Services Department for organizational restructuring.

Monitoring

- Developed simplified monitoring formats to assess extension activities at all national and regional levels. Conducted periodic site visits nationwide and reported findings to Director of Extension Services. Served as liaison to Policy, Planning, Monitoring, and Evaluation Department of the Ministry of Agriculture. Evaluated transportation and communication by and among field officers. Submitted quarterly and annual reports to Director of Extension. Served as the extension counterpart to the World Bank's extension representative in monitoring activities of Pilot Farmers' Association in Sekyiama, a rural Ghanaian village.

In 1995 this model department was awarded the "Best Department Award" by the Secretary of Agriculture as well as a $40 million World Bank loan for the implementation of the national extension project. 1999 to 2002.

Project Officer: "31st December" Women's Movement (NGO). Served as a consultant on a grassroots nationwide NGO project designed to promote the economic self-sufficiency of rural and urban Ghanaian women. Assessed and made recommendations for enhancement, redirection, and financial support of indigenous projects designed to promote women's entrepreneurial abilities. Developed a proposal for a UNIFEM-funded ($1 million) project that provided hand-dug wells in villages in the Central Region of Ghana. Represented the organization on the Ghanaian Association of Private and Voluntary Organizations in Development (GAPVOD), Ghana's national organization of NGOs. August, 1999 to November, 1999.

Agricultural Economist: Agricultural Services Rehabilitation Project and Department of Foreign Economic Relations under the Ministry of Agriculture, Accra, Ghana. Assisted in developing proposals to international funding agencies (World Bank, FAO, USAID, IFAD) for support of agricultural programs. Undertook feasibility studies for the introduction of various agricultural projects funded by international agencies to support small-scale farmerholder projects in Northern and Volta regions. Projects analyzed agricultural potential along with the infrastructural base for project implementation (research, technology transfer, production, marketing outlets, processing, and distribution of farm produce. Study resulted in developing systems for health care, education, and agricultural cooperatives. Represented the Ministry of Agriculture at various bilateral and multilateral commission meetings. Worked with trade ministries of other African countries on negotiated trade agreements; assisted in evaluation of cost and price of agricultural products (pineapples, cocoa, and coffee) and foreign trade items (petroleum and heavy agricultural machinery).

Collective/State/Private Farm Researcher/Analyst/Participant: Ukraine and Moldavia. Studied, analyzed, and evaluated the comparative advantages and disadvantages of the collective, state, and private farm systems. Made policy recommendations for reorganizing the organizational structure of the three farm systems as well as for improving the quality and quantity of farm produce. Worked in all phases of farm operations. An on-going five-year study/project as part of a major undergraduate and graduate study program, 1993-1998.

EDUCATION

M.S. in Agricultural Economics, 1998
Odessa Agricultural Institute, Odessa, Ukraine

> Specialized in farm management and production economics. Program involved practical work, study, and organization development experience on five state, collective, and private farms over a five year period. Completed master's thesis on reducing agricultural production costs.

Advanced and Ordinary Level Certificates, General Sciences

> Mawuli School, Ho, Volta Region, Ghana, 1992
> Our Lady of Apostles Secondary School, Ho, Volta Region, Ghana, 1990

LANGUAGES

Multilingual. Completely fluent in Russian, English, and Twi – speaking, reading, and writing. Can work in all three languages.

FLIGHT ATTENDANT

MARILYN CARROLL   Home: 999-999-1782
2933 Stewart Drive   Work: 999-999-8765
Greensboro, NC 29999   Carrollm@aol.com

OBJECTIVE: A flight attendant position where demonstrated communication, organization, promotion, sales, and supervision skills will be used in promoting excellent customer service, and where enthusiasm, friendliness, judgment, maturity, humor, and dress and appearance are important to getting the job done.

AREAS OF EFFECTIVENESS:

Communications/Promotion
Coordinated press relations, developed advertising and promotional literature, and persuaded community leaders to sponsor programs and hire personnel. Maintained customer relations, promoted product line, and developed communication approaches for marketing publications worldwide. Promoted a variety of product lines, from food and clothing to stationery and gift items, at national and regional trade shows. Hosted receptions for community membership drives.

Selling
Several years experience selling clothing, food, stationery, books, computer software, educational videos, and gift items through trade shows, retail outlets, and direct-mail. Owned and operated a high quality jewelry business specializing in custom service; attained 100% customer satisfaction at all times. Especially enjoy meeting customers, demonstrating products, finalizing sales, and following-up customer relations.

Organizing
Directed a successful nine-year community fund raising program which resulted in completely discharging financial obligations. Involved in researching museum activities and selecting new historical sites. Sponsored and coordinated annual events for community leaders. Planned and implemented a successful political campaign. Organized the design and manufacture of custom-made jewelry. Developed art work for publications.

Supervising
Supervised major community projects and fund raising efforts. Hired and supervised employees involved in jewelry and publication businesses. Organized and supervised trade show activities, campaign workers, and young people.

WORK HISTORY:

Tyler Publications, Lincoln, NE, 2002-2005. Customer service representative and computer operator involved with maintaining customer relations, processing orders, accounting, and sales.

Community Savings Bank, Lincoln, NE, 2000-2001. Customer service involving opening new accounts, maintaining confidentiality, and handling deposits.

Mega Jewelry Co., Lincoln, NE, 1994-1999. Owner/operator involved in the sales and custom design of jewelry as well as day-to-day business operations.

Denver Merchandise Mart and Trade Center, Denver, CO, 1989-1993. Trade show sales representative.

BARRY A. MITCHELL
1234 Riverwoods Drive
Savannah, Georgia 56321
(404) 555-1212

OBJECTIVE

Health Care Facilities Director position encompassing the administration of multi-site operations; personnel training and staff development programs; and organization providing retirement living with continuing care capability.

BACKGROUND SUMMARY

Over 20 years experience developing expertise in:

- Training
- Strategic Forecasting
- Events Planning
- Recruiting
- Financial Management
- Customer Service
- Team Building
- Geriatric Assisted Living
- For Profit Operations
- State HRS & Federal OBRA Regulations

ACHIEVEMENTS

- Instituted first managed rehabilitation operation in Georgia at Sunset Towers to complement different levels of assisted care including: adult day care services, a geriatric fitness center, and a home care agency.

- Developed a program to assist life care residents who had depleted their funds. By enrolling them in a Medicaid program Sunset Towers was able to relieve their financial obligation while ensuring them continued quality care.

- Effected cash flow turnaround, increased annual revenues form $6.5 million to $14.5 million while increasing customer satisfaction and quality of life benefits for a multi unit retirement facility.

- Chaired a Political Action Committee to assist nursing home administrators lobby representatives and senators to enact nursing home legislation.

- Managed all club operations at Garrison Creek Golf & Country Club the year prior to, and during the 1984, GGA Championship tour event.

EXPERIENCE

SUNSET TOWERS, Savannah, GA   1986 - Present
Executive Director
Manage the activities of this 596 unit retirement community which includes a 150-bed skilled nursing facility. Control an operational budget of $13 million. Establish standards of service to customer while increasing revenues and profits. Supervise a professional staff of 315 employees.

CARMEL'S MANAGEMENT SERVICES, Pasadena, FL   1977 - 1986
Food Service Director
Began employment as a steward. Progressed to area and traveling manager, eventually managed all aspects of contract food services including specialty, hospitality, country club, and health care. Developed policy and procedures manuals for the retirement facilities food service accounts.

EDUCATION

BS, Food Service, The Culinary Institute, Atlanta, Georgia   1974

AFFILIATIONS

The Goodman Association
Georgia Health Care Association
All Saint's Hospital Committee

KEITH CARBON
5632 Cochran Street
West Valley, MA 63542
(517) 555-1212

OBJECTIVE

Communication Instructor/Trainer position involving creating presentations; leading seminars/workshops; writing speeches; and preparing individuals for public speaking engagements for a proprietary seminar or management consulting firm.

BACKGROUND SUMMARY

Over four years experience developing expertise in:

- Training
- Coaching
- Speech Writing
- Classroom Instruction
- Creating and Leading Seminars
- Public Speaking
- Proposal Writing

ACHIEVEMENTS

- Led seminars and workshops on interpersonal skills, multi-cultural relationships, and business communications for Public Speaking, Inc., Pasadena, FL.
- Coached CEOs, television anchors, sales reps, physicians, attorneys, and NFL football player on the art of speaking in front of groups and cameras.
- Created presentations and wrote speeches as both a member and instructor of university speech and debate teams.
- Received national recognition for competitive speaking.

EXPERIENCE

Public Speaking, Inc.   Pasadena, FL
Communications Consultant   1995 - 1996
Created and led training seminars; developed organizational proposals; and instructed/coached/prepared individuals for public speaking engagements.

EDUCATION

Tallahassee University   Tallahassee, FL
Speech Communication Instructor   1994 - 1995
Taught speech courses; evaluated and graded students' speeches, organized and developed lesson plans; presented speeches to be used as references.
Speech and Debate Coach
Organized speech tournaments; constructed competitive speeches and coached speech team members; budgeted for and reported expenditures.

Numerous Restaurants (from deli to fine dining)   1985 - 1994
Bartender/Food Server/Shift Supervisor/New Employee Trainer
Sold and served food and beverages; developed employee work schedules, trained new employees; greeted and seated guests.

COMPUTER & LANGUAGE

MA, Speech Communication, Tallahassee University, Tallahassee, FL   1995
BS, Speech Communication, Florida College, Parkside, FL   1994
AA, General Studies, Springfield College, Springfield, MA   1992

SKILLS

WordPerfect 6.1,WordPerfect Presentations 3.0, Windows 95, Procomm 2.0, Microsoft Word 7.0, Word Works, Page Maker, Corel Draw 6.0, Quattro Pro, ClarisWorks 2.1, MacWrite, MacDraw, MacPaint, Spreadsheet, Database, and Internet & World Wide Web connectors: Netscape, Mosaic, and Indylink. Fluent in Hebrew. Working knowledge of Spanish.

AFFILIATIONS

National Public Speaking Association
American Public Speaking Association
International Communicators Society

JERRY RUDACKER
3645 Calvert Street
Baltimore, MD 20745
(410) 555-1212

OBJECTIVE

General Manager position encompassing golf/proshop/facilities operations; full service food, beverage, and banquet services, personnel training and staff development programs; and capital improvements/expense forecasting and strategic planning for a prestigious member-owned country club.

BACKGROUND SUMMARY

Over 10 years experience developing expertise in:

- Training
- Recruiting
- Team Building
- Strategic Forecasting
- Financial Management
- Membership Marketing
- Events Planning
- Customer Service
- For Profit Operations
- Fine Dining/Banquet/Party Supervision

ACHIEVEMENTS

- Increased membership by instituting an Ambassador program; introduced fine dining, food and beverage quality standards; and established staff structuring at the Bent Tree Country Club.
- Introduced a distinguished lecture program featuring President Gerald R. Ford, Henry Kissinger, David Stockman, Jean Kirkpatrick among others at the Baltimore City Club to the delight of the Baltimore Chamber of Commerce.
- Effected cash flow turnaround, from a $30,000 loss to a profit of $110,000 after first 12 months, and improved revenues by over 9% each year thereafter for National Club Corporation at the Cantonsville City Club.
- One of four individuals representing 60 clubs in the region to be nominated for National Club Corporation Manager of the Year, 1991.
- Created a warm and inviting atmosphere among employees, members, and the Board/Trustees at every club by using a "hands-on" management style.

EXPERIENCE

Links Golf Management   Baltimore, MD
General Manager, Bent Tree Country Club, Baltimore, MD   1995 - 1996
Directed the activities of this former privately owned thirty year old, 350 member club on behalf of a management consulting organization. Prepared the 1996-2000 strategic plan and capital expense forecast. Supervised golf/proshop, course facilities, fine dining, and banquet/party operations.

National Club Corporation (NCC)   Baltimore, MD
Club Manager, Baltimore City Club, Baltimore, MD   1993 - 1995
Managed a prestigious 2,000 member downtown city club to ensure efficient and profitable operation. Actively participated in expanding the membership, improving cash flow, and establishing member equity. Did the financial and strategic planning.

Club Manager, The Cantonsville City Club, Cantonsville, MD   1987 - 1993
Developed the club into a catalyst for business growth in downtown Cantonsville. As the sole employee of NCC, established standards for service to members while increasing revenues and profits. Planned and directly supervised fine dining and entertainment. Established a Distinguished Lecture Series with banquet format.

Associate Club Manager, The River Club, Savannah, GA   1985 - 1987
Completed the associates training program earning NCC rookie of the Year award. Supervised kitchen operations; purchased food products, beverages, and wines.

EDUCATION

BA, Communications, The University of Maryland, Baltimore, MD   1985
Certified Club Management & Operations Trainer, NCC, Catonsville, MD   1994

Jeff B. Tatum
45 111ᵗʰ Street, Apt. 202
Washington, DC 20027
(202) 555-1212

OBJECTIVE

A position utilizing my skills in **Sales and Marketing, Program Development, Project Management, Promotional Events** and **Presentations** in order to:
- increase sales through refining services and heightening market penetration
- expand organization's impact, profitability and client base
- plan and implement programs to enhance public awareness and company image.

QUALIFICATIONS

- Sales/Management
- Market Development
- Customer/Client Relations
- Negotiations
- Key Account Management

- Project Management
- Program Development
- Leadership/Motivation
- Staff Development
- Recruiting/Interviewing

- Promotional Events
- Presentations
- Coaching/Training
- Community Relations
- Image Development

WORK HISTORY

Owner
  Depend on Us, Inc., VA   1997 - Present
Account Executive
  Washington Pistols Arena Football, League, DC   1996 - 1997
Head Men's Basketball Coach / P.E. Teacher
  East Riverside High School, DC   1993 - 1996
Basketball Scout
  Berkley Scouting Service, VA   1992 - 1993
Assistant Basketball Coach
  Mason College, VA   1990 - 1992
Head Basketball Coach
  Dunham Junior College, MD   1986 - 1990
Assistant Basketball Coach
  University of Maryland at College Park, MD   1983 - 1986

EDUCATION

Master's Degree in Physical Education
  Dupree University
Bachelor of Science Degree in Physical Education
  Maryland State University

PERSONAL

• Willing to Travel • Willing to Relocate • Golf • Coaching • Biking •

Chandler M. Taylor
246 Lightning Avenue
San Jose, CA 99876
(876) 555-1212

OBJECTIVE

A position utilizing my skills in **Business and Commercial Law, Strategic Problem Solving, Market Analysis** and **Market Development** in order to:

- represent clients to maximize business potential while safeguarding interests
- identify, avoid or troubleshoot potential impediments to organizational profitability
- assess and expand growth in marketplace.

QUALIFICATIONS

- Business/Commercial Law
- Contract Negotiations
- Insurance/Property Law
- Litigation Strategies
- Risk Management

- Strategic Problem Solving
- Project Management
- Consulting
- Motor Sports Industry
- Writing/Editing

- Market Development
- Research & Analysis
- Client Relations
- Leadership/Supervision
- Agency Agreements

WORK HISTORY

Billings, Johnson & Morgan, LLP, San Jose, CA   1996 - Present
   Attorney
Young, Goldman & Schmidt, Springfield, VA   Summer 1995
   Summer Associate
Miller, Jones, Simpson & Delp, San Jose, CA   Summer 1994
   Summer Associate
MicroTech, Boulder, CO   Summer 1993
   Marketing Representative
Miller-Jenkins Corporation, Waco, KY   Summers 1989 - 1992
   Marketing Intern

EDUCATION and PROFESSIONAL

Juris Doctor   1996
   University of California, School of Law. Los Angeles, CA
   Notes Editor, *California Journal of International & Comparative Law*
   Bill Davis Moot Court Team

Bachelor of Arts in Psychology, *Cum Laude*   1993
   Parkside Junior College, San Diego, CA
   President, Class of 1993

Invitation to Serve: Advisory Board for Sports Business Program at San Jose Technology Institute
   Parker Business School, Global Affairs (official appointment pending final program formation).

Member: American Bar Association: State Bar of California; San Jose Bar Association (Sports Section).

Admissions: Superior and State Courts of California. Court of Appeals of California; Supreme Court of California; U.S. District Court for the Northern District of California; U.S. Tenth Circuit Court of Appeals.

PUBLICATIONS

Identifying Agents for Depositions Under Federal Civil Procedure Rules. CIV Journal, Vol. 8, No. 2 , May 1998.

Proper Investigatory Surveillance. CIV Journal, Vol. 10, No. 32, March 1997.

Advantages of a Limited Liability Partnership (LLP), Intra-law firm publication, May 1994.

Flood Relief Manual. FEMA inspired source book for volunteer attorneys to assist 1994 earthquake victims.

COMPUTER SKILLS

- Windows 95 • WordPerfect ,7.0 • Lotus 1-2-3 • Microsoft Word • Excel • PowerPoint • Westlaw • Lexis

ACHIEVEMENTS

Business and Commercial Law

Negotiated Sponsorship Contract between USAUTO All Pro Team client (Sunny Racing Group) and union-automotive nonprofit entity (UAF-HM). Assessed proposed contract; utilized motor sports and legal knowledge to explain ramifications and implications; recommended changes to protect team interest and enhance marketability position; negotiated changes with sponsoring entity. **Results:** Secured favorable terms: improved team visibility and changes increased market exposure through sponsored show-car exhibits at USAUTO Salem Cup race events.

Defended lawsuit against large insurance clients for breach of contract, fraud and tortious interference with business arising out of complex off-shore captive insurance devised litigation approach; deposed numerous parties and witnesses; researched, analyzed, prepared and argued full range of motions; assisted in mediation, settlement negotiations and trial. **Results:** Obtained full defense; saved clients over $3 million dollars; shielded sensitive internal business operations from public eye and scrutiny; reduced risk of further litigation.

Reduced potential multi-million dollar exposure for large client sued for breach of contract, fraud, bad faith and retention. Analyzed client's business practices; designed approach to receive immediate response from client; formulated defense strategy; drafted and argued discovery motions; evaluated and appraised discovery requests from opponent on client's business; determined extent of compliance. **Results:** Client prevailed on every discovery motion; significantly reduced client expense and employee time and energy required to locate, evaluate and produce documents, computer print-outs and other requested materials; protected client from public dissemination of extremely sensitive internal information.

Strategic Problem Solving

Generated state-by-state compendium of law regarding methods of wine promotion for international wine marketing; including use of store coupons, in-store division of large beverage campany. Identified promotional categories, in-store tastings, sweepstakes, combination packaging and supermarket sales; researched laws of all fifty states; applied laws to promotional and sales methods; designed comprehensive quick glance chart with appended supporting statutes and regulations. **Results:** Wine division saved time and resources by relying on information to develop permissible promotional activities in each state; reduced potential fines stemming from noncompliance.

Prevented plaintiff from obtaining products liability judgment against large appliance manufacturer client. Evaluated merits of complaint; investigated case and statutory law: determined client had been sued without justifiable cause; demanded dismissal. **Results:** Obtained dismissal, saved client time, legal expense and potential damage award; guarded client from inevitable negative product publicity and corresponding adverse market reaction.

Defended large insurance client in coverage lawsuit seeking over $3 million in alleged damages for environmental clean up of two EPA sites. Researched and analyzed case history; determined winnable defense that would not adversely affect client in future; convinced client not to settle as had 5 other defendants: pursued strategy. **Results:** Court granted summary judgment; established new California caselaw for late notice defense in insurance claims coverage disputes.

Market Analysis/Development

Recruited USAUTO Late Model Stock driver for management by USAUTO All Pro Team client. Interviewed and assessed driver's accomplishments and potential; discussed marketability of driver and recommended consideration; advised client on duties, responsibilities and scope of authority over driver; drafted letter of intent, negotiated and prepared agent contract between client and driver. **Results:** Created mutually beneficial and successful professional relationship; client saved recruitment expense by having attorney with motor sports knowledge assess driving skills and marketability.

Advised NHRA Pro Stock Truck Team (SunCoast Motors) on implementing effective marketing strategies to maximize sponsorship opportunities. Researched alternative methods; assessed opportunities: prioritized strategies: presented tactical sponsorship plan to owner and implementation team. **Results:** received several promising sponsorship leads for 1999 race season.

Marketed computer equipment and services for MicroTech. Initiated contact: consulted on current utilization: developed rapport: educated prospective and existing clients on advantages of upgrading current computer systems and utilizing support services: persuaded on value of company's products and services: briefed technical sales force on needs. **Results:** Elevated interest in computer system upgrades and support services: increased company leads.

Ashley L. Johnson
2200 Lincoln Drive
Fairfax, VA 22345
(703) 555-1212

OBJECTIVE

A position utilizing my skills in **Information Technology Management, Strategic Problem Solving, Consulting** and **Business Liaison Relations** in order to:

- improve operating efficiency and effectiveness through management, staff development and fiscal accountability
- design and implement cutting edge technology to increase organization's profitability
- maximize business affiliations through enhanced service and sophisticated negotiations.

QUALIFICATIONS

- Information Technology Management
- Software/Hardware Engineering
- System Crash Prevention
- Systems Analysis/Procedures
- Contingency Systems Planning
- ISO-9002

- Business Liaison Relations
- Government Relations
- Customer/Client Service
- Organizational Development
- Leadership/Motivation
- Training/Presentations

- Strategic Problem Solving
- Crisis Management
- Consulting
- Operations Management
- Business Operations Analysis
- Budget Management

PROFESSIONAL EXPERIENCE

Technology Source, Inc.	1998 - Present
Computer Operations Manager	
AppleMac	1996 - 1998
Americas Field Development Unix Program Manager	
ACI	1995 - 1996
Regional Operations Senior Systems Administrator	
TWN International	1995 - 1995
Information Technology Manager	
Applaud Systems	1993 - 1995
Business Recovery Specialist	
All Seasons Hotel	1988 - 1990
U.S. Secret Service Security Liaison	

EDUCATION, HONORS and CIVIC

University of Richmond, VA
  Bachelor of Science in Criminal Justice, *Magna Cum Laude*

Virginia Technology & Training Center
  Unix Systems Administration Certification

Recognition Society of the Handicap Student (RSTHS)-Co-Founder
National Health Corps-CPR/First Aid Instructor, Disaster Relief Volunteer

COMPUTER SKILLS

Operating Systems: SCO, HP-UX, AIX, SOLARIS, SYSTEMS V, DYNIX, DG-UX
Servers and Mainframes: HP, IBM, Sequent, DEC, Data General, Sun
PC's: IBM, NEC. HP, AT&T, DELL, MICRON
Networks: TCP/IP, TSO/IMSP PES, MAUS, SQL, DECNet, CCMail, MSMail
Software Applications: ENCORE Property Management Systems. MSWord, EXCEL, Windows for Workgroups, ECCO, Quicken, Peachtree Accounting for Windows, Lotus 1-2-3, Access, HP Service Guard. HP LVM. Corel WebMaster.

ACHIEVEMENTS

Information Technology Management

Initiated maintenance programs to stabilize data center for value added reseller. Designed and implemented software to alert users of problems; scheduled quarterly hardware system checks; renegotiated support agreements; managed staff and third party vendors; coauthored ISO 9000 Disaster Recovery Plan. **Results:** Improved and stabilized servers reducing system downtime; increased system performance.

Developed, customized and implemented technical training program for AppleMac. Assessed training requirements; motivated staff; designed Unix and DMIL curriculum; engineered career development plans; initiated new course content; scheduled instructors; purchased supplies. **Results:** Educated approximately 2000 employees at all levels.

Negotiated hardware/software contracts within three months after being named Unix Program Manager. Evaluated needs; designed and updated hardware configurations; recommended and implemented support processes and procedures; trained personnel; monitored quality assurance and contractual agreements. **Results:** Purchased & leased and initiated new hardware and software configurations below budget; enforced default clause of contract netting approximately $25,000 in refunds.

Led team in evaluation of prereleased operating systems to avoid conflicts with existing software products. Collected and analyzed data from participating departmental members; identified problem areas; conducted meetings to formulate solutions; recommended improvements and enhancements; monitored implementation of suggested changes. **Results:** Prevented issuance of insufficient technology.

Analyzed and **recommended** strategies to systematize technology updates in workplace for increased employee retention as member of AM senior level task force. Assessed work environment; investigated past and current documentation relating to job distress; conceptualized matrix for ranking complexity of software changes or releases; recommended proprietary software tools to facilitate knowledge and understanding. **Results:** Strategies accepted and being implemented.

Strategic Problem Solving/Consulting

Implemented phase one of server upgrades for Technology Source within 5 days of hire. Assessed status; made time line recommendations; delegated tasks; identified potential problem areas; scheduled third party vendor to assist; oversaw and troubleshot. **Results:** Enhanced system performance.

Investigated software product that caused system to crash (core dump). Gathered data from system network and customer; formulated core dump pattern; researched calls and source code; performed tests; coordinated resources to resolve issue; spearheaded labs in redesigning source code in high availability software. **Results:** Corrected software's interaction with kernel within 6 months.

Managed down systems for high availability customers in large technology firm. Diagnosed problems; designed recovery plans; coordinated resources to resolve issues; generated reports; interpreted data; monitored system activity; recommended customers purchase higher service level agreements. **Results:** Reviewed and stabilized between 150-200 customers' machines per month; saved millions of dollars for customer and company; increased service revenues by 5-10%.

Reduced theft 72% within 3 months of transfer for major retailer. Reviewed theft detection; purchased surveillance equipment; educated employees; readjusted schedules; initiated network among other retailers. **Results:** Increased apprehension of shoplifters and dishonest employees; increased employee awareness regarding internal and external theft.

Business Liaison Relations

Facilitated meetings to resolve hardware compatibility issues between third party vendor, prominent customer and major computer company. Diagnosed problems; developed alternative scenarios; scheduled and conducted meetings between CEOs and senior level management initiated and monitored action plan. **Results:** Hardware replaced; customer satisfaction increased; customer purchased higher service level agreement.

Conceptualized, designed and **implemented** procedures to increase customer satisfaction for governmental and secured site customers. Consulted with customers; researched needs and available resources; developed standard operating procedures; presented both internally and externally. **Results:** Facilitated expedited transfer of information; enhanced corporate image; increased revenues.

Coordinated interaction between Secret Service, Special Forces, hotel staff and other agencies during 1988 Presidential Campaign. Researched employees' background, scheduled staff coverage; established/implemented timelines and routes; installed special communications systems; facilitated meetings; surveyed and conducted control during diplomatic movements. **Results:** Successfully transported President and candidates, their spouses, families and staff.

Directed development of first 300 hour Security Officer training course for technical school. Developed course guidelines; evaluated content; motivated development staff, obtained state certifications without modification; coached on instructional techniques; created benchmarks. **Results:** Successfully deployed state certified course for Security Officers in 47 states.

Sales Representative

BETTY JOHNSON
52 Old Country Road
Braintree, MA 02854
(517) 555-1212

OBJECTIVE

A sales representative position leading to management using proven skills in the areas of communicating, overcoming, negotiating and achieving in a progressive, growth oriented company.

QUALIFICATIONS AND BACKGROUND

14 years progressive responsibility and experience in:

- Achieving
- Overcoming
- Organizing
- Focusing

- Communicating
- Negotiating
- Preparing
- Learning

SELECTED ACHIEVEMENTS

NEGOTIATED eight computer reservation system contract renewals. Analyzed wants and needs of the client; developed specific proposals that met client needs without expensive incentives. **Results:** Renewed seven out of eight contracts within a four month period with one pending; attained 87.5% retention.

MANAGED all daily operations of a $4m travel agency. Arranged all travel concerns for corporate travel; initiated and maintained communication with corporate representative; oversaw 3 employees; hired and trained agent. **Results:** Successfully arranged travel for 800 corporate executives generating $4m in sales.

ACHIEVED full time account representative status from a part time customer service agent position. Independently learned **all** aspects of account representative position; initiated training from managers for responsibilities needed in position; undertook additional job responsibilities; initiated an on call status for existing position. **Results:** Promoted to account representative position in less than three years competing with employees who had as much as 15 years seniority.

OVERCAME concerns of a group of customers based on comments by competitors. Listened to the concerns; identified product; informed superiors; persuaded customers to meet with superiors to examine the benefits of the product. **Results:** Re-established open communication; secured opportunity to discuss renewal of contract.

EXPERIENCE

One Star Systems (MA)   1997-Present
Sales Manager
Maintained agency base of 44 accounts in Massachusetts and New York; prepared proposals; negotiated renewal and new computer reservation system contracts; processed amendments to contracts; resolved problems for customers; advised and sold various products; organized seminars and training.

EXPERIENCE

Worldwide Blower Pac   1997
Sales Support/Customer Service
Contacted engineers to get planholders' lists; called contractors to determine bidding intentions on upcoming projects; taxed scopes and quotes to contractors; made changes on computer for scopes and quotes for the estimating engineer; produced blue prints; compiled EXP quotes for engineers; answered phones and directed calls; called travel agent for air fare; computed freight charges for inbound and outbound; posted invoices on computer.

St. Francis (MA)   1989-1997
Certified Dietary Manager
Ensured that special therapeutic diets were prepared by the Massachusetts Diet manual; purchased food and supplies according to need; negotiated price points with vendors; directed and supervised dietary personnel in the preparation and serving of an adequate diet while meeting nutritional needs; controlled food inventories by maintaining adequate records for donated, purchased and government commodities.

El Tacolleta Restaurant   1988-1989
Bar Manager
Presented in store training program which increased operational efficiency; conducted performance evaluations/salary reviews and coordinated pay increases based on merit.

El Tacolleta Mexican Restaurant   1985-1988
Service Manager
Supervised, scheduled and trained a staff of 60 employees; planned and scheduled large parties and banquet reservations; maintained customer and employee relations which enhanced the product quality, service and customer satisfaction.

EDUCATION

B.S. Restaurant Hotel and Institutional Management   Boston University   1985
Certified Dietary Manager   New York State University 1991

HONORS AND ACTIVITIES

Sports Scholarship 1980
Starter Scholarship 1984

Adam Winston
48 Paul Street
Brunwick, ME 03918
(302) 555-1212

OBJECTIVE

Customer Service Management position using proven skills of organizing, planning, record keeping and succeeding in a fast paced, growth oriented company where customer satisfaction is a top priority.

QUALIFICATIONS AND BACKGROUND

Over 9 years of progressive responsibility and expertise in:

- Team Building
- Record Keeping
- Organizing Meetings
- Planning

- Purchasing Raw Materials
- Inventory Management
- Scheduling Production
- Forecasting

ACHIEVEMENTS

PLANNED and **COORDINATED** all responses to sales and customer service inquiries. Answered questions about manufacturing, shipping, quality control, and special orders, quoted pricing and availability, confirmed information on orders; analyzed production schedules, backlogs, and production forecasts; negotiated production schedule on behalf of customer; proposed alternatives as needed. **Results:** Helped to increase sales representatives' new business by an average of $500,000 per representative; received customer service appreciation award.

ORGANIZED scheduling of daily plant production. Analyzed pending orders and due dates; schedule production and product mix to meet customer delivery requirements and maximize efficiency of plant resources; scheduled communication meetings; planned future production; tracked shipping of orders; processed requisition of critical materials to meet customer demands as well as Just In Time inventory objectives. **Results:** Increased production efficiency, decreased down time and 10% reduction of critical materials inventory.

PRODUCTION of highest quality product by directly overseeing that ISO9000 and specific company quality standards are met on every manufacturing run. **Results:** Low rate of customer complaints and credits while promoting the quality abilities of our company to current customers as well as new prospects. Less than 1% of manufacturing credits as a percentage of sales. Established new 8 hour production benchmark for division.

SUCCEEDED in the implementation of an outsourcing program for a difficult manufacturing run. Determined ergonomic liability for our employees; sought outside vendors who could perform work safely; calculated outsource cost versus retaining work in house; chose select vendors; implemented program; maintained business relationship. **Results:** Decreased cases of reported Carpal Tunnel Syndrome; allowed machines to run at faster, more productive speeds, allotted time for more orders in production scheduling, promoted positive community image.

EXPERIENCE

Eastco Corporation (ME) — 1995-Present
Production Control Manager — 1998-Present
Schedule Plant production equipment. Requisition all packaging, paper and miscellaneous production materials. Create daily and long range schedules; direct production control meetings to stimulate communication, maximize production and meet customer demands.

Production Supervisor — 1996-1998
Served as Second Shift Production Supervisor for Envelope Department. Duties included direction and management of unionized employees to ensure that customer satisfaction, safety, quality, productivity, and maintenance goals were maximized.

Customer Service Representative — 1995-1996
Customer Service Representative for Bangor Envelope Plant. Responsibilities included coordination with customers, sales, and plant personnel of quotations, orders, order status, scheduling, artwork and deliveries.

Agricultural Insurance (ME) — 1990-1994
Insurance Agent
Served as licensed property, casualty, life and health insurance agent. Duties included the solicitation and closing of new business as well as providing customer service assistance for existing clients.

Franklin Inc. (VT) — 1992
Intern
Product and sales analyst for engineering plastics and polymers. Produced timely sales and data reports for production planning and forecasting. Developed computer program in Dbase IV which enabled marketing to determine the profitability of various product pricing strategies.

Franklin Inc. (VT) — 1991
Intern
Responded to information needs within rubber department. Maintained marketing information systems facilitating effective managerial planning and decision making, using the corporate mainframe, Lotus 1-2-3, SAS, and various other PC software applications.

EDUCATION/ADVANCED TRAINING

Advanced training in:

Safety Standards	IS09000	Interviewing Skills
Public Speaking	SAP	Warehouse Management
Diversity Training	Lotus 1-2-3	International Finance
Customer Service	D-Base III & IV	French

B.S. Management	University of Vermont	Burlington, VT

AFFILIATIONS
United Way

William Ronner
95 King George Drive
Chicago, IL 63897
(775) 555-1212   •   Email: wronner@anywhere.net

OBJECTIVE

To provide executive leadership in a medium-sized business and create superior shareholder value by growing market share as well as improving revenues, profitability and customer satisfaction.

PROFESSIONAL QUALIFICATIONS

Experienced senior manager accustomed to P&L responsibility for single and multi-location organizations with revenues up to $300,000,000. Led underperforming company to national market presence through creative marketing. As executive with Fortune 1000 corporation, directed marketing and product management of leading-edge product portfolios. Skilled leader capable of identifying and resolving challenges organizations encounter in determining correct environment and processes and converting those challenges into opportunities. Demonstrated passion for finding, serving and keeping customers. Successful at establishing multi-party business alliances and negotiating positive business relationships.

ACHIEVEMENTS

Led an underperforming computer technology company confronted with diminishing resources and insufficient skill sets to develop positive national recognition. Created sales force, developed strategic initiatives, implemented operational plans, introduced new products, built business relationships and established a winning culture and successful record the company today enjoys. Grew net revenues 28% and net market share 32%.

Chaired acquisition/assimilation team during negotiations for $55,000,000 (net revenues) business. Concluded purchase 30 days ahead of plan and 17.9 % below financial model target. Saved $7,600,000 in acquisition costs.

Formed third-party alliances expanding product placement for the company and two major customers. Increased product sales for all parties and enabled one of the company's wavering product lines to profitably continue in the market .

Developed sales/marketing plans and incentive programs for field operations that improved net sales and profits while providing increased financial/professional rewards for the sales staff. Reduced sales personnel turnover 30 % and lowered sales training costs for new staff.

Drove customer retention 19% over a 30-month period by developing industry surveys, analyzing processes and establishing baseline customer satisfaction index. Introduced improvements leading to increased customer focus.

Established alliance with nationally-recognized development company to provide program design and implementation tools, leading to improved product quality and time-to-market and saving $155,000 in direct costs.

Developed long-range needs assessment and business plans during formation of new business which improved order accuracy of 200-person team 35% within the first six months of implementation.

Improved average time-to-market for product line by 21.4 % and reduced business unit costs to serve customers by more than $2,000,000 for the fiscal year.

William Ronner
Page 2

ACHIEVEMENTS CONT'D

Cross-trained and assimilated over 400 employees into parent company operations, matching experience/skill sets to key positions. Reduced operating costs 21% first year and avoided duplication.

Achieved sales club status the first year assigned to the corporation's poorest performing sales territory where its largest competitor was headquartered.

Established open communications in a company with history of organizational conflict. Initiated weekly meetings, encouraging employees to express ideas and other solutions. Created newsletter to inform work force of the company's progress and celebrate "wins." Demonstrated how information positively supported the efforts of everyone.

Identified opportunity and led re-engineering processes enabling company to emerge among the first operations to automate field sales activities. New technology expedited order processing and improved accuracy.

Acquired high profile, class "A" office facilities in major technological development center for 61% of average cost plus no-cost leasehold improvements. Saved $149,000 over five-year term.

Founded organization to provide support to family members and others experiencing loss during child custody proceedings. Grew local membership to 300 persons first year, appearing on numerous television and radio news/human interest programs and creating national recognition for the organization.

EXPERIENCE

President & Chief Operating Officer, **CarCom Technology**, Chicago, IL

Led $3,000,000 company during period of unprecedented growth by revising business objectives and plans in accordance with current conditions and initialing and directing marketing alliances with key business leaders.

The Miller & Miller Company, Springfield, IL

> *Director & General Manager,* **Marketing, Retail Sales Enterprise - Automotive Systems Division,** Springfield, IL. Determined marketing product management strategies for dealership sales applications and services for $400,000,000 division of $1.2B corporation.

> *Director*, **Management Systems and Services - Automotive Systems Division**, Springfield, IL. Created, staffed new operation to re-engineer corporate processes and procedures for warehousing, manipulating, using data supporting targeted marketing/sales initiatives.

> *National Director,* **Administration, Planning and Statistics - Automotive Systems Division,** Springfield, IL. Managed sales administration/planning staff. Developed, implemented sales compensation plans, objectives, sales tracking/analysis processes for 200 sales representatives, managers, officers.

> *Regional Sales Manager* - **Chicago Region**. Directed 21 field sales representatives in six-state territory.

> *Assistant General Sales Manager,* Springfield, IL
> *Marketing Manager* - **Parts & Service Applications**, Springfield, IL
> *Sales Representative,* San Diego, CA
> *Manager* - **Customer Service & Support**, Bowling, IN
> *Instructor* - **Parts Inventory Control Systems**, Bowling, IN
> *Assistant* **Manager** - **Customer Service & Support**, Bowling, IN

WILLIAM CONNOLLY

8879 Scrabble Road   (338) 555-1212
Oakdale, CA 67089   bconnolly@contactme.com

OBJECTIVE

Communications manager responsible for all internal and external communications in relation to public affairs, community relations and media relations. Special skills include editorial and opinion writing, and news management.

QUALIFICATIONS

Award-winning writing, editing and communication skills. Proven team leader, organizer and consensus builder. Creative problem solver and innovator. Short and long-term planner and project leader. Effective manager and motivator. Teacher, trainer and mentor. Proficient at analyzing and simplifying complex issues. Efficient and decisive, especially under deadline pressure. Comfortable with issues of diversity.

SELECTED ACHIEVEMENTS

- Directed investigation into campaign spending in California. Organized reporters, developed story ideas, established deadlines and edited all copy. Won first place award for investigative reporting from the Metropolitan Newspapers of America. Submitted in the Pulitzer competition.

- Wrote hard-hitting weekly editorials analyzing local policy and taxation issues and recommending course of action. Editorials shaped public policy and won eight professional awards, including five first place, in eight years.

- Analyzed staffing organization following corporate downsizing reducing staff by 25 percent. Reorganized assignments and shifted work load for more efficient and improved news coverage. Won three awards for general excellence, including one first place.

- Won Journalist of the Year Award in 1994 from among 125 editorial employees. Cited for staff reorganization and development, readership development plan, four individual awards, publication of eight special projects and community leadership in five organizations.

- Analyzed spending patterns at Oakdale High School before a tax referendum. Published series of stories and editorials detailing patterns of overspending and taxation. Tax referendum was defeated resulting in a tax savings for residents.

- Researched and wrote an investigative report on the environmental dangers of Leaking Underground Storage Tanks after an underground vault exploded due to leaking gasoline. Won two awards for investigative reporting.

- Directed breaking news coverage of the flood of the Los Valjos River which was honored for best breaking news story by the California Sun.

WILLIAM CONNOLLY ... **Page 2**

SELECTED ACHIEVEMENTS
(continued)

- Planned annual Reader Development action plans by surveying readers, conducting focus groups, resulting in improved news coverage, op-ed pages, new feature ideas and continuing reader involvement and marketing.

- Initiated an employee recruitment program, including minority recruitment, by attending numerous job fairs and conferences. Leadership resulted in establishment of a recruitment committee and appointment as chairman of committee on diversity.

- Trained up to 12 reporters on improving reporting and writing skills. Focused on story organization, clarity, editing, research and investigation. All became award winners for reporting and writing.

- Motivated two experienced reporters who were not performing up to their abilities by increasing responsibilities, performance expectations and training. Both have won awards and are performing to their abilities.

- Managed day-to-day operations for two editorial offices publishing 17 newspapers with 33 employees and a combined circulation of 70,000 readers.

EMPLOYMENT HISTORY

PIONEER PRESS, Oakdale, CA   1986-Present
  Associate Editor, Northwest Group, 1996-present
  Managing Editor, Tree Bark , 1990-present
  Managing Editor, Fall Leaves, 1986-1990

METRO LIFE CITIZEN, Wacan, CA   1981 - 1986
  Assistant City Editor, 1984 - 1986
  Sports Editor, 1982 - 1984

LIFETIME PAPER, Berwyn, CA   1979 - 1981
  News Reporter

EXPERIENCE

DAVIEN UNIVERSITY, Riverton,CA   1996 - Present
  Adjunct Professor of Journalism

EDUCATION

CALIFORNIA UNIVERSITY, Springbrook, CA
  Master of Science, Journalism
  State House Beat; Editor for Illinois Courant, Graduate School publication.

OAKDALE COLLEGE, Oakdale, CA
  Bachelor of Arts, English
  Daily Sun news staff for three years; Sigma Pi Rho Honorary Society

Danny Sajid Vajpayee

237 Donelson Pike #305   Home (615) 367-4923
Nashville, Tennessee 37214   Work (615) 871-8600

FOOD & BEVERAGE MANAGEMENT

Qualified through professional training and experience to lead fast-paced, high-volume food and beverage operations within hotel, restaurant, and other food service environments. Strong qualifications in communication, team building, and team leadership. Effective motivator and trainer. Dedicated to continuous improvements in quality, productivity, efficiency, and customer service. Computer skills include Microsoft Meeting Matrix, Excel, and Word. Fluent in English and Zulu; conversational French. Key strengths include:

- Food & Beverage Operations
- Space Planning, Design, & Set-Up
- Customer Service

- Staffing, Training, & Scheduling
- Event Planning, Catering, & Banquets
- Inventory Management

Professional Training / Education

CERTIFIED HOSPITALITY SUPERVISOR – 2000
The Educational Institute of the American Hotel & Motel Association

POST-GRADUATE DIPLOMA – HOTEL MANAGEMENT – 1999
International College of Hospitality – Brig, Switzerland

BACHELOR OF ARTS – 1992 – University of Durban-Westville, South Africa

Food & Beverage Experience

NASHVILLE HOTEL & CONVENTION CENTER – Nashville, Tennessee   1999 – Present
Supervisor / Banquet Captain / Banquet Coordinator / Management Trainee

- Direct special event and banquet affairs for this facility with 2,883 guestrooms and over 600,000 sq. ft. of convention space. Currently completing 18-month Food and Beverage Division Training Program.
- Supervise and direct up to 300 temporary support staff to ensure adequate service coverage.
- Create and design detailed space and floor plans for banquets, dinners, receptions, and other special events using *MS Meeting Matrix* software.
- As on-site liaison with captains, catering managers, and banquet set-up managers, coordinate the planning, development, and delivery of customized service functions.
- Assist with floor management and catering for up to 6,000 persons/day on one floor.
- Provide ongoing support to management to determine server schedules (using *Excel* software) complete check entries, close out banquet office at night, and related areas.

Additional Experience

ARVIDA SECONDARY SCHOOL – Durban, South Africa   1996 – 1998
Head of Humanities Department / Senior Geography Teacher

UNIVERSITY OF DURBAN-WESTVILLE – Durban, South Africa   1993 – 1995
Coordinator & Tutor / Academic Program for Disadvantaged Communities

VARIOUS SECONDARY SCHOOLS – Durban, South Africa   1980 – 1993
Secondary School Teacher / Examinations Officer

Cyril DeParté Freeman
19 Seymour Avenue, Edison, NJ 08817
732-339-0777 ▪ cfreeman@hatmail.com

Accounting / Audit Professional

Highly motivated, disciplined accountant with 8 years' experience in major foreign banking institutions. Quick learner who readily accepts challenges. Skilled at tracking data and solving complex problems. BBA Degree in Accounting. Experienced in hands-on supervision and training. Expertise in:

✓ Accounts Receivable	✓ Accounts Payable	✓ Computerized Accounting
✓ General Ledgers / Journals	✓ Bank Reconciliations	✓ Financial Forecasts
✓ Credit / Collections	✓ Financial Analysis / Reporting	✓ Audit Preparations

Strong individual contributor and leader who performs at a high level of accuracy and productivity. Proven track record of mastering computerized accounting software and office systems applications.

Legal Alien – Unlimited Stay – Authorized to Work

PROFESSIONAL EXPERIENCE

NATIONAL BANK OF NIGERIA, Lagos, Nigeria   February 2000 – June 2001
Regulatory arm of the Republic of Nigeria created to protect depositors' funds following a chaotic civil war period. Turnaround situation. 175 employees. Annual revenues of $10 million - $100 million.

Manager – Accounts Division
Managed daily general accounting operations: A/R, A/P, general ledger, financial analyses, financial statement preparation, corporate banking services, corporate insurance accounting, reporting and documentation. Oversaw 12-member accounting staff including training, supervision and development.

- Reorganized the Accounts Division into 3 functional areas: Financial Accounting, Reconciliation, and Budgeting. Redesigned workflows and programs, realigned key accounting positions, consolidated similar functions, and established and enforced customer processing time limits. **Result:** Increased productivity, improved efficiency and upgraded quality of operations.

- Supervised monthly bank reconciliations performed by Reconciliation Officers, ensuring no errors. Analyzed and reconciled complex monthly financial statements: P&L statements, balance sheets ($150 million), and income ($100 million). Balanced fixed asset register and sub-ledgers to GL.

- Launched massive debt collection campaign as Acting Manager of Credit and Collections with responsibility for 25 borrowing accounts valued at $2 million. Improved credit portfolio bringing in $500K in one quarter. Earned President's "Top Performer Cash Award" for collections turnaround.

- Led initiative to uncover fictitious overtime, yielding 30% staff cost savings ($1.5 million annually).

- Key player in preparing and coordinating external audits, assuring accounts were free of any material misstatements prior to audit review. Served as liaison between management and auditors.

- Verified discrepancies, wrote financial reports and projections for multi-million dollar revenues, and presented findings to management. Chosen to prepare National Bank's $4 million annual budget.

- Successfully managed demanding workload. Completed projects accurately and on schedule.

Cyril DeParté Freeman
732-339-0777 ▪ cfreeman@hotmail.com   **Page 2**

PROFESSIONAL EXPERIENCE

NIGERIAN DEVELOPMENT & INVESTMENT BANK (NDIB), Lagos, Nigeria   1998 – 2000
Privately owned financial institution engaged in a full range of investment and commercial banking services including commercial loans, savings and checking accounts, bond services, international and Western Union money transfers, foreign exchange trading, vault services and pre-export financing. 100 – 160 employees. Annual revenues of $2 million - $10 million.

Chief Accountant / Assistant Comptroller
- Pioneered the selection and introduction of a fully integrated accounting software application – Bank Manager – which accommodated both the retail ledger and the general ledger. Personally served as Systems Administrator assigning passwords and security access levels to users. **Result:** Significant improvement in the quality, accuracy and usefulness of financial data for daily operating management and long-range business planning.

- Updated policies and procedures for general accounting, financial reporting, cash management, and financial analysis. Implemented the flexibility required to respond to emerging growth needs.

- Chosen to coordinate external audits, ensuring that unaudited financial statements were prepared according to generally accepted accounting procedures and that the audits ran smoothly.

NIGERIAN MERIDIEN BANK LIMITED (NMBL), Lagos, Nigeria   1992 – 1996
Privately owned commercial bank with 180 employees and $10 million - $50 million annual revenues.

Chief Accountant, Washington Insurance Company – Division of NMBL (1995 – 1996)
- Promoted to serve on turnaround team to realign financial situation of 100% NMBL-owned company. Consistently met or exceeded corporate goals encompassing accounting, financial reporting and internal auditing. Annual revenues rose from $1 million to $5 million within 2 years.

- Designed and implemented a series of standards, policies and systems to more efficiently manage accounting / financial data collection, analysis and reporting.

Lending Officer / Assistant Manager – Credit & Marketing Dept. (1993 – 1995)
Management Trainee (1992 – 1993)

BANK AMERICA, N.A. / NIGERIAN MERIDIEN BANK LIMITED   1985 – 1991
Computer Operator / Systems Supervisor

EDUCATION & TRAINING
BBA Degree – Accounting, University of Nigeria, Lagos, Nigeria – 1991

Professional seminars and financial career development in:
✓ National Bank Accounting & Auditing (2000) .   ✓ Credit Analyses & Risk Evaluation (1994)

COMPUTER SKILLS

Windows NT	MS Office 2000	Bank Manager	Sage
Windows 98	MS Access 2000	Banker 80	BAS
MS Excel 2000	MS Word 2000	MIDAS	Internet / Email

FRANK ROBBINS

34 Peak Crescent
Byron Bay NSW 2456
• (02) 9898 7878
• pramul@bigpool.com

E-BUSINESS MANAGEMENT
CONSULTING

BUSINESS DEVELOPMENT

TECHNOLOGY EXPANSION

- Financial Services
- Information Technology
- Telecommunications
- Government/Non Profit
- Health
- Retail & Wholesale

High-impact innovator. 6+ years experience consulting with global market leaders to develop business strategies, align management vision, and introduce cutting edge e-business technologies that deliver genuine results. Distinguished from contemporaries as possessing an intrinsic understanding of "what works" and the pragmatic realism that strategically translates plans into action.

CUSTOMER FOCUSED • COST CONSCIOUS • SOLUTION ORIENTED

KEY CREDENTIALS

- Alliance & Partnership Building
- Application & Product Development
- Project Management
- E-Business Consulting
- Strategy Development
- International & Domestic Market Expansion
- Budget Management/Resource Allocations
- Risk Assessments & Recommendations

- Board Presentations/Public Speaking
- Marketing Communications & Strategies
- E-Procurement/Supply Chains
- Intellectual Capital Development
- Consultative/Solution-Based Sales & Support
- E-Business Readiness Assessments
- Business Development/Market Expansion
- Benchmark & Goal Setting

SELECTED ACCOMPLISHMENTS

- Propelled unknown start-up company into an international player in the e-business market.
- Acknowledged e-business authority; trademarked and established e-business methodologies.
- Aggressively sought acceptance for recognition in the global business community; acclaimed by Open Market (USA) as the only non-US company competent in e-commerce implementations.
- Achieved first worldwide appointment by IBM Global Services to offer IBM's e-business readiness and opportunity assessment programs.
- Developed knowledge base adopted by universities and students for research and course unit study.
- Personally negotiated and secured IBM and Compuware as channel partners for e-business education services.
- Pioneered Asia-wide program for Unisys contributing $8M to top-line revenues.
- Spearheaded innovative "Go To Market" program for IBM, realizing 3.2% market share increase.
- Established a worldwide community forum for collaboration/problem solving and thought leadership on issues surrounding e-business, b2b e-commerce, and e-marketplaces.

CAREER SUMMARY

Business Consultant/Founder, *Multimedia Facts On-Line,* Australia, NY 1995-Present
Product Marketing Manager, *CloseNet,* Sydney Australia 1995
Marketing Manager – Asia, *HAL Asia-Pacific,* Hong Kong, New Zealand 1991-1993
Product Manager, *NTB,* Australia, New Zealand 1988-1991
Product Manager, *QWB,* New Zealand 1988-1989
Technical Sales Support, *Hotodo Computers,* New Zealand 1987-1988
Systems Executive, *Ballarat Industries,* India 1985-1987
Programmer/Sales Executive, *Hardtech,* India 1984-1985

QUALIFICATIONS

MBA, *Grand India University, India (1984)*

EXPERIENCE- AMPLIFIED

Business Consultant/Founder, *Multimedia Facts On-Line,* Australia, NY 1995-Present
Launched and grew to international recognition, fledging e-business practice, providing intellectual leadership to multimillion dollar companies worldwide. Consultancy has excelled in offering direction in strategy development, technological expansion, project management, and process reengineering services, delivering immediate and impressive revenue contributions and increased market share.

Over time have analyzed business performances, reengineered unproductive or unprofitable work practices, and positioned business strategically for each new growth phase. Expanded consultancy to offer e-business education, marketing and sales support services, and intellectual leadership.

<u>Selected Projects/Highlights/Results:</u>

Alliance & Partnership Building. *Clients: HAL; CloseMart (USA); ComputalAsia-Pacific.*
- Secured world's 1st e-business partner recognition for HAL E-Business Advisory Services.
- Gained recognition as an expert in CloseMart web-based e-commerce products.
- Negotiated successfully with HAL and Computal to offer recognized e-business education.

Application Development/Project Management. *Clients: CloseMart, First Bank, Telstra, John Smith Wines & Spirits, Internet Globe, World Federation of E-Finance.*
- Designed and developed e-commerce ready online prototype for marketing demonstrations and sales support (CloseMart USA).
- Established technical support documentation for First Bank's e-commerce hosting and payment enablement service.
- Launched e-companies: *Hotsport* and *Kid'sPlace;* project managed e-commerce implementation.
- Designed/developed Active X based website, recognized as one of top 50 ActiveX sites worldwide.

E-Business Planning & Strategy Consulting. *Clients: Seaset Telephone & Telegraph (Canada), Unitel, Austrade, BNQ Investments, Cable & Wireless Optus, Hallman.*
- Reviewed existing e-commerce strategies, assessed potential market opportunities, analyzed financials, conducted feasibility studies, recommended new models, and developed business cases for senior management acceptance.

E-Business Education. *Clients: ComputalAsia-Pacific, HAL Australia, Supertrade, DataP Systems, CFR & ComBit Conferences.*
- Delivered customized training courses and e-business education sessions throughout Australia, Singapore, Hong Kong, and Korea. Lectured and presented pre/post sales information, e-Sense methodologies training, and e-business strategy framework sessions to customers, employees, and senior executives.

E-Procurement, Supply Chain & Trading Partner Enablement Programs. *Clients: NETBiz (USA), City Sleuth (USA), HAL, BNQ General, DataP Systems, QNJ Insurance.*
- Developed and delivered program allowing buyer organizations to secure commitments from trading partners quickly – at low cost and low risk. Conceived business strategies for private b2b exchange, analyzed existing models, and produced reports on solutions and recommendations.

Marketing Strategy & Services. *Clients: CloseMart, ComputalAsia-Pacific, Chase Manhattan Bank, Telstra, AusPost, Department of Energy, ProMan Technology.*
- Provided services for prototype development, beta program development, brand enhancement, industry analysis, marketing research, and customer acquisition strategies.

Sales Support/Business Development. *Clients: HAL Australia, ComputalAsia-Pacific, FREE Group, Cable & Wireless Optus, Microfort Australia.*
- Offered sales support via lead generation programs. Qualified opportunities, developed solid relationships, and identified new prospects.

REFERENCES

Available Upon Request.

John McCleary Josephson
176 Woodhaven Drive, Eatontown, NJ 07724
732-927-5555 Home ▪ jmjoseph@hetmail.com

OBJECTIVE

Entry-level Mechanical Engineering position utilizing my experience and knowledge in engineering science process improvement and technical support.

PROFILE

☑ Mechanical Engineering Technology Diploma. Diverse technical, analytical, and problem-solving skills and experience including field work.

☑ Proven leadership abilities and a "make it happen" attitude that leads to the achievement of team and individual goals.

☑ **Computer Skills:** ArcView GIS V3.1, Vocarta, GW basic, Quattro, Lotus, Fortran 77, Pascal, Alice Pascal, Win 98, Office 2000, WordPerfect, DOS.

☑ **Technical Skills:** GIS mapping, GPS systems, AutoCAD, MSDS, WHMIS.

☑ **Qualifications Training:** Radiation protection (Orange Badge, AECB).

EDUCATION

Diploma in Mechanical Engineering Technology 1998
Yorktown University, Yorktown, Ontario, CANADA

Specific Mechanical Technology Program coursework included:
Fundamentals of Statics, Dynamics, Mechanics of Materials, Fluid Mechanics, Heat Transfer, Thermodynamics, and Machine Design.

RELEVANT EMPLOYMENT

Field Technician, Applied Engineering, Ltd. (*civil engineering*) 1999 – 2000
Madison, Ontario, CANADA

▪ Conducted pavement management study of 14,000 kilometers within Canada, New Jersey, New York, Virginia and Nevada. Performed semi-automated collection of pavement data utilizing ultrasonic and laser sensors, as well as video logging, and submitted improvement reports.

▪ Mapped all concrete and signage in Reno County, Nevada using voice-to-data technology in GIS mapping interfacing with GPS systems.

Water Lancing Crew, Corley & Davids, Inc. (*energy services*) 1998
Yorktown, Ontario, CANADA

▪ Worked in teams of 2 managing computer-assisted robotic steam generator cleansing (low volume, high pressure) of the Yorktown Nuclear Generating Station, increasing efficiency of heat transfer pipes.

Facilities Technician, The Hunter Group (*chemicals manufacturing*) 1997
Blackstone, Ontario, CANADA

▪ Provided facilities support for this chemical purification plant, assisting in the pumping, bottling and warehousing of organic solvent upgrades.

RECENT EMPLOYMENT

Data Coordinator, Eatontown Urology (*healthcare services*) 2000 – present
Eatontown, NJ

▪ Track urology patient data for long-term clinical research drug studies. Accurately input information from 3 nurses, utilizing proprietary database.

▪ Routinely manage information from 4 drug studies simultaneously (10+ patients per study), interfacing daily with physicians, drug companies and monitors. Transmit patient information via the Internet, ensuring security.

Willing to travel or re-locate within the tri-state area.

THÉODORE JODOUIN
54 Émile Avenue
Brockville, ON F1J-7Y9
CANADA

Home: (519) 555-0987   Work: (519) 454-6682

GLOBAL BUSINESS DEVELOPMENT
New Ventures / Project Management / International Relations

Dynamic project management career with over 11 years within international arenas. Expert legal strategist promoting growth, funding, support, and implementation of proposals within developed and emerging nations. Persuasive and skilled negotiator possessing superb communication abilities in English, French, Italian, Portuguese, and Mandarin Chinese. Strong proficiencies in:

- Business Strategy & Strategic Planning
- Financial Management
- International Business Relations
- Multi-Site Project Management

- Multicultural Team Building & Leadership
- Capital & Operating Budgets
- Executive Negotiations & Presentations
- Corporate & International Law

Lawyer and member of Law Society of Upper Canada.

KEY INTERNATIONAL PROJECTS

❑ Spearheaded planning and inception as **National Office Director** of a CN$3M, high-profile **housing project in West Bank/Gaza**. Led consultations between all stakeholders including: World Bank (WB), International Financial Corporation (IFC), and National Mortgage and Housing Corporation (NMHC).

❑ Directed **international negotiations** with Chinese authorities (Ministry of Construction and Shanghai's Sanshi District Government) in conjunction with Canadian Department of Foreign Affairs, Industry, and Trade in order to secure **Canada-China housing demonstration project in Shanghai**.

❑ Assumed **implementation and direction** of housing finance **project in Gabon**, including establishment of liaisons between Canadian Embassy, Gabonese Officials, and BBEK Construction (Canadian Firm).

❑ Worked in **co-ordination with CIDA** to establish **Slovakia National Housing Agency Project.**

❑ **Negotiated contractual arrangement** with "Développement International Millére (DIM)" and NMHC to **ensure completion of Housing Finance project in Bali.**

PROFESSIONAL EXPERIENCE

NATIONAL MORTGAGE AND HOUSING CORPORATION , Toronto, ON   1998- present
(Ambassador of Canadian Expertise helping Canadian companies export their building prowess within international arenas)

HOUSING EXPORT DEPARTMENT
Project Manager – International Projects (1999 – present)

High-profile leadership position participating on special task force launching new international department. Utilized superior analysis abilities to accomplish advisory services as well as hands-on involvement in strategic, operating, organizational and financial affairs. Demonstrated diplomatic decorum by operating at senior official level as Canadian envoy for newly created department.

Co-ordinated and supervised all highly technical procedures while maintaining liaisons with appropriate stakeholders. Responsible for extensive negotiations, maintaining keen awareness of cultural diversity and international relations issues.

- Instrumental in launching NMHC's first national tender call, screening qualified Canadian builders for large international project. Responsibilities included drafting of TOR's, leading selection committee, organizing trade mission, and advising stakeholders regarding defining issues (legal, business, political, and cultural).
- Extensive experience negotiating and partnering with international organizations including World Bank (WB), International Financial Corporation (IFC), and Canadian International Development Agency (CIDA).

THÉODORE JODOUIN
Page 2

HOUSING EXPORT DEPARTMENT
Project Manager – International Projects (Cont.)

♦ As National Office Project Director, successfully negotiated CIDA contracts totaling in excess of CN$3M for inception and implementation phases of international housing project, including financial management and HR allocation.
♦ Organized and co-ordinated management-level orientation training and briefing sessions within international milieus.
♦ Orchestrated international trade missions to establish feasibility studies and research utilized in formulating final proposals and contractual agreements.
♦ Solely responsible for project management duties including building of financial projections, writing of TOR's/Statements of Work/ MOU's/ financial reports, drafting of clauses for consultants and subcontractors, and negotiating funding agreements from foreign officials, Ministry of Housing, and the Ministry of Finance.

LAND MANAGEMENT DIVISION
Research Officer – Business and International Development (1998)

Researched international business, drafting series of powerful documents utilized to transition organization into becoming advocate for exportation of Canadian housing industry. Papers included:
◆ Risk Management in International Contracts ◆ Chinese Organizations Dealing with Foreign Investments
◆ Doing Business in China (Information Package) ◆ Joint Venturing in China
◆ Summary of Federal & Financing & Assistance Programs for Exporters

EARLY LEGAL EXPERIENCE

Progression through series of positions building on litigation and corporate law expertise. Responsibilities hinged on multi-party contract negotiations involving legal due diligence while ensuring optimum client relationship management. Early exposure to international scene through work with Canadian government's highest legal arenas. Employers included:

Geoffrey Miller Law Offices, Gloucester, ON (1997)

Shawn Micheal Law Firm, Ottawa, ON (1993-1997)

Supreme Court of Canada, Ottawa, ON (1990-1992)

House of Commons, Ottawa, ON (1989 – summer intern)

EDUCATION / PROFESSIONAL DEVELOPMENT

Bachelor of Education (Cum Laude), University of Carleton, Ottawa, ON   1995
Baccalaureate of Laws (LLB), University of London, London, ON   1991
Bar Admission Exams, Law Society of Upper Canada   1993
Bachelor of Arts (Political Science), St Thomas University, Fredericton, NB   1990
(Major: International Relations)

◆ **Project Management,** McGwir International Executive Institute (2000) ◆ **Mortgage Lending for Residential Housing**, Real Estate Institute of Canada (1998) ◆ **International Housing Finance**, Wharton Real Estate Centre, University of North Bay (1997) ◆ **Mandarin Chinese**, University of Toronto (1995)

COMPUTER EXPERTISE

◆ AmiPro I & II ◆ Lotus 1-2-3 ◆ Freelance ◆ Liaison
◆ Microsoft Project Management ◆ MS Word ◆ MS Excel ◆ Internet

Extensive References Available Upon Request

RICHMOND T. CARTER

32 Sanjing West Road ▫ Changzhou, Kiangsu, China
Residence 8852 2017 3919 ▫ Business/Mobile 0852 4701 9442

richcarter@ghuan.cz.js.cn

WORLD CLASS MANUFACTURING

Supply Chain & Distribution Management / Manufacturing Engineering
Business Process Reengineering / Purchasing & Materials Management

Highest-ranking country executive in large global manufacturing operations throughout Europe and Asia. Expert in hi-tech, high-volume manufacturing environments in the US and abroad with full P&L, capital expenditure and executive staffing accountability. Extensive distribution network with major OEMs in the computer hardware and electronic component market, with high-profile achievements including building manufacturing plants and installing operations for 4 of the largest disk drive manufacturers in the world.

Multinational Boards of Directors
Renowned International Conference Speaker

PROFESSIONAL EXPERIENCE

Exilor Peripherals; Irvine, CA   **1996 – 2000**
Billion-Dollar Multinational Disk Drive Manufacturer

President, Asia Operations

Challenge: Redesign all manufacturing processes to include robotics assembly, cell concept and Kan Ban manufacturing methods. Chartered to transition the culture and operations into "Six Sigma" disciplines and restructure to a batch-mode manufacturing process.

Achievements

- Directed multi-site plant operations for high-volume manufacturing facilities in Singapore, South Korea, Malaysia and the Peoples Republic of China. Combined revenues exceeded $1 billion, with 13 executive reports and 5,000 employees. Improved output volume from 300,000 per month to over 1,000,000 per month in one year. Accelerated production from under 385,000 units per quarter to over 4 million, increasing gross margins 300%.

Southern Digital Corp; San Diego, CA   **1990 – 1996**
Billion-Dollar Multinational Disk Drive Manufacturer

Vice President, Asian Operations (1990-1996)

Challenge: Charged with the organizational redesign and implementation of sophisticated Western manufacturing strategies to position country operations for aggressive growth and expansion initiatives.

Achievements

- Introduced JIT methodology, substantially increasing inventory turns and saving $250 million the first year. Reduced scrap $23 million in less than 24 months and ultimately reduced scrap levels to .65%. Designed and implemented "End-of-Life" strategies for disposition of obsolete materials.

- One of only two Western executives assigned to the Singapore National Productivity Board designed to set-up training grants and programs for various Asian businesses and industry. Negotiated tax incentives for new and existing US companies with local Asian governments. Negotiated a 23-year tax-free status for three multinational companies and saved Southern Digital $50 million in annual tax obligations.

Professional Experience continued...

Landview Corporation; Denver, CO 1983 – 1989
Billion-Dollar Multinational Disk Drive Manufacturer

Vice President Singapore Operations (1985-1989)
    Challenge: Lead multinational cross-functional team through research, design and execution strategies to expand into the Asian market.

Achievements

- Established communications with government officials to define permitting, zoning, code requirements and labor standards. Under strict government monitor, time constraints and compliance issues, managed all activities of the ground-up construction of a 300,000 square foot manufacturing facility. Led cross-cultural team of contractors, engineers, technologist and laborers to complete project 60 days ahead of schedule and 15% under budget.

- Designed and installed the plant's production and operating systems, and assembled a highly qualified leadership team of manufacturing executives from the US, Europe and Asia. Directed a group of 8 first-line reports in the development of HR policy and procedure. Hired and trained over 5,000 employees and introduced class 10 clean rooms.

- During the first 12 months of operation, received numerous awards for meeting extremely challenging deadlines and revenue goals. Won the "Eye of the Tiger" award from the Asian Business Advisory Counsel (ABAC) for the most innovative solutions to increase growth in one year.

PRESENTATIONS

Kennedy School Of Business – Harvard University,
"US Multinational Companies in Asia"

East Asian Executive Leadership Conference – Harvard University
and Nanyang Technology University – Singapore
"Supply Chain Management Concepts"

Pepperdine University and University Of Paris
International Management Series for Graduate Students

BOARD OF DIRECTORS

Republic Of Singapore National Productivity Board
Singapore Technical Training Committee
Singapore Data Storage Institute

EDUCATION

Hawkeye Institute Of Technology; Denver, CO
Associates of Applied Science – Electrical Engineering, 1987

DeVry Institute of Technology; Chicago, IL
Associates of Applied Science – Industrial Engineering, 1982

EDUARDO CADENAS

Phone: (919) 620-2886   121 Johnson Mill Road, Apt. 11
Cell: (919) 545-9632   Email: cadenas414@aol.com   Durham, North Carolina 27712

CHIEF FINANCIAL OFFICER – INTERNATIONAL MARKETS
Start-up, High-Growth & Multinational Corporations

Corporate Finance Executive with over 15 years' experience leading the financial, treasury, general accounting, and human resource management of world-class multinational corporations. Diverse financial experience across advanced technology and telecom industries. Multilingual, with expertise in the Central and Latin American markets. Consistently delivered strong and sustainable financial gains in highly competitive business markets worldwide through expertise in:

- Strategic Financial & Business Planning
- Financial Modeling
- Corporate Banking & Lending
- International Banking Relations
- Risk & Investment Management

- Transaction Structuring & Negotiations
- Merger & Acquisition Review
- Corporate Treasury Management
- Debt Restructuring & Reduction
- Financial Reviews, IPO & SEC Reporting

PROFESSIONAL EXPERIENCE

COMMUNICATIONS.COM   January 2000 to Present

A 2½-year-old, $5 million capital-infused Internet company specializing in a full range of Latin American e-commerce business solutions for small- and medium-sized businesses in Latin America. Communications.com develops, markets, licenses, and supports a suite of high performance software products allowing customers to deploy Internet-based business applications facilitating B2C and B2B e-commerce.

Chief Financial Officer

Corporate CFO leading the development of all financial, treasury and accounting models plus S-1 IPO filing documentation. Assumed responsibility for human resources and led development of HR infrastructure, benefit programs and payroll functions. Developed nine-person management team overseeing a staff of 40 professionals.

- Established appropriate procedures to comply with SEC regulations, including implementation of corporate policies and procedures for quarterly reviews and annual audits.
- Created all aspects of corporate financial reporting systems, cash management systems, and corporate treasury functions.
- Aggressively facilitated completion of a 2½ year audit being conducted by a Big Five accounting firm within two months to meet scheduled IPO launch date.
- Assisted senior executives in negotiation and completion of agreements with strategic partners and international banks throughout the US and Latin America.
- Assisted in negotiating multinational on-line credit card transaction contracts with VISA's international and local networks.

CASTILLA USA PUBLISHING COMPANY, INC.   1998 to 1999

A $300 million, privately-held multinational publishing company based in Spain with a portfolio of 20 entities in 15 countries throughout North and South America (2000 employees) generating in excess of $150 million annual revenues.

Chief Financial Officer

Corporate Financial Executive recruited to lead formation and financial management of a Miami-based holding company overseeing all 20 of the Americas entities. Coordinated corporate treasury functions, capital budgets, cash management systems, debt restructuring, and financing. Oversaw 15 Directors of Finance. Consolidated and executed all financial reporting functions to Spain's holding company.

- Established standardized financial models, reporting systems, and budgeting processes for all 20 entities, including implementation of a Microsoft SQL-based data warehouse with online analytical tool capabilities.
- Developed and managed critical relationships with international banking institutions to fund Americas operations.
- Led aggressive restructuring, consolidation, and renegotiation of all existing corporate indebtedness and slashed the number of lending institutions from 45 to 5, yielding a $1.2 million interest savings.
- Conducted merger and acquisition feasibility reviews, advised executive management teams, and led financial integration/consolidation.

EDUARDO CADENAS Page 2

PROFESSIONAL EXPERIENCE (Continued)

WORLDWIDE HOLDINGS, INC. (WHI) 1994 to 1998

A $500 million holding company with a portfolio of premier video, audio, data, and programming service entities throughout 20 countries worldwide.

Vice President / Chief Financial Officer – CCN Communications (1997 to 1998)

Executive member of a four-person management team selected to lead start-up of a Latin American cable television network.

- Established entire corporate infrastructure including finance, treasury, accounting, operations, human resources, and administration, as well as programming acquisitions.
- Directed financial planning functions and presented final results to Board of Directors and investors.
- Structured transactions and contracts and managed negotiations with operational facility, production company, talent, and artists.

Chief Financial Officer-Latin America – WHI (1995 to 1997)

CFO overseeing all financial, accounting, and audit functions for Latin American investments in excess of $250 million throughout five countries. Reported directly to President of Latin America.

- Coordinated financial reporting functions for WHI properties in Mexico, Venezuela, Brazil, Peru, and Chile in accordance with GAAP and International Accounting Standards.
- Conducted due diligence processes and made final recommendations regarding acquisitions or investments prior to presentation to Board.
- Instrumental in assisting WHI properties in obtaining local financing for operational management and expansion.
- Negotiated with international banks to consolidate debt funding worldwide.

MADRID TELECOM CORPORATION 1990 to 1994

An $8 billion industry-leading manufacturer of telecom equipment and wireless products.

Manager, Finance – Latin America (1993 to 1994)
Director of Finance – Madrid Subsidiary (1993)
Manager of Offshore Accounting (1990 to 1993)

Managed financial operations throughout Latin America and provided support to Vice President of Sales in Central America, Venezuela, Peru, and Argentina.

- Designed a collection system with local banks as part of a joint venture with a major company in Colombia.
- Designed and implemented local accounting functions for Colombia, Venezuela, Brazil, and Argentina offices.
- Designed and implemented an entire billing and collections system supporting annual revenues of $36 million for a telephone company with over 250,000 lines.
- Assisted in the execution of expatriate program including housing, legal and tax matters.
- Set up an Oracle accounts payable/receivable system and slashed receivables 85% within 10 months.

DELOITTE & TOUCHE 1985 to 1990

Senior Accountant-Audit Division

Five years' experience with an industry-leading consulting firm. Participated in audits of international banks, financial institutions, non-profit organizations, captive leasing companies, local government, and public companies.

EDUCATION

BS, Finance and Marketing, Rockhurst College, Kansas City, Missouri, 1984
CPA, North Carolina and Missouri

COMPUTER SKILLS

ProSystem Accounting, Oracle, Platinum, QuickBooks, Microsoft Excel, Lotus, Access, MAS 90, Peachtree

Carlos Juan Santiago

USA
56 Second Ave.. Suite No. 3324, Tampa, FL 12345
Fax 555-555-5555

carlos.santiago@peras.com

Brazil
Amalfa #355 Los Condes, Rio De Janeiro
Phone (H) 55-2-222-2222 • Phone (B) 55-2-555-5555
Fax (B) 55-2-111-1111 • Cell 55-2-0-000-0000

International Marketing Professional

Fortune 100 strategic business / marketing specialist and expert on Latin American markets. Currently Marketing Director for Procter and Gamble, Brazil, managing the full market-cycle from concept, to development, to market.

Respected as a dynamic business builder, hands-on leader, and creative solutions provider, delivering impressive bottom-line impact. Thrive under the challenge of planning and managing demanding assignments. Energized by the development of entrepreneurial marketing strategies that generate maximum results.

Use systematic, bottom-line approach to development — engage in cross-departmental research and author future-forward marketing plans to determine products' viability. Have produced a continuous stream of profitable marketing initiatives, cost-reducing measures, and innovative solutions.

Entirely fluent in English and native Spanish. Broad background in international cross-cultural relationship building. Working and living experience in the United States and Latin America. Accustomed to the rigors of frequent business travel.

Areas of Expertise

- Strategic marketing
- Global market study / research
- Product / market identification
- Business plan creation
- Short- and long-term forecasting

- Long-term market analysis
- Competitive and value analysis
- Profitability, EVA, ROI analysis
- Multimillion-dollar budgets
- On-time and on-budget projects

- Project management
- Solutions sales / marketing
- Cross-function teaming
- Marketing materials design
- Boardroom presentations

Recent Marketing Milestones

Led outstanding results in P&G's beauty care business in Brazil, behind excellent performance in hair care, increasing Pantene's volume +54% and sales +64%. (2000)

Revitalized feminine care category in Brazil with volume and sales of the Always brand up by +16% and +18% respectively over previous year. (1999-2000)

Managed several new category launches for Latin American subsidiaries, creating new market segments for Secret cream antiperspirant, Pringles potato chips, and Pampers baby wipes. (1999-2000)

Restored profitability of P&G's Latin American personal cleansing business, delivering above target results, improving profits by +56% over previous year, and creating first-ever profits for a P&G Latin American sub-region. (1999)

Carlos Juan Santiago
page 2 of 4

Recommended a trade program in Venezuela to improve the diapers and hair care businesses in the Drugstore channel. With an annual sales potential of $5 million, initiative became a P&G top priority. (1999)

Led P&G's sales improvement in diapers in Venezuela, lifting unit price by +15% over previous year. (1998)

Turned around P&G's Venezuelan bleach business. Elevated sales by 85% and reversed negative profit margins, achieving 10% margin by June 1997, versus -16% margin in last six months of 1996. (1997)

Increased P&G's diaper volume 28% above previous year to $4.3 million, with profit improvements of 100%, and cost savings of $1.7 million by recommending an expansion of an optimized diaper product. (1995)

Representative Marketing Initiatives

Revitalized subsidiaries' second largest business.

Category had experienced a two-year downward trend, losing 30% in past 18 months.

Proposed plan to increase sales by 60% in three years. Championed plan through P&G channels and pushed local team hard to quickly relaunch one of the product lines.

Plan's key elements included relaunch of top-performing product line using better technology and new advertising... introduction of new product presentations, adding 3% to 7% incremental business... revising pricing strategy... leadership of the sales platform recovery behind two major price increases in 12 months... a progressive plan to increase unit level sales by +25% from its base... implementation of a business plan to recover wholesaler / distributor business (25% of category volume)... relaunch of the basic performing brand behind better technology and re-establishment of marketing support.

- **Bottom-line**
  Top performing line grew 16%... total category trend was stabilized, declining only 4% in the last 12 months vs. 15% decrease in previous two years... pricing leads were followed by category competitors.

Improved results of strong, yet stalled, category.

Category was not growing past its 50% share.

In response, implemented holistic marketing program with strong media support to all product lines... proposed pricing above what was needed to recover inflation and devaluation... implemented a promotional program to surpass competition and significantly grow business out of the basement of a 35% share key category channel... managed a product line relaunch using better technology and a new advertising campaign.

- **Bottom-line**
  Recorded record-high profits... improved unit price by 15%... increased market share by two points over previous year.

JACQUES PHILIPPE

500 Maple Avenue, Lincoln, Nebraska 68508

Residence: 402-555-1212   JPhilippe3@email.com   Fax: 402-555-2121

SENIOR LEVEL MANAGEMENT / INTERNATIONAL BUSINESS DEVELOPMENT

Global Sales & Marketing · Turnaround Leadership · P & L Accountability

Results-oriented **Multinational Business Executive** driving innovation by creating and implementing unique market entry strategies. Expert international sales and marketing skills achieving consistent records of aggressive growth in industries with slow buying cycles. Ability to access top officers of targeted companies, recruit in-country sales professionals, create top-performing sales support offices, and establish prominent local brands. Officer/shareholder of travel company and advertising agency. Multilingual in French, English, and German. French citizen with work permits in 15 countries.

PROFESSIONAL EXPERIENCE

FANFARE, INC., Omaha, Nebraska   1996 to Present

Privately owned US-based manufacturer of cleaning maintenance products with operations in US and Europe, staffing 650 employees and reporting $50 million annual sales with 15% in exports.

DIRECTOR, INTERNATIONAL SALES

Manage high-growth international sales and marketing operations with full P&L responsibility for newly built European manufacturing plant. Administer annual $550 thousand international division operating budget. Establish and meet international sales goals exceeding $5 million per year for parent company and international subsidiary. Supervise European sales office, organizing and leading marketing activities related to global markets. Appointed United Kingdom subsidiary Officer, collaborating with subsidiary Managing Director on issues of personnel, administration, production planning, inventory requirements, and manufacturing process improvements. Redesigned company image from that of pure manufacturing group to a leading-edge company offering business solution systems and specialized expertise.

- Installed transfer-pricing policies between parent company and United Kingdom subsidiary. Result: Reduced import duties 18% and overall corporate tax liability $75 thousand in 2000.

- Assisted in reversing negative performance of international subsidiary within 12 months, contributing to record profits in 1998. Result: Exceeded 8% of sales after tax in 1999.

- Grew sales 75% from 1997 to 1999 by restructuring territories to strengthen European distribution including the initiation of direct sales in major European markets. Result: Steep margin increases.

- Triggered 90% increase in sales in 1996 by securing 2 new accounts with exclusive 5-year contracts valued at $1 million per annum. Result: Stimulated subsidiary turnaround profitability.

- Recommended $300 thousand new production equipment investment to boost expansion with new products in new markets. Result: 65% of equipment capacity sold within 6 months with ROI on track to be under 24 months.

- Established, staffed, and supervised European sales office, successfully hiring outside talents with proven industry track records. Built high-performing, self-motivated, autonomous sales staff that achieved consistent under-spending despite sharp sales increase and requirement for more resources.

JOHNSON HYGIENE PRODUCTS, INC., Essex, United Kingdom   1989 to 1996

Wholly owned subsidiary of Garçone, a French-based company of $850 million sales per annum, employing 70 people and reporting $10 million sales in 1996 with 70% in exports.

EXPORT SALES MANAGER, 1993 to 1996
COMMERCIAL ADMINISTRATION MANAGER, 1989 to 1993

Directed export sales for leading world manufacturer of hygiene and sanitary equipment. Exceeded goals by selling to top officers of key accounts. Collaborated with marketing director to launch new products. Appointed distributors and provided ongoing support. Planned and directed international trade shows. Organized and presented technical training for customer sales representatives. Built effective management information system by introducing PC-based office software. Implemented new key accounts database system with exhaustive account details, revenue analysis, short- and medium-term product needs, plus other key elements to drive future account strategy.

- Increased value of territory from $650 thousand in 1993 to $1.7 million in 1996.
- Accelerated sales growth 27% over 3 years despite loss of 2 major accounts representing 34% of all export sales in 1996.
- Recommended $125 thousand investment to successfully adapt standard range of products to specifications for export market.
- Captured largest single distributorship in company history valued at $450 thousand per annum within 12 months of activity in Japan.
- Closed largest single stock order sale in South Africa valued at $75 thousand.
- Consistently exceeded sales goals for 3 years with 20% under-spending in departmental operating budget.

ADDITIONAL EXPERIENCE:
FOOD & BEVERAGE CONTROLLER, HOTEL INTERNATIONAL, Nice, France   1989
MARKET RESEARCH ASSISTANT, UNITED TELESALES, Paris, France   1987 to 1988

EDUCATION

BACHELOR OF SCIENCE (US equivalent)   1989
Business Administration/General Management
French Academy of Business, Paris, France

Hautes Études Commerciales (Business school preparatory course)   1986
Mierse College, Nice, France

PROFESSIONAL ACTIVITIES

Affiliations
- Textile Rental Service Association
- Textile Service Association

Presentations
- *"Joys and Challenges of International Business Careers,"* Guest Speaker International Business Immersion Week, University of Nebraska, 3/96
- *"Concept Selling – the Four-Step Sales Process,"* Guest Speaker International Cleaning Products Asia Show, Singapore, 8/98

BERN HERTENSTEIN, M.D.
87 Lawrence Road
Trenton, New Jersey 98000
Residence: (555) 555-5555
E-mail: bernhert@compaserv.com

PROFILE

Pharmaceutical Research & Development Management Professional with expertise in the design and management of clinical trials for OTC skin care, sunscreen and cosmetic product lines. Clinical and managerial competencies combine with thorough knowledge of dermatological and other pharmaceuticals plus bioengineering. Strengths include marketing support, product innovations, product training, relationship building and contract negotiations. Successful in cultivating relationships with opinion leaders in the field of dermatology as well as with clinical test institutes and clinical research organizations (CROs) in the U.S. and Europe, collaborating on clinical studies. Adept in international arenas and cross-cultural communications with business experience in Europe, United States and Japan. Bilingual in English and German. Computer literate.

EDUCATION & TRAINING

M.D., in Dermatology, *graduated magna cum laude*, 1979-1986
University of Hamburg, School of Medicine, Hamburg, Germany

- Thesis: *"Comparative Study of Systemic and Local Side Effects of Prednicarbate Conventional Corticosteroids with Halogen Groups"*

Internship – Internal Medicine and Anesthesiology, 1985-1986
General Hospital, Hamburg, Germany

Completed University Entrance Qualification (B.S. equivalency in U.S.), concentration in Economics
Albright Gymnasium, Hamburg, Germany

PROFESSIONAL HISTORY

PHARMADORF INC.   Trenton, New Jersey
A $150 million U.S. subsidiary of a multi-billion dollar, German-based pharmaceutical, cosmetic and OTC skin care products company with 68 subsidiaries worldwide. Pharmadorf is #1 market leader in skin care products throughout Europe.
Director, Medical and Scientific Affairs • 1999 to Present

Develop, conduct and manage an average of 20 clinical studies per month, ranging from several weeks to 3 years; supervise research staff. Assess test results and provide scientific support of claims and new indications for existing as well as new skin care product lines. Research, audit, negotiate contracts and supervise independent product test sites. Team with Marketing and Consumer Affairs Departments to provide scientific, advertising/promotion and customer relations support. Perform analyses of new technologies and potential applications for new product development initiatives. Manage $1.5 million budget for all clinical testing in the U.S.

Contributions:

- **Designed and instituted procedures for conducting safety and efficacy studies on all products in the U.S. Managed clinical studies for 21 product launches since 1996.**

- **Sourced, conducted comprehensive audits and negotiated contracts with 10 new independent sites for product testing throughout the U.S. and Canada.**

- **Cultivated and maintain productive relationships with dermatology industry experts/leaders, resulting in successful product promotion in "Dermatologic Surgery, Cutis, Cosmetic Dermatology" and other publications.**

BERN HERTENSTEIN, M.D. - Page 2

Director, Medical and Scientific Affairs *continued...*

- Trained marketing and sales professionals on various product lines, expanding their product knowledge and contributing to successful marketing/sales results.
- Partnered with company's Japanese joint venture to source, develop and conduct clinical trials to meet the needs of the Japanese market.

Manager, Medical and Scientific Affairs – Munich, Germany • 1993 to 1999

Designed, conducted and directed clinical research on the safety and efficacy of company's medical skin care product line (25 different products) at European headquarters in Germany. Managed budget and staff of research professionals. Developed strategies for new and existing cosmetic and pharmaceutical skin care products, including scientific support for claims and indications. Provided scientific, medical and product development support to Marketing Department.

Contributions:

- Initiated and managed joint international research projects (new product efforts) with Clinical Research Organizations in England, Germany and the U.S.
- Conducted and led clinical studies for 6 new product launches over 3-year period.
- Introduced new technologies and applications for new OTC pharmaceutical products.

PHARMASCHEIN AG   Hamburg, Germany

A multi-million dollar global company specializing in pharmaceutical, herbal and vitamin product lines.

Manager, Medical and Scientific Affairs/Medical Marketing Advisor • 1990 to 1993

Diverse scope of management responsibilities included designing and conducting clinical studies to support new and existing product lines, overseeing regulatory affairs, serving as medical advisor and facilitating product training. Accountable for providing all scientific and medical support regarding any aspect/issue of each product.

Contributions:

- Directed clinical trials on over 28 products and fostered positive relationships with regulatory agencies.
- Collaborated with the Marketing Department in development of product brochures, ensuring scientific accuracy in product claims and indications.
- Presented product training seminars to sales teams; provided medical consultation as advisor to the Marketing Department of another company division.

SCHERSON AG   Berlin, Germany

Scientific Assistant in Experimental Dermatology • 1987-1990

Managed research project entitled, "Comparative Study of Systemic and Local Side Effects of Various Corticosteroids," published in *Yearbook of Dermatology* in 1990.

Additional Experience: Department of Clinical Chemistry, General Hospital, Hamburg, Germany (1986-1990).

PROFESSIONAL MEMBERSHIPS

Society of Investigative Dermatology
International Society for Bioengineering and the Skin

References Available on Request.

FERNANDO C. RUIZ

235 W. 77th St. ▪ New York, NY 10023 ▪ Home: 212-382-7777 ▪ Cell: 917-848-6666 ▪ fcruiz@yahoo.com

INTERNET MARKETING EXECUTIVE

Strategic and Tactical Marketing ▪ **Web Architecture** ▪ **Site Optimization** ▪ **Sales Support Strategy**

Master of Business Administration ▪ **Bachelor of Science, Electrical Engineering**

✓ Ten years' experience blending marketing and product development skills to develop state-of-the-art online marketing, software, and hardware product initiatives that build brand identity and drive sales.

✓ Visionary change agent with proven success redefining value propositions to deliver novel products and services that capture new market share.

✓ Savvy business strategist and analytical thinker who speaks the language of the customer and the developer and matches customer needs with innovative cost-effective business applications.

✓ Influential and flexible leader and project manager with ability to meet aggressive deadlines and build, retain, and motivate multi-disciplinary teams in environments where priorities change quickly.

Core Competencies

Solutions Marketing ▪ Requirements Gathering ▪ Business Analysis/Feasibility Studies ▪ Niche Marketing
Market Research ▪ Strategic Partnerships ▪ Product Development ▪ Product Launch ▪ Project Management
E-Commerce ▪ Web Development and Marketing ▪ Custom Applications ▪ Beta Testing ▪ Business
Development ▪ Talent Acquisition and Management

PROFESSIONAL EXPERIENCE

Tel-Gen Telecommunications, New York, NY   **1999 to 2005**

Director of Internet Marketing, *(2001 to 2005)*
Spearheaded global internet strategy for Tel-X product, the dominant player in the market with more than 30 million customers worldwide and revenues over $900 million. Pioneered multi-year, $4.5 million project to overhaul content and infrastructure including content management system, B2B/B2C store, portal, search engine, and custom applications for 50+ websites. Restructured business processes and orchestrated complete renovation of site information architecture, design, and content. At peak, managed team of 15 business analysts, project managers, and content developers and a $1.8 million budget.

Website Optimization
▪ Transformed underutilized, inefficient site to more robust, user-friendly medium. Conducted extensive market research to redesign 9,000 pages of content and maximize ease of site navigation.

▪ Boosted site visits by 300% over two-year period.

▪ Accelerated site "stickiness" over 200%; increased average length of visit from four to ten minutes.

▪ Dramatically enhanced distributor resource section of site visit statistics from 30-40 views per month to 100 per day in first six weeks following launch.

Solutions-Selling Opportunities
▪ Built resource subscription site to support product knowledge and proactively address cell phone users; complimentary feature became one of most popular features of site.

▪ Grew referrals to channel partners and designed portal for sales representatives, dealers, and distributors allowing them to download latest product information for use in individual marketing campaigns.

▪ Developed store manager online professional development application to augment in-person training program.

Process Improvement
▪ Established content management system and related business authoring processes that reduced site maintenance time and freed up two members of maintenance team to work on new development.

FERNANDO C. RUIZ, page two

PROFESSIONAL EXPERIENCE (continued)

<u>Management Development</u>
- Experienced virtually no turnover on team over four-year period.
- Grew staff over 250% during tenure.
- Leveraged extensive knowledge of marketing, sales, and engineering to eliminate silos between business units and build cohesive teams.

Product Manager (1999 to 2001)
Defined product features and design requirements for Tel-Gen's telecommunications products and website. Key member of cross-functional development teams responsible for researching industry leaders, policy makers, and end-users and planning/executing market launch activities.

- Realized 400% jump in site visits following site enhancements for cell phone products despite an almost invisible budget.
- Created first-of-their-kind support pages including usage ideas, software downloads, frequently asked questions, and dealer referrals as well as developer and community programs.
- Validated customer needs using formal and informal research methods and represented end-user requirements to development team.
- Forged partnership with engineering graduate program at Columbia University. Students gained real-world experience by refining, prototyping, and testing future product concepts, many of which were developed into Tel-Gen brand products.

Cell-Tel Telecommunications, Jersey City, NJ   1997 to 1999

Product Development Manager
Created and implemented product strategy for U.S. market. Represented Cell-Tel USA at worldwide research and development meetings to set global telecommunications product strategy.

- Negotiated and managed relationships with alliance partners to develop and market new product features.
- Defined product functionality for the CTL-1000, the first cell phone with color graphics.
- Developed CTL Advisory Committee user panel to solicit product feedback from influential industry leaders.

Tele-Star Corporation, White Plains, NY   1995 to 1997

Product Development Marketing Manager (1996 to 1997) · *Product Specialist* (1995 to 1996)
Managed product lifecycle for Star 2000 communications products. Created and executed marketing and sales support programs encompassing advertising, public relations, trade shows, and collateral materials. Led team of two product and product marketing specialists.

- Increased overall brand share to 60% by introducing mid-range products at key price points to supplement an 80% leadership position in the high-end of category.
- Created first television advertising campaign for Star 2000 supporting market specific sell-thru at retail channel partners.
- Introduced several product innovations including conference call feature and alarm clock.

EDUCATION

M.B.A., Columbia University, New York, NY   2000
Dean's Award for Academic Excellence (GPA 3.9)

B.S., Electrical Engineering, University of Arkansas, Fayetteville, AK   1995

DENISE NELSON

4600 Harrison Avenue NW
Washington DC 20012

dnelson@yahoo.com

202-555-2500
202-499-4512

FUNDRAISING/BUSINESS DEVELOPMENT EXECUTIVE
STRATEGIC PLANNING • PROGRAM DEVELOPMENT • DIVERSITY MANAGEMENT

Creative, visionary with 15+ years' experience in executive-level financial planning, programmatic initiatives, and international development programs. Employ energetic leadership style and "out-of-the-box" thinking to create innovative capital campaign programs. Expertise in diversifying donor sources and securing high levels of funding from corporations, national foundations, government agencies, and individuals. Outstanding relationship manager leading by example and motivating others to excellence. Received "Award for Museum Leadership" for exhibiting outstanding vision and leadership in program development.

Professional strengths and qualifications include:

- Strategic Alliances
- Program Development
- Global Markets
- Public Relations
- Budget Development
- Planned Giving

- Reorganizations
- Corporate Image Enhancement
- Contract Negotiations
- Staff Coaching
- Training Programs
- Programmatic Initiatives

- Fiscal Management
- Research and Development
- Consultation
- Mission Statements
- Marketing Direction
- International Programs

Fosters strong network of viable contacts at nation's largest private, corporate, and government foundations.

CAREER HISTORY

George Washington University Law Center, Washington, DC
Internationally recognized law school offering nation's largest and most comprehensive legal curriculum.

2000–present

ASSOCIATE DIRECTOR OF ADVANCEMENT, MAJOR GIFTS
Capital Campaign Goal: $1,000,000

Solicit and expand annual contributions from growing pool of law alumni located in East Coast region. Challenged to influence conservative senior management in formulating new development strategy from "scratch". Reinforced relationships with alumni by implementing annual women's forum and boosting participation at annual reception of National Bar Association (NBA). Manage ongoing alumni relations, represent law center at various conferences and seminars throughout the year.

Selected Accomplishments:

- Accomplished 50% and 20% increase in annual contributions by African-American and female alumni respectively.
- Boosted annual attendance at NBA reception 150% by revising fee structure; increased annual donations 25% by generating renewed interest in law center activities and programs.
- Accomplished annual campaign goal 100% in FY 2002 and surpassed goal 20% in FY 2003.
- Originated and implemented $50,000 scholarship fund based on center's largest gift from single donor.
- Raised $500,000 in six-month period by introducing new scholarship fund targeting female alumni.

-continued-

Africare, Washington, DC   1998–1999
Thirty-four year old nonprofit organization, which provide over $450 million in aid to 35 African countries.

DIRECTOR OF ADVANCEMENT
Capital Campaign Goal: $15,000,000

Led long-term planning and strategic efforts to diversify company's funding sources and alleviate its dependency on annual fundraising dinner. Developed and organized educational forums to increase awareness of Africa and related development issues. Established expanded network of national leaders and representatives in foundations, private sector, government, social, and faith-based organizations. Solicited additional funds through grant proposals and fundraising events.

Selected Accomplishments:
- Reached personal campaign goal 100% in first 12 months.
- Securing additional $4 million in contributions by forging new relationships with National Endowment for Democracy and Bill & Melinda Gates Foundation.

Broadcast Capital Fund, Washington, DC   1996–1997
Former leading venture capital company, which financed acquisition and construction costs for 3,000+ minority-owned broadcast companies.

DIRECTOR OF ADVANCEMENT
Capital Campaign Goal: $1,000,000

Identified and acquired reliable financing sources for private equity fund serving female and minority-owned broadcasters. Facilitated relationship with Small Business Administration, reviewed loan proposals, and performed due diligence. Administered $3 million client portfolio.

Selected Accomplishments:
- Realized annual campaign goal 100% during declining business operations and eminent business closure.

Congressional Black Caucus Foundation, Washington, DC   1993–1996
Research, educational, and public policy institution committed to improving social, economic, and political conditions for African-Americans.

DIRECTOR OF DEVELOPMENT
Capital Campaign Goal: $500,000

Directed financial, fundraising, and capital development programs for all major organizational initiatives. Identified lack of diversity in funding sources and expanded scope of government and private donors. Advocated widespread community outreach programs to reinforce organization's bi-partisan mission. Performed as Executive Director for legislative conference drawing over 20,000 participants.

Selected Accomplishments:
- Launched foundation's first "international exchange" program uniting US Congress members and South African parliamentary members. Granted $500,000 for program's first year of operations.
- Diversified funding sources and financial portfolio 30% through $1 million of private grants and contributions.
- Juggled conflicting agendas and objectives for 40 Congress members and representatives.
- Collaborated with consultants to develop strategic five-year plan and resources for long-term financial growth.

-continued-

Historical Society of Washington, (now City Museum) Washington DC   1990–1993
Cultural institution dedicated to preserving history of District of Columbia and its residents.

DIRECTOR OF DEVELOPMENT
Capital Campaign Goal: $500,000
Directed all aspects of program development, annual fundraising, major gift solicitations, and planned giving for museum. Facilitated event planning and served as primary contact for board of directors and volunteers. Maintained $250,000 budget and supervised five employees.

Selected Accomplishments:
- Strengthened overall institutional funding sources 20%, bringing in over $750,000 annually.
- Maximized limited human capital and technology resources to increase financial assistance without additional expenditure.
- Selected members and assembled company's first diversity committee to address program creation and audience retention concerns. Re-energized community involvement by creating diverse programs.
- Received Smithsonian's "Award for Museum Leadership" for displaying outstanding vision and leadership.

EARLY FUNDRAISING EXPERIENCE planning and implementing fundraising policies and procedures nonprofit organizations, including Arena Stage, largest nonprofit producing theatre.

EDUCATION AND TRAINING

Juris Doctor
GEORGE WASHINGTON UNIVERSITY, Washington, DC

Certificate in International Human Rights Law Programme
OXFORD UNIVERSITY, United Kingdom,

Master in African-American Studies
CLARK ATLANTA UNIVERSITY, Atlanta, GA

Bachelor in English
LONG ISLAND UNIVERSITY, Brooklyn, NY

Representing and Managing Tax Exempt Organizations • Representing and Managing Private Foundations
The Seven Habits of Highly Effective People • Transformational Leadership

MEMBERSHIPS AND AFFILIATIONS

Founding member and trustee emeritus, National Center for Black Philanthropy
Board member, Robbins Center for Cross Cultural Communication
National Association of Female Executives

ROGER A. JACKSON

59 Charles River Drive • Alexandria, VA 22310 • 703-332-0130 • rjackson@yahoo.com

NETWORK ADMINISTRATOR / SENIOR HELP DESK ANALYST

PROFESSIONAL PROFILE

Hardworking, highly certified Network Administrator with six years' experience in local area networking, operating systems, software applications, and intranet technologies. Employ innovative, technological programming to enhance work productivity and improve systems utilization. Able to effectively support multiple networks with beginning and advanced users. Knowledgeable technical expert assigned to lead company-wide training programs.

Professional strengths include:

- Network Administration
- Firewalls
- Technology Integration
- Installations

- Network Configuration
- TCP / IP Administration
- System Configuration
- Software Upgrades

- Video Card Technology
- Ethernet Connections
- Test Equipment
- Database Administration

- Staff Training
- Troubleshooting
- Passwords
- MIS Systems

CERTIFICATIONS, TRAINING, AND SEMINARS

Certifications: A+ • MCSE • MCSA • Microsoft Windows NT • NT Workstation • NT Server • NT Server in Enterprise • Network Essentials.

Seminars: McAfee Security • Microsoft Exchange.

Significant professional development through advanced education, professional organizations, and technology publications.

TECHNICAL PROFICIENCIES

Operating Systems: Microsoft Windows 2000 / 98 / 95 • Windows NT Server v4.0 • Windows XP • Windows NT Workstation • Windows 3x • Novell NetWare v5 • Red Hat Linux v6.1

Software: Microsoft Office XP / 2003 / 2000 / 97 • Microsoft Internet Server • BackOffice • Microsoft Works • Kronos • Adobe Acrobat • Adobe PageMaker • Adobe Photoshop • Novell Network • FoxPro • Association Plus Lawson

Hardware: Network Cabling (UTP, STP, Coaxial) and Connectors • SCSI / IDE Hard Drives • PCI and PCMCIA Interface Cards • CD-ROM • Floppy Drives • Modems • Sound Cards • Net Gear • 10 BaseT Ethernet Hubs Net Gear 10 / 100 MBPS Dual Speed Hubs • CPU's System Boards • Dell Workstation • NEC Workstation • Memory CD-R • CD-RW • Flash Drive • Zip Drives • Printers • Motherboard • Scanners

CAREER SYNOPSIS

American Association of Physical Therapists, Washington, DC   1998–present
NETWORK ADMINISTRATOR/SENIOR TECHNICAL SUPPORT SPECIALIST

Maryland Department of Technology Services, Towson, MD   1992–1998
HELP DESK TECHNICIAN (1996–1998)
MANAGER (1992–1996)

United States Marine Corps (Honorable Discharge)   1987–1992

-continued-

ROGER A. JACKSON   **Page Two**

CAREER HISTORY AMPLIFIED

American Association of Physical Therapists
NETWORK ADMINISTRATOR/SENIOR TECHNICAL SUPPORT SPECIALIST   1998–present

Apply technical expertise in computer hardware and peripherals repair, systems analysis, software requirements, and network upgrades to 26 departments. Configure, troubleshoot, and maintain 737 desktops computers and 55 laptops. Make management recommendations on system improvements, computer replacements, and software purchases.

Selected Accomplishments:
- Raised staff competency levels 25% by designing and conducting Microsoft Office technical training classes.
- Improved work productivity 15% by removing over 1,900 computer network viruses in 17-month period.
- Cut company's educational costs 40% by incorporating interactive web training modules.

Maryland Department of Technology Services
HELP DESK TECHNICIAN   1996–1998

Administered hardware repair, troubleshooting, and preventative maintenance for computers, printers, and scanners. Guided and assisted 500 end users by telephone, e-mail, and in-person with various technical issues.

Selected Accomplishments:
- Reduced lost work time by repairing network system in 25+ overtime hours.
- Increased project completion time 35% by establishing and implementing centralized help desk system.
- Boosted information sharing and project management capabilities through newly formed help desk.

MANAGER   1992–1996

Managed daily operations for armory warehouse. Authorized internal purchases for chemical agents, weapons, and body armor. Devised and implemented system improvement programs for inventory handling. Accountable for $5 million departmental budget.

Selected Accomplishments:
- Decreased "lost" or "misplaced" inventory items 65% by executing automated, user-friendly database program.
- Maximized work productivity 25% by producing employee scheduling and task assignment tracking forms.
- Increased inventory tracking and distribution by designing Microsoft Access program.
- Improved access to non-sensitive materials by modifying inventory layout and storage.
- Enhanced inventory control and processing by creating standard policies and procedures manual.
- Demonstrated advanced system configuration, software installation, and database administration skills to land promotion as help desk technician.

United States Marine Corps   1987–1992

Served 5-year rotational tour with armed forces. Managed safety, maintenance, and preventive care for military vehicles and equipment. Awarded "*Good Conduct*" medal and honorary discharge.

REFERENCES FURNISHED UPON REQUEST

SAMUEL MARKS
6500 Livingston Road, Oxon Hill, MD 20745
Home: 301-549-6541 ~ Cell: 240-332-0310 ~ E-mail: sam_mounsey@hotmail.com

SYSTEMS ADMINISTRATOR
INFORMATION SYSTEMS MANAGEMENT ▪ WIRELESS NETWORKS MANAGEMENT ▪ LONG-TERM IT PLANNING

Hard working, motivated Systems Administrator with technical capabilities in network administration, system configuration, technology integration, and software upgrades. Experience includes troubleshooting hardware, software, and operating systems for multiple user networks. Successful at developing programs and technological initiatives that streamline operations, increase productivity, and reduce operating costs. Recognized for efficient project management skills and ability to interact with novice and advanced computer users.

Technical strengths and areas of competency include:

- Security Access
- Extranet
- Database Design
- Help Desk

- Technical Guidance
- Network Security
- Applications Software
- Technical Assistance

- Troubleshooting
- Network Architecture
- Database Security
- Software Upgrades

- User Training
- Passwords
- Client Relations
- IP Addresses

Hardware / Operating System Platforms: IBM AS / 400, Dell, Apple Macintosh, KVM switches, USB ports, modems, expansion boards, and hubs.

Operating Systems: Microsoft Proxy Server, Microsoft Windows XP, 2000, and NT.

Data Structure / Database: Microsoft Access and SQL Server.

Software Programs: Microsoft Office, XP, 2000, Lotus Notes, FrontPage, and Dreamweaver.

PROFESSIONAL EXPERIENCE

SYSTEMS ADMINISTRATOR / IT COORDINATOR
Spring Valley Community College, Temple Hills, MD   2003–present

Recruited to completely revamp school's computer environment, identify system requirements, and install new and upgraded software programs. Manage and oversee maintenance and service of 275 desktop computers and 13 laptops. IT scope encompasses domain authentication, internet configuration, web page design, and user training. Recommend hardware and software solutions consistent with company's growing technology needs.

- Protected company data against power failure by establishing dual database backup system.
- Improved system security by creating a standard operating manual outlining operational policies and procedures for computer usage.
- Increased staff productivity 97% by configuring a backup, reserve computer for utilization during system failures.
- Eliminated repeated occurrence of software piracy by instituting new user policies and improving software license compliance.
- Lowered software purchase costs 10% by implementing proper software upgrades and removing excessive hardware and network devices.
- Provided technical insight and advice for computer system and software purchases.
- Performed successfully at workload capacity equivalent to three IT professionals.

-Continued-

SAMUEL MARKS   Page Two

PROFESSIONAL EXPERIENCE continued

IT CONTACTOR   2002
Compu-Pro Staffing Inc, Clinton, MD

Brought onboard to assist marketing companies with ongoing help desk support, network communication troubleshooting, system configuration, and roaming profile management.

- Increased system security by channeling web filtering and network security software through legacy switches and routers.

COMPUTER TECHNICIAN   2000
The United States Census Bureau, Forestville, MD

Initially hired to collect and process census data for over 5,000 people in Washington DC metropolitan area. Strengths in IT and programming skills led to increased responsibilities and accountability for 75 office computers. Handled computer maintenance, troubleshooting, software integration, and software upgrades.

- Preserved accuracy and timeliness of data by recovering vital databases lost during power outage and computer failure.
- Gained broad knowledge of state-of-the-art technology, equipment, and systems.

JUNIOR SYSTEMS PROGRAMMER   1997–1999
Marshall Systems Technology, Silver Spring, MD

Member of cross-function code development group tasked with writing Y2K program compliance codes. Worked closely with staff gathering functional requirements, participating in technical design sessions, and implementing Y2K application components. Developed codes utilizing Java, C++, and all assembly language; applied codes to upgrade existing computer systems toward operational efficiency with "2000" dates.

- Assigned time-sensitive project, which involved upgrading 200 legacy systems to Y2K compliance.

JUNIOR SYSTEMS INTERN   Summer 1996
American University, Washington, DC

Served as computer support intern for university's Risk Management department. Managed all database entries and performed data migrations and rollouts. Assisted users with Windows, DOS 3.0, and Microsoft Office troubleshooting techniques. Addressed and corrected any system interface issues.

- Reduced lost files 25% by implementing Excel-based tracking system for risk management cases.

EDUCATION

BACHELOR in COMPUTER SCIENCE TECHNOLOGY   2001
Washington State University, Seattle, WA
Honors: National Honor Society, Deans List and Who's Who Among American College Students

PERSONAL INTERESTS

DESIGNING WEB PAGES …BUILDING COMPUTERS…TEACHING COMPUTER BASICS…UPGRADING HARDWARE

JACKIE SMITH

11408 Dana Avenue
Silver Spring, MD 20904

smithj@hotmail.com

Home: 301-505-2829
Cell: 301-475-8889

CORPORATE TRAINER ~ SALES COACH ~ TRAINING MANAGER

Strategic Business Alliances / Innovative Sales Tactics / Customized Training Programs

High-energy, creative finance professional offering over 15 years' experience in sales management, marketing, and new business development. Expertise includes strengths in consultative selling and relationship building. Performance-driven leader with particular talent for coaching and motivating sales teams to outstanding revenue results.

Professional strengths and qualifications:

▪ Sales Training	▪ Sales Team Management	▪ Strategic Alliances	▪ Relationship Building
▪ Business Development	▪ Community Relations	▪ Public Relations	▪ Sales and Marketing Campaigns
▪ Marketing Strategy	▪ Publicity Programs	▪ Networking	▪ Client Needs Assessments
▪ Revenue Growth	▪ Client Presentations	▪ Cold Call Sales	▪ Creative Sales Techniques
▪ Staff Development	▪ Recruiting	▪ Client Retention	▪ Brand Marketing

Received numerous company awards for excellence in sales performance, community relations, and leadership

CAPABILITIES AND VALUES OFFERED

Sales Training: Develop and implement training curriculum effectively blending sales skills and product knowledge with corporate marketing strategy.

Brand Marketing: Enhance company image through consistent relationship building and strategic partnerships.

Recruiting: Identify human capital needs, interview candidates, and hire qualified personnel and support staff.

Client Presentations: Introduce and promote new products and services through creative sales presentations.

Staff Development: Coach and mentor sales staff on professional and personal development issues.

Community Relations: Maximize relationships with current network of business, corporate, and community leaders in Metropolitan DC area.

CAREER HISTORY

Moneytree Bank, Greenbelt, MD   2002–2004
SMALL BUSINESS ADVOCATE

Challenge: Target small businesses and build $20 million loan and deposit portfolio in highly competitive banking environment.

Developed innovative sales and marketing strategies to penetrate new customer segments in Greater Washington area. Trained 25 branch managers on selling additional banking products and services to current and prospective clients. Created and conducted seminars demonstrating techniques in prospects, cold calls, lead generation, and consultative sales. Designed instructional materials, integrated role-plays, facilitated group discussions, and incorporated hands-on exercises to ensure training effectiveness.

Contributions and Results:
- Played instrumental role in growing small business portfolio from zero to $10 million in eight-month period.
- Led sales team to achieve $500,000 monthly production goal in under 90 days.
- Transformed company's visibility and recognition in community through active partnerships with networking, community, and civic firms.
- Devised and implemented, "Million Dollar Club", an incentive program for sales representatives reaching $1 million annual loan volume.
- Accomplished highest level of revenue production among peers in region.

-continued-

JACKIE SMITH   Page Two

Bank of Washington, Washington, DC   1998–2002
Mid-Atlantic Supplier Diversity & Development Regional Market Manager (2000–2002)

Challenge: Influence conservative management team to increase dollars spent with minority suppliers and vendors in Mid-Atlantic region.

Identified minority and women-owned participants for bank's $30 million contracting and procurement program. Drove new business development and marketing outreach activities with community-based, non-profit, and industry-affiliated organizations. Consulted with bank presidents in three states on monthly business objectives and current contracting goals.

Contributions and Results:
- Increased bank product sales 40% by leveraging relationships with existing minority suppliers and vendors.
- Realized 20% of procurement budget in contracting opportunities, which exceeded annual corporate goal of 15%.
- Spearheaded development of mentor protégée program, which teamed smaller subcontractors with prime vendors in procurement program.
- Captured company's top quality awards, "Meeting Overall Regional Goals" and "Overall Participation on External Procurement Boards."

Relationship Manager (1998–2000)

Challenge: Facilitate bank conversion process for current clients and grow existing non-profit portfolio in Washington, DC.

Directed and managed relationship development, customer-focused sales, and client needs assessments for 40 national, non-profit organizations. Coordinated extensive marketing campaigns to retain existing commercial clients. Accountable for growing portfolio profitability 20% annually.

Contributions and Results:
- Raised portfolio profitability 30% by adding non-profit businesses and upselling banking services and products to current customer base.
- Strengthened client relationships by exhibiting high level of competence and professionalism.
- Obtained "Best Deposit Growth on Team" award for growing loan deposits 25% in nine-month period.

Sunnyville Bank, Laurel, MD   1989–1997
Business Banking Officer (1997)
Credit Analyst (1996–1997)
Financial Services Investment Officer (1992–1995)
Customer Service Representative (1990–1991)
Bank Teller (1989–1990)

Fast-tracked through increasingly responsible positions to pinnacle role as **Business Banking Officer** directing sales process for companies earning under $5 million. Juggled conflicting agendas of merging companies to execute comprehensive sales plan and marketing direction for eight branch managers. Taught effective sales techniques including prospects, lead generation, and value-added sales.

Contributions & Results:
- Assisted managers increase sales productivity 15% and achieve monthly production goals.
- Motivated ten licensed branch representatives to accomplish $7.5 million regional goal during role as Financial Services Investment Officer.

EDUCATION AND TRAINING

BBA – Finance, Hampton University, Hampton, VA, 1992
Spin Sales Training by Huthwaite, Inc. ▪ Omega Sales Training ▪ Cohen Brown Sales Training

---

PROFESSIONAL AFFILIATIONS

Business Network International ▪ Toastmasters ▪ Urban Financial Services Coalition ▪ Washington Association Financial Management Roundtable ▪ MD/DC Minority Supplier Development Council ▪ Women's Business Owners Association Tidewater Minority Supplier Development Council ▪ Women's Business Enterprise National Council

7

Resume Worksheets

THE FOLLOWING WORKSHEETS ARE designed to help you systematically generate a complete database on yourself for writing each resume section. We recommend completing the forms **before** writing your resume.

Generate the Right Data on Yourself

You will be in the strongest position to write each resume section after you document, analyze, and synthesize different types of data on yourself based on these forms. Each form will assist you in specifying your accomplishments and generating the proper resume language. Since you are likely to have more experience/education than the number of worksheets provided here, make several copies of these worksheets if necessary to complete the exercises.

Try to complete each form as thoroughly as possible. While you will not include all the information on your resume, you will at least have a rich database from which to write each resume section. Our general rule is to go for volume – generate as much detailed information on yourself as possible. Condense it later when writing and editing each resume section.

The final worksheet focuses on detailing your **achievements**. In many respects, this may be the most important worksheet of all. After you complete the other worksheets, try to identify your seven most important achievements. The language generated here will be important to both writing your resume and handling the critical job interview. You should be well prepared to clearly communicate your qualifications to potential employers!

Employment Experience Worksheet

1. Name of employer: _____

2. Address: _____

   _____

3. Inclusive dates of employment: From _____ to _____.
                                          month/year   month/year

4. Type of organization: _____

5. Size of organization/approximate number of employees: _____

6. Approximate annual sales volume or annual budget: _____

7. Position held: _____

8. Earnings per month/year: (not to appear on resume) _____

9. Responsibilities/duties: _____

   _____

   _____

   _____

10. Achievements or significant contributions: _____

   _____

   _____

   _____

   _____

11. Demonstrated skills and abilities: _____

   _____

   _____

12. Reason(s) for leaving: _____

   _____

Military Experience Worksheet

1. Service: _____

2. Rank: _____

3. Inclusive dates: From _____ to _____.
                              month/year   month/year

4. Responsibilities/duties: _____

   _____

   _____

   _____

   _____

5. Significant contributions/achievements: _____

   _____

   _____

   _____

   _____

   _____

   _____

6. Demonstrated skills and abilities: _____

   _____

   _____

   _____

   _____

   _____

   _____

7. Reserve status: _____

Educational Data

1. Institution: _____

2. Address: _____

    _____

3. Inclusive dates: From _____ to _____.
    month/year   month/year

4. Degree or years completed: _____

5. Major(s): _____ Minor(s): _____

6. Education highlights: _____

    _____

    _____

7. Student activities: _____

    _____

    _____

8. Demonstrated abilities and skills: _____

    _____

    _____

9. Significant contributions/achievements: _____

    _____

    _____

10. Special training courses: _____

    _____

    _____

11. G.P.A.: _____ (on _____ index)

Community/Civic/
Volunteer Experience

1. Name and address of organization/group: _____

    _____

    _____

2. Inclusive dates: From _____ to _____.
                         month/year   month/year

3. Offices held/nature of involvement: _____

    _____

    _____

    _____

    _____

4. Significant contributions/achievements/projects: _____

    _____

    _____

    _____

    _____

    _____

5. Demonstrated skills and abilities: _____

    _____

    _____

    _____

    _____

    _____

Additional Information

1. Professional memberships and status:

   a. _____

   b. _____

   c. _____

   d. _____

2. Licenses/certifications:

   a. _____

   b. _____

   c. _____

   d. _____

3. Expected salary range: $ _____ to $ _____ (do not include on resume)

4. Acceptable amount of on-the-job travel: _____ days per month.

5. Areas of acceptable relocation:

   a. _____   c. _____

   b. _____   d. _____

6. Date of availability: _____

7. Contacting present employer:

   a. Is he or she aware of your prospective job change? _____

   b. May he or she be contacted at this time? _____

8. References: (name, address, telephone number – not to appear on resume)

   a. _____   b. _____

   _____   _____

   _____   _____

   c. _____   d. _____

   _____   _____

   _____   _____

9. Foreign languages and degree of competency:

   a. _____

   b. _____

10. Interests and activities: hobbies, avocations, pursuits

   a. _____

   b. _____

   c. _____

   d. _____

Circle letter of those which support your objective.

11. Foreign travel:

	Country	Purpose	Dates
a.	_____	_____	_____
b.	_____	_____	_____
c.	_____	_____	_____
d.	_____	_____	_____
e.	_____	_____	_____

12. Special awards/recognition:

   a. _____

   b. _____

   c. _____

   d. _____

13. Special abilities/skills/talents/accomplishments:

   a. _____

   b. _____

   c. _____

   d. _____

Detail Your Achievements

Definition: An "Achievement" is anything you enjoyed doing, believe you did well, and felt a sense of satisfaction, pride, or accomplishment in doing.

ACHIEVEMENT # ____: _____

_____

1. How did I initially become involved? _____

_____

_____

_____

2. What did I do? _____

_____

_____

_____

3. How did I do it? _____

_____

_____

_____

4. What was especially enjoyable about doing it? _____

_____

_____

_____

_____

Index

The Authors

FOR MORE THAN TWO DECADES Ron and Caryl Krannich, Ph.Ds, have pursued a passion – assisting hundreds of thousands of individuals, from students, the unemployed, and ex-offenders to military personnel, international job seekers, and CEOs, in making critical job and career transitions. Focusing on key job search skills, career changes, and employment fields, their impressive body of work has helped shape career thinking and behavior both in the United States and abroad. Their sound advice has changed numerous lives, including their own!

Ron and Caryl are two of America's leading career and travel writers who have authored, co-authored, or ghost-written more than 70 books. A former Peace Corps Volunteer and Fulbright Scholar, Ron received his Ph.D. in Political Science from Northern Illinois University. Caryl received her Ph.D. in Speech Communication from Penn State University. Together they operate Development Concepts Incorporated, a training, consulting, and publishing firm in Virginia.

The Krannichs are both former university professors, high school teachers, management trainers, and consultants. As trainers and consultants, they have completed numerous projects on management, career development, local government, population planning, and rural development in the United States and abroad. Their career books focus on key job search skills, military and civilian career transitions, government and international careers, travel jobs, and nonprofit organizations and include such classics as *High Impact Resumes and Letters*, *Interview for Success*, and *Change Your Job, Change Your Life*. Their books represent one of today's most comprehensive collections of career writing. With nearly 3 million copies in print, their publications are widely available in bookstores, libraries, and career centers. No strangers to the Internet world, they have written ***America's Top Internet Job Sites*** and ***The Directory of Websites for International Jobs*** and published several Internet recruitment and job search books. They also have developed career-related websites: www.impactpublications.com, www.winningthejob. com, www.exoffenderreentry.com, and www.veteransworld.com. Many of their career tips have appeared on such major websites as www.monster.com, www.careerbuilder. com, www.employmentguide.com, and www.campuscareercenter.com.

Ron and Caryl live a double life with travel being their best kept *"do what you love"* career secret. Authors of over 20 travel-shopping guidebooks on various destinations around the world, they continue to pursue their international and travel interests through their innovative ***Treasures and Pleasures of...Best of the Best*** travel-shopping series and related websites: www.ishoparoundtheworld.com and www.travel-smarter. com. When not found at their home and business in Virginia, they are probably somewhere in Europe, Asia, Africa, the Middle East, the South Pacific, the Caribbean, or the Americas following their other passion – researching and writing about quality antiques, arts, crafts, jewelry, hotels, and restaurants as well as adhering to the career advice they give to others: *"Pursue a passion that enables you to do what you really love to do."*

As both career and travel experts, the Krannichs' work is frequently featured in major newspapers, magazines, and newsletters as well as on radio, television, and the Internet. Available for interviews, consultation, and presentations, they can be contacted as follows:

> Ron and Caryl Krannich
> krannich@impactpublications.com

Contributors

THE RESUME EXAMPLES INCLUDED in this book come from several sources. Many were developed by the authors from their work with numerous students and clients. All military-related resumes are drawn from their work with transitioning military personnel. These and many other examples are showcased in *Military Resumes and Cover Letters* by Carl S. Savino and Ronald L. Krannich (Impact Publications, 2004).

Most of the international-related resumes were developed by professional resume writers who contributed to *Best Resumes and CVs for International Jobs* by Ronald L. Krannich and Wendy S. Enelow (Impact Publications, 2002). Many of these contributors are members of three professional resume writing organizations (NRWA, PARW, and PRWRA) which we identified on page 2. If you need assistance in writing a resume, we recommend contacting members of these organizations who may also offer career coaching and related job search services.

Most of the classic achievement-oriented resumes are drawn from the files of Bernard Haldane Associates (now BH Careers International) and are showcased in *Haldane's Best Resumes for Professionals* (Impact Publications, 1999).

Two professional resume writers contributed examples on pages 196-206:

Abby M. Locke, MBA (pages 198-206)
Premier Writing Solutions
Tel. 1-877-582-4085 (Washington, DC)
Website: www.premierwriting.com
E-mail: info@premierwriting.com

Barbara Safani (pages 196-197)
Career Solvers
980 Madison Avenue
New York, NY 10021
Tel. 212-579-7230 or 866-333-1800
Website: www.careersolvers.com

Career Resources

THE FOLLOWING CAREER RESOURCES are available directly from Impact Publications. Full descriptions of each title, as well as several downloadable catalogs and specialty flyers, can be found on our website: www.impactpublications.com. Complete the following form or list the titles, include shipping (see formula at the end), enclose payment, and send your order to:

IMPACT PUBLICATIONS
9104 Manassas Drive, Suite N
Manassas Park, VA 20111-5211 USA
1-800-361-1055 (orders only)
Tel. 703-361-7300 or Fax 703-335-9486
Email address: info@impactpublications.com
Quick & easy online ordering: www.impactpublications.com

Orders from individuals must be prepaid by check, money order, or major credit card. We accept telephone, fax, and email orders.

Qty.	TITLES	Price	TOTAL
Featured Title			
_____	Nail the Resume!	$17.95	_____
Other Titles By Authors			
_____	101 Secrets of Highly Effective Speakers	$15.95	_____
_____	201 Dynamite Job Search Letters	$19.95	_____
_____	America's Top Internet Job Sites	$19.95	_____
_____	America's Top 100 Jobs for People Without a Four-Year Degree	$19.95	_____
_____	America's Top Jobs for People Re-Entering the Workforce	$19.95	_____
_____	Best Jobs for the 21st Century	$19.95	_____
_____	Best Resumes and CVs for International Jobs	$24.95	_____
_____	Change Your Job, Change Your Life	$21.95	_____
_____	Complete Guide to Public Employment	$19.95	_____
_____	Directory of Websites for International Jobs	$19.95	_____
_____	Discover the Best Jobs for You	$15.95	_____
_____	Dynamite Salary Negotiations	$15.95	_____
_____	The Ex-Offender's Job Hunting Guide	$17.95	_____
_____	Find a Federal Job Fast	$15.95	_____
_____	Get a Raise in 7 Days	$14.95	_____
_____	Haldane's Best Answers to Tough Interview Questions	$15.95	_____
_____	Haldane's Best Cover Letters for Professionals	$15.95	_____

____	Haldane's Best Resumes for Professionals	$15.95	____
____	High Impact Resumes and Letters	$19.95	____
____	I Want to Do Something Else, But I'm Not Sure What It Is	$15.95	____
____	Interview for Success	$15.95	____
____	The Job Hunting Guide: Transitioning From College to Career	$14.95	____
____	Job Hunting Tips for People With Hot and Not-So-Hot Backgrounds	$17.95	____
____	Job Interview Tips for People With Not-So-Hot Backgrounds	$14.95	____
____	Jobs for Travel Lovers	$19.95	____
____	Military Resumes and Cover Letters	$21.95	____
____	Nail the Cover Letter!	$17.95	____
____	Nail the Job Interview!	$13.95	____
____	Nail the Resume!	$17.95	____
____	No One Will Hire Me!	$13.95	____
____	Salary Negotiation Tips for Professionals	$16.95	____
____	Savvy Interviewing: The Nonverbal Advantage	$10.95	____
____	The Savvy Networker	$13.95	____
____	The Savvy Resume Writer	$12.95	____

Testing and Assessment

____	Aptitude, Personality, and Motivation Tests	$17.95	____
____	Career Tests	$12.95	____
____	Discover the Best Jobs for You	$15.95	____
____	Discover What You're Best At	$14.00	____
____	Do What You Are	$18.95	____
____	Finding Your Perfect Work	$16.95	____
____	Gifts Differing	$16.95	____
____	I Could Do Anything If Only I Knew What It Was	$14.95	____
____	I Don't Know What I Want, But I Know It's Not This	$14.00	____
____	I Want to Do Something Else, But I'm Not Sure What It Is	$15.95	____
____	I'm Not Crazy, I'm Just Not You	$16.95	____
____	Now, Discover Your Strengths	$28.00	____
____	The Pathfinder	$15.00	____
____	What Should I Do With My Life?	$14.95	____
____	What Type Am I?	$14.95	____
____	What's Your Type of Career?	$18.95	____

Attitude and Motivation

____	100 Ways to Motivate Yourself	$14.99	____
____	Attitude Is Everything	$14.95	____
____	Change Your Attitude	$15.99	____
____	Reinventing Yourself	$18.99	____

Inspiration and Empowerment

____	7 Habits of Highly Effective People (2nd Edition)	$15.00	____
____	7 Habits of Highly Effective Teens	$14.00	____
____	The 8th Habit: From Effectiveness to Greatness	$26.00	____
____	101 Secrets of Highly Effective Speakers	$15.95	____
____	Awaken the Giant Within	$15.00	____
____	Change Your Thinking, Change Your Life	$24.95	____
____	Dream It Do It	$16.95	____
____	Eat That Frog!	$19.95	____
____	Finding Your Own North Star	$14.95	____
____	Goals!	$14.95	____
____	It's Only Too Late If You Don't Start Now	$15.00	____
____	Live the Life Your Love	$12.95	____
____	Life Strategies	$13.95	____
____	Magic of Thinking Big	$13.00	____
____	Maximum Achievement	$14.00	____
____	Power of Positive Thinking	$12.95	____
____	Power of Purpose	$20.00	____

_____ Purpose-Driven Life	$19.99	_____
_____ Self Matters	$14.00	_____
_____ Who Moved My Cheese?	$19.95	_____

Career Exploration and Job Strategies

_____ 5 Patterns of Extraordinary Careers	$17.95	_____
_____ 25 Jobs That Have It All	$12.95	_____
_____ 50 Best Jobs for Your Personality	$16.95	_____
_____ 50 Cutting Edge Jobs	$15.95	_____
_____ 95 Mistakes Job Seekers Make & How to Avoid Them	$13.95	_____
_____ 100 Great Jobs and How to Get Them	$17.95	_____
_____ 101 Ways to Recession-Proof Your Career	$14.95	_____
_____ 200 Best Jobs for College Grads	$16.95	_____
_____ 250 Best Jobs Through Apprenticeships	$24.95	_____
_____ 300 Best Jobs Without a Four-Year Degree	$16.95	_____
_____ America's Top 100 Jobs for People Without a Four-Year Degree	$19.95	_____
_____ Best Entry-Level Jobs	$16.95	_____
_____ Best Jobs for the 21st Century	$19.95	_____
_____ Career Change	$14.95	_____
_____ Change Your Job, Change Your Life (9th Edition)	$21.95	_____
_____ Cool Careers for Dummies	$19.99	_____
_____ Directory of Executive Recruiters	$49.95	_____
_____ Five Secrets to Finding a Job	$12.95	_____
_____ A Fork in the Road: A Career Planning Guide for Young Adults	$14.95	_____
_____ Great Careers in Two Years	$19.95	_____
_____ High-Tech Careers for Low-Tech People	$14.95	_____
_____ How to Get a Job and Keep It	$16.95	_____
_____ How to Get Interviews From Classified Job Ads	$14.95	_____
_____ How to Succeed Without a Career Path	$13.95	_____
_____ Job Hunting Guide: College to Career	$14.95	_____
_____ Job Search Handbook for People With Disabilities	$17.95	_____
_____ Knock 'Em Dead	$14.95	_____
_____ Me, Myself, and I, Inc.	$17.95	_____
_____ Monster Careers	$18.00	_____
_____ Quick Guide to Career Training in Two Years or Less	$16.95	_____
_____ Quick Prep Careers	$18.95	_____
_____ Quit Your Job and Grow Some Hair	$15.95	_____
_____ Rites of Passage at $100,000 to $1 Million+	$29.95	_____
_____ Suddenly Unemployed	$14.95	_____
_____ What Color Is Your Parachute?	$17.95	_____

Career Directories

_____ Almanac of American Employers	$199.95	_____
_____ Associations USA	$75.00	_____
_____ Enhanced Occupational Outlook Handbook	$39.95	_____
_____ Job Hunter's Sourcebook	$160.00	_____
_____ Occupational Outlook Handbook	$16.90	_____
_____ O*NET Dictionary of Occupational Titles	$39.95	_____
_____ Professional Careers Sourcebook	$150.00	_____
_____ Vocational Careers Sourcebook	$150.00	_____

Internet Job Search

_____ 100 Top Internet Job Sites	$12.95	_____
_____ America's Top Internet Job Sites	$19.95	_____
_____ Career Exploration On the Internet	$24.95	_____
_____ Cyberspace Job Search Kit	$18.95	_____
_____ Directory of Websites for International Jobs	$19.95	_____
_____ Guide to Internet Job Searching	$14.95	_____
_____ Haldane's Best Employment Websites for Professionals	$15.95	_____

Resumes and Letters

_____	101 Great Tips for a Dynamite Resume	$13.95 _____
_____	175 Best Cover Letters	$14.95 _____
_____	201 Dynamite Job Search Letters	$19.95 _____
_____	Best KeyWords for Resumes, Cover Letters, & Interviews	$17.95 _____
_____	Best Resumes and CVs for International Jobs	$24.95 _____
_____	Best Resumes for $75,000+ Executive Jobs	$16.95 _____
_____	Best Resumes for $100,000+ Jobs	$24.95 _____
_____	Best Resumes for People Without a Four-Year Degree	$19.95 _____
_____	Best Cover Letters for $100,000+ Jobs	$24.95 _____
_____	Blue Collar Resumes	$11.99 _____
_____	College Grad Resumes to Land $75,000+ Jobs	$24.95 _____
_____	Competency-Based Resumes	$13.99 _____
_____	Cover Letters for Dummies	$16.99 _____
_____	Cover Letters That Knock 'Em Dead	$12.95 _____
_____	Cyberspace Resume Kit	$18.95 _____
_____	e-Resumes	$11.95 _____
_____	Expert Resumes for People Returning to Work	$16.95 _____
_____	Gallery of Best Cover Letters	$18.95 _____
_____	Gallery of Best Resumes	$18.95 _____
_____	Haldane's Best Cover Letters for Professionals	$15.95 _____
_____	Haldane's Best Resumes for Professionals	$15.95 _____
_____	High Impact Resumes and Letters	$19.95 _____
_____	Military Resumes and Cover Letters	$21.95 _____
_____	Resume Shortcuts	$14.95 _____
_____	Resumes for Dummies	$16.99 _____
_____	Resumes in Cyberspace	$14.95 _____
_____	Resumes That Knock 'Em Dead	$12.95 _____
_____	The Savvy Resume Writer	$12.95 _____

Networking

_____	A Foot in the Door	$14.95 _____
_____	How to Work a Room	$14.00 _____
_____	Masters of Networking	$16.95 _____
_____	Networking for Job Search and Career Success	$16.95 _____
_____	The Savvy Networker	$13.95 _____

Dress, Image, and Etiquette

_____	Dressing Smart for Men	$16.95 _____
_____	Dressing Smart for Women	$16.95 _____
_____	Power Etiquette	$14.95 _____

Interviews

_____	101 Dynamite Questions to Ask At Your Job Interview	$13.95 _____
_____	Haldane's Best Answers to Tough Interview Questions	$15.95 _____
_____	Interview for Success	$15.95 _____
_____	Job Interview Tips for People With Not-So-Hot Backgrounds	$14.95 _____
_____	Job Interviews for Dummies	$16.99 _____
_____	KeyWords to Nail Your Job Interview	$17.95 _____
_____	Nail the Job Interview!	$13.95 _____
_____	The Savvy Interviewer	$10.95 _____
_____	Sweaty Palms	$13.95 _____

Salary Negotiations

_____	Dynamite Salary Negotiations	$15.95 _____
_____	Get a Raise in 7 Days	$14.95 _____
_____	Get More Money On Your Next Job	$17.95 _____
_____	Salary Negotiation Tips for Professionals	$16.95 _____

Ex-Offenders in Transition

____	9 to 5 Beats Ten to Life	$15.00 ____
____	99 Days and a Get Up	$9.95 ____
____	Ex-Offender's Job Hunting Guide	$17.95 ____
____	Man, I Need a Job	$7.95 ____
____	Putting the Bars Behind You (6 books)	$57.95 ____

Government Jobs

____	Book of U.S. Government Jobs	$21.95 ____
____	FBI Careers	$18.95 ____
____	Post Office Jobs	$18.95 ____
____	Ten Steps to a Federal Job	$39.95 ____

International and Travel Jobs

____	Back Door Guide to Short-Term Job Adventures	$21.95 ____
____	Careers in International Affairs	$24.95 ____
____	Directory of Websites for International Jobs	$19.95 ____
____	International Job Finder	$19.95 ____
____	Jobs for Travel Lovers	$19.95 ____
____	Teaching English Abroad	$15.95 ____

VIDEOS

Interview, Networking, and Salary Videos

____	Best 10¼ Tips for People With a Not-So-Hot Past	$98.00 ____
____	Build a Network for Work and Life	$99.00 ____
____	Common Mistakes People Make in Interviews	$79.95 ____
____	Exceptional Interviewing Tips	$79.00 ____
____	Extraordinary Answers to Interview Questions	$79.95 ____
____	Extreme Interview	$69.00 ____
____	Make a First Good Impression	$129.00 ____
____	Seizing the Job Interview	$79.00 ____
____	Quick Salary Negotiations Video	$149.00 ____
____	Why Should I Hire You?	$99.00 ____

Dress and Image Videos

____	Head to Toe	$98.00 ____
____	Tips and Techniques to Improve Your Total Image	$98.00 ____

Resumes, Applications, and Cover Letter Videos

____	The Complete Job Application	$99.00 ____
____	Effective Resumes	$79.95 ____
____	Ideal Resume	$79.95 ____
____	Quick Cover Letter Video	$149.00 ____
____	Quick Resume Video	$149.00 ____
____	Resumes, Cover Letters, and Portfolios	$98.00 ____

Assessment and Goal Setting Videos

____	Career Path Interest Inventory	$149.00 ____
____	Career S.E.L.F. Assessment	$89.00 ____
____	Skills Identification	$129.00 ____
____	You DO Have Experience	$149.00 ____

Attitude, Motivation, and Empowerment Videos

_____	Down But Not Out	$129.00	_____
_____	Gumby Attitude	$69.00	_____
_____	Looking for Work With Attitude Plus	$129.00	_____

SOFTWARE

_____	Job Browser Pro 1.4	$359.00	_____
_____	Multimedia Career Center	$385.00	_____
_____	Multimedia Career Pathway	$199.00	_____
_____	Multimedia Personal Development Series	$450.00	_____
_____	OOH Career Center	$349.95	_____

SUBTOTAL _____

Virginia residents add 5% sales tax _____

POSTAGE/HANDLING ($5 for first
product and 8% of SUBTOTAL) _$5.00_

8% of SUBTOTAL -- _____

TOTAL ENCLOSED -------------------------------------- _____

SHIP TO:

NAME _____

ADDRESS: _____

_____

_____

PAYMENT METHOD:

❑ I enclose check/money order for $ _____ made payable to IMPACT PUBLICATIONS.

❑ Please charge $ _____ to my credit card:

❑ Visa   ❑ MasterCard   ❑ American Express   ❑ Discover

Card # _____ Expiration date: _____/_____

Signature _____

Keep in Touch . . .
On the Web!

www.impactpublications.com
www.winningthejob.com
www.exoffenderreentry.com
www.veteransworld.com
www.ishoparoundtheworld.com
www.travel-smarter.com